About the authors

Timothy F. Braun is an assistant professor of biological sciences at the State University of New York College at Oswego.

Lisa M. Glidden is an associate professor of political science at the State University of New York College at Oswego.

UNDERSTANDING ENERGY AND ENERGY POLICY

Timothy F. Braun and Lisa M. Glidden

Zed Books
LONDON

Understanding Energy and Energy Policy was first published in 2014 by Zed Books Ltd, 7 Cynthia Street, London N1 9JF, UK

www.zedbooks.co.uk

Set in Monotype Plantin and FontFont Kievit by Ewan Smith, London
Index: ed.emery@thefreeuniversity.net
Cover designed by www.roguefour.co.uk
Cover image © Nicholas Eveleigh/Getty

A catalogue record for this book is available from the British Library
Library of Congress Cataloging in Publication Data available

ISBN 978-1-78032-935-2 hb
ISBN 978-1-78032-934-5 pb
ISBN 978-1-78032-936-9 pdf
ISBN 978-1-78032-937-6 epub
ISBN 978-1-78032-938-3 mobi

CONTENTS

FIGURES AND TABLES

Figures

Tables

ABBREVIATIONS AND ACRONYMS

A	amp
AC	alternating current
AD	anaerobic digestion
BTU	British Thermal Unit
BWR	boiling water reactor
CCS	Carbon Capture and Sequestration
CHP	combined heat and power
CO_2e	CO_2 equivalent
co-gen	co-generation
DC	direct current
DRC	Democratic Republic of Congo
EGS	Enhanced Geothermal System
EPA	Environmental Protection Agency (US)
EROeI	Energy Return On energy Investment
EU	European Union
FIT	feed-in tariff
GDP	gross domestic product
GHG	greenhouse gas
GLOW	Great Lakes Offshore Wind
GW	gigawatt
HF	hydraulic fracturing ('fracking')
ICJ	International Court of Justice
IPCC	Intergovernmental Panel on Climate Change
ITER	International Thermonuclear Experimental Reactor
K A CARE	King Abdullah City for Atomic and Renewable Energy
kWh	kilowatt-hour
LCOE	Levelized Cost of Electricity
LIFTR	liquid fluoride – thorium cycle
LNG	liquefied natural gas
LNT	linear no-threshold
METI	Ministry of Economy, Trade, and Industry (Japan)
mSv	milliSievert
MTBE	methyl-tertbutylether
MW	megawatt
NISA	Nuclear and Industrial Safety Agency (Japan)
NRC	Nuclear Regulatory Commission (US)

NYPA	New York Power Authority
OPEC	Organization of the Petroleum Exporting Countries
ppm	parts per million
PTC	Production Tax Credit
PV	photovoltaic
PWR	pressurized water reactor
rem	Roentgen equivalent man
ROI	Return On Investment
RPS	Renewable Portfolio Standard
STTS	solar thermal with thermal storage
UNFCCC	UN Framework Convention on Climate Change
V	voltage
WCD	World Commission on Dams

ACKNOWLEDGMENTS

We owe thanks to many people who had a part in making this book become a reality. The book is developed from a course that Lisa created with Dr Alok Kumar, Professor of Physics at SUNY Oswego. She is grateful to a Curriculum Innovation Grant that supported the course's creation, and to Dr Walter Opello, who first put her in touch with Alok Kumar. This course has been offered twice, first co-taught with Alok Kumar, and then co-taught with Dr Timothy Braun, Assistant Professor of Biological Sciences, the book's co-author. We are thankful to SUNY Oswego's commitment to interdisciplinarity, shared by most of the academic departments on campus, which made offering the course possible. We are also very thankful to the two cohorts of students who took part in and provided feedback on the course, and the current students in Global Environmental Politics, who helped choose the book cover.

We also owe a debt of gratitude to many of our colleagues and students. Dr Kestutis (Kestas) Bendinskas, Associate Professor of Chemistry at SUNY Oswego, kindly agreed to review some of the chemistry discussions, and suggested helpful revisions. Patricia Tifft, administrative assistant for political science, helped with graphics and images, especially the Appendix. Jim Russell (Public Affairs) and Casey Raymond (Department of Chemistry) took time out of their busy schedules to find photos of the geothermal field installation. Julie Blissert, Director of Public Affairs, responded quickly with permissions requests, and even caught a typo for us. At the beginning of this book project Stephon Boatwright, one of our undergraduates, served as a research assistant. We appreciate a Summer Scholar's Grant that was able to support Stephon's work. Toward the end of this project, Alexander Lykins, also one of our undergraduates, provided research assistance and data collection. We are grateful to both of them for their contributions. Of course, any errors remain our own. We are also thankful to Laura Brazak, one of our undergraduates who is also a professional photographer, for taking professional author's photos of us, and for her many ideas on promoting this book.

We are immensely grateful to Dr Duane Braun, Professor Emeritus of Environmental, Geographical, and Geological Sciences at Bloomsburg University, and the father of one of the authors, for lightning-fast turnaround time reviewing our chapters, providing suggestions, and helpful language revisions. We greatly appreciate the support our families – Ruth and Duane Braun, and Joann and Ed Glidden – have provided in general, but especially in this last year of research and writing.

Finally, we would like to thank the editorial team at Zed Books, especially Kim Walker, our editor through most of this project, Tamsine O'Riordan and Kika Sroka-Miller, our first and transition editors, and Ken Barlow and Jakob Horstmann, fantastic commissioning editors. It has been a pleasure working with all of you.

For Anna, Lily, and Ben – here's hoping we can leave your generation with fewer problems.

INTRODUCTION

On 10 May 2013 scientists at the Mauna Loa Observatory in Hawaii reported that the average daily reading for carbon dioxide (CO_2) in the atmosphere reached 400 parts per million (ppm) (Gillis 2013). Increasing CO_2 concentration in the atmosphere is primarily coming from human use of fossil fuels. For many, 400 ppm is seen as a threshold heralding mankind embarking upon a dangerous new era of increasing global temperature and climatic disruption, the Anthropocene.[1] Climate scientists use computer models to predict the impact of climate change, in an attempt to figure out how many degrees Celsius the Earth will warm, and what impact the warming will have on global climate. While there is some uncertainty in the models, climatic shifts are likely, leading to some areas becoming drier and others wetter. Also, the climate may become more variable than it has been as it shifts toward a new state. According to a recent report, 'impacts from climate-related extremes, such as heat waves, droughts, floods, cyclones, and wildfires, reveal significant vulnerability and exposure of some ecosystems and many human systems to current climate variability' (IPCC 2014: 7).

Consider, however, that all of recorded human history and technological development, going back to the dawn of agriculture, fits in the last 12,000 years after the end of the last ice age. This period was relatively calm from a climatic standpoint, and current thinking posits that this climatic stability was required for the development of agriculture and complex society – in short, human civilization. Also, consider that humans are putting multiple stresses on the Earth, not just global warming. We are also losing topsoil for agriculture, fresh water for drinking and agriculture, and stressing the oceans with pollution and overfishing. There is the very real question of how much stress the natural systems of Earth can take before a critical threshold is breached and wide-scale failures are seen. To avoid this possibility we need to move to living as part of a sustainable ecosystem. One of the hurdles to sustainable living is to de-carbonize our energy systems, to move humankind off fossil fuels. Ways to accomplish de-carbonization will be one of the major focuses of this book.

The last time the CO_2 concentration was at 400 ppm in the atmosphere was in the Pliocene era, between three and five million years ago, when the Earth's average temperature was three or four degrees Celsius (5.4–7.2 degrees Fahrenheit) warmer than today and sea levels ranged from 16 to 131 feet higher than today (Monroe 2013). The international community, meeting at

Durban, South Africa, in its annual round of climate talks in 2011, agreed CO_2 should not surpass 450 ppm, which models say will be accompanied by a two degree Celsius increase in the Earth's average temperature. There is no plan currently in place to stop us from reaching that impending threshold, although the international community is meeting in Lima, Peru, in late 2014 to lay the foundation to craft a new climate agreement.

In 2013 the International Energy Agency released a special issue of its *World Energy Outlook*, which 'urged governments to swiftly enact four energy policies that would keep climate goals alive without harming economic growth' (OECD/IEA 2013a). They recommend a combination of efficiency measures, moving to renewable energy from inefficient coal-fired power plants, reducing methane, and phasing out fossil fuel subsidies (ibid.). Despite the recommendations, countries around the world have made uneven progress toward crafting energy policies that take into account those recommendations. Climate change presents additional policy challenges because of 'displaced hardship.' The countries likely to be most affected by climate change are not those that need policy shifts. The chapter on how policy decisions are made will explain this challenge in greater detail. Climate scientists are in agreement that we are not sufficiently reducing the amount of CO_2 being introduced into the atmosphere that will allow us to continue current development patterns.

Publics around the world are concerned about climate change (World Public Opinion 2009). A Pew Research Center poll conducted in October 2012 found that 67 percent of Americans believed that 'there is solid evidence of global warming,' while 42 percent believed that warming was caused by human activity (Pew Research Center 2012: 1). Those concerned about global warming were happy to note the numbers were on the rise from the previous poll in 2009, but were still *lower* than those polled in 2006, when 77 percent of Americans believed that there was 'solid evidence of global warming' (ibid.: 1). Whether one believes that global warming is real but natural or has been caused by human activity, a country's energy policy is about more than its carbon emissions. It is also about the energy sources it uses for electricity generation, to power its transportation sector, to power its industries and heat its homes. Yet we cannot even engage in the debate about energy policy without understanding some basic science and the range of energy policy choices possible and practical.

As citizens, we need to understand the science behind the types of energy that support our lifestyle and how it works, in order to have a useful voice in the debate over our countries' energy policies. But the question is, are we scientifically literate enough to understand the potential policy choices before us? This book provides readers with explanations of the science of various energy sources for electricity generation and an understanding of policy choices across the globe. We examine non-renewable and renewable energy sources – from burning fossil fuels, to power created through nuclear reactions, to solar/

wind energy, geothermal energy, biofuels, and water (hydro- and tidal power). Alongside the scientific explanations of electricity generation are energy policy case studies of countries using the type of energy source. We draw on cases from the global North and South,[2] from countries that are resource poor and resource rich. Our goal is to provide the reader with a basic understanding of energy systems, an introduction to how different countries approach energy policy, and the means to critically examine arguments about energy policy; in other words, to be a scientifically literate, engaged, citizen.

We hope readers will draw four lessons from this book. On the policy side, the case studies illustrate that policies tend to grow organically or on an ad hoc basis as a reaction to a crisis or challenge. The resulting status quo might seem normal, but it is not necessarily rational, effective, or the only way of doing things. The second policy lesson is that there is more than one way of accomplishing a goal. We present a range of case studies because seeing the diversity of policies and situations allows us to broaden the scope of what we think is possible. On the science side, in order to make effective policy, we have to understand the science behind the energy sources we use. We hope readers will come away with an understanding of fundamental physical theories, such as thermodynamics, in order to understand the physical constraints, what energy systems can and cannot do. The second science lesson is that units of measurement matter. We must be aware of what units of measurement are being used in a comparison of different systems and whether those units are appropriate or not. In short, we need to analyze the facts before us, and think critically about them, not take them at face value.

This chapter is divided into two sections. Section one introduces readers to global energy issues. It examines how much power is produced and consumed worldwide, and by country. We demonstrate that what information we choose to examine provides very different pictures of energy issues and potential solutions. Section two examines the concept of consensus understanding in the sciences, which is important to many aspects of energy policy and specifically as applied to the issue of climate change. Many countries have climate change adaptation or mitigation policies, and some countries have crafted energy policies that would allow them to significantly reduce their carbon footprints (see case studies in following chapters).

Global energy issues

Energy use is connected to development. Broadly speaking, the more developed a country is, the more energy it uses to power its homes, cars, industries, businesses, and gadgets.[3] Our economies and our lifestyles rely heavily on energy use, but we face several economic, environmental, political and technological challenges from many of our energy sources. These challenges are discussed in greater detail in the following chapters.

At the 1992 Earth Summit in Rio de Janeiro, Brazil, the international community agreed to work together to address climate change. As a result, the United Nations Framework Convention on Climate Change (UNFCCC) was created in 1994. Countries that are parties to – that is, signed – the UNFCCC drafted the Kyoto Protocol in 1996. Countries were divided into two groups – Annex I and non-Annex I.[4] Annex I countries were wealthier and more industrialized, and would be required to lower their CO_2 emissions. Non-Annex I countries were less wealthy and less industrialized, and would not be required to lower emissions under the Kyoto agreement, which ended in 2012. The Kyoto Protocol's division of countries into those two groups was meant as recognition that the amount of CO_2 in the atmosphere was primarily a result of the 200 years of industrialization and development by the Annex I countries. Since wealth and higher standards of living accompanied industrialization, non-Annex I countries should not have to put aside those aspirations.

There were a few mechanisms put into the Kyoto Protocol that would give the opportunity for non-Annex I countries to industrialize in a more sustainable way. For instance, a market would be created for CO_2, and each country would be allotted a certain amount of pollution credit. If that country reached its CO_2 cap, it would have to buy more pollution credits from a country, likely a non-Annex I country, with extra credits to sell. In this way non-Annex I countries would get money for developing technologies that were more sustainable and less polluting, and Annex I countries would have a monetary incentive to move to cleaner technologies and decrease emissions. This is commonly known as a cap-and-trade system.[5]

The Kyoto Protocol's differentiated CO_2 emissions limits intended to introduce fairness into the treaty. However, not all parties viewed the Kyoto Protocol as fair. We can understand different articulations of fairness more easily if we look at the different ways one can measure energy consumption. What we choose to measure affects what we identify as problems, and what solutions

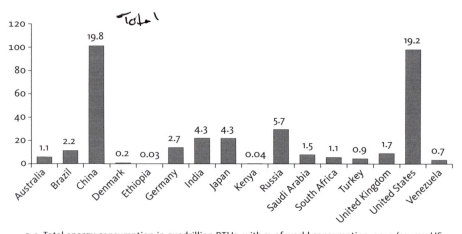

0.1 Total energy consumption in quadrillion BTUs, with % of world consumption, 2010 (*source*: US Energy Information Administration, *International Energy Statistics*)

we propose, so it is really important to understand what the numbers are measuring, what the numbers are telling you, and what they are not telling you. Several charts illustrate this point. Figure 0.1 shows total energy usage for a selection of countries, many of which we use as case studies in later chapters. The numbers in the chart are quadrillion British Thermal Units, because that is how the US Energy Information Agency reports energy consumption.

One BTU is 'about the amount of energy in the tip of a match' (Wilcoxen 2009). One kilowatt hour, the unit we use more often than BTU in this book, is equivalent to 3,412 BTUs. Most countries consume so many BTUs that we use the measure of quadrillion. One quadrillion BTUs is 'about equal to the amount of energy in 45 million tons of coal, or 1 trillion cubic feet of natural gas, or 170 million barrels of crude oil' (ibid.).

As you can see in Figure 0.1, China (non-Annex I) and the United States (Annex I) dwarf the other countries in terms of energy consumption. This is one of the reasons why the USA thought that China should not be exempt from having to curb CO_2 emissions. From the US perspective, China would gain a competitive economic advantage if it did not have to buy pollution credits. China is rapidly growing, its products compete with US-made goods, and it would have an unfair advantage. President Clinton signed the Kyoto Protocol, but never submitted it to the US Congress for ratification; President George W. Bush effectively unsigned the USA from the treaty. One response to those kinds of unfairness claims can be drawn from the data in Figure 0.2, which shows energy usage for those same countries, but instead of looking at the country in total, we look at the country per capita.

As you can see from Figure 0.2, if you divide the total energy consumption by the number of people living in that country, we get quite a different picture. The message we draw from the graph showing energy consumption by country, Figure 0.1, is that the USA and China are clearly the two actors

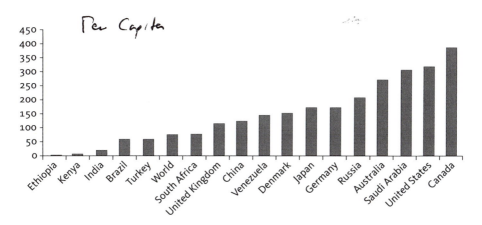

0.2 Total energy consumption per capita in millions of BTUs, 2010 (*source*: US Energy Information Administration, *International Energy Statistics*)

in the world that need to make major changes. If we look at those figures on a per capita basis, however, the countries that seem to bear the most responsibility are Canada, the USA, and Saudi Arabia. China's large emissions make much more sense if we think about how many people are accounting for those emissions.

There is another way to spin energy consumption. Carbon intensity is the amount of carbon emissions produced relative to economic output (Morales 2013). A country like the USA has a large economy, as measured by its gross domestic product (GDP), but if you look at the USA's carbon intensity, it has been declining as the USA has become more efficient in terms of energy usage. China's energy policy of 2012 notes that its goal is to improve its carbon intensity to be more in line with that of developed countries. The problem with using carbon intensity as a measure is that a country's carbon intensity can decrease at the same time as its carbon emissions increase, because the country's economy grows and its energy usage becomes more efficient. In terms of addressing climate change, using measures of carbon intensity goes nowhere because CO_2 emissions still generally rise, although some argue that in a developing country with a huge economy like China improving carbon intensity is worthwhile (Friedman 2009).

Figure 0.3 shows energy intensity for the same group of countries using the countries' gross domestic product (GDP), which is the value of the goods and services produced in the country that year. The monetary value used for the calculation of energy intensity was adjusted in two ways in order to make a more meaningful comparison. First, the US Energy Information Administration collects data across many years, so it chose a benchmark year and converted the dollars[6] for all years into what the value of those dollars would have been in 2005. Secondly, instead of using the market exchange rate in the country,

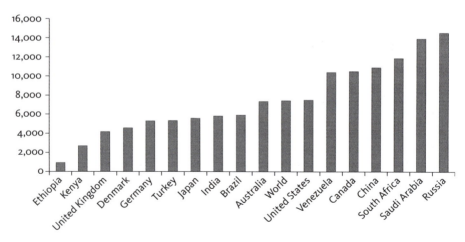

0.3 Energy intensity – total energy consumption per dollar of GDP (BTU per year 2005 US dollars, purchasing power parities), 2010 (*source*: US Energy Information Administration, *International Energy Statistics*)

they used purchasing power parity exchange rate, which is a measure that economists use to account for different costs of living across countries.

Once again, by analyzing energy consumption in a different way, we get a very different picture of where we should focus CO_2 emissions policies. To use a specific example so that we can see the relationship between energy intensity and CO_2 emissions, let us look at a few of these countries over time. All of the countries listed in Table 0.1 have been improving their efficiency, as noted by their declining energy intensity numbers. However, the overall CO_2 emissions have risen during that same time period.

TABLE 0.1 Energy intensity and CO2 emissions from energy consumption (million metric tons)

Country	Energy intensity 1990	CO₂ emissions 1990	Energy intensity 2000	CO₂ emissions 2000	Energy intensity 2010	CO₂ emissions 2010
Brazil	5,530	237	6,383	344	5,948	451
China	20,523	2,178	11,986	3,272	10,902	7,997
India	7,482	579	7,442	991	5,838	1,601
Russia	22,236 (total USSR)	3,821 (total USSR)	20,686	1,499	14,544	1,642
United States	10,525	5,040	8,810	5,863	7,505	5,637

Note: Energy intensity is total primary energy consumption per dollar of GDP (BTU per year, 2005, US dollars – purchasing power parities)

Source: US EIA, *International Energy Statistics*, 2013, www.eia.gov/cfapps/ipdbproject/iedindex3.cfm? tid=92&pid=47&aid=2&cid=regions&syid=2007&eyid=2011&unit=BTUPUSDM

Note again that what we choose to measure tells us different stories about what the problem is and who is responsible, and gives us differing policy prescriptions.

Any industrialized country requires large amounts of energy to function. This energy, though, comes in different forms and is used in different ways from country to country. We will spend considerable time talking about generating electricity in this book. However, for most countries electricity generation is only a portion of total energy usage. Other large sectors of energy usage are transportation, industry, and heating/cooling buildings. To dramatically affect a nation's overall energy use requires addressing all of the ways that energy is used. Look, for example, at the breakdown of energy consumption in France and India. Table 0.2 shows what powered different sectors of France's economy, and Table 0.3 shows the breakdown for India. Affecting just one sector will have only a limited effect on a country's energy security, energy independence, emissions, or other factors the country deems important enough to direct its energy policy.

Tables 0.2 and 0.3 do not tell us about the amount of energy used in France and India. Nor do they tell us how efficiently those countries use energy to

TABLE 0.2 France, final energy consumption by sector by energy source, 2010 (%)

	Electricity (generation sources: 75% nuclear, 11% fossil fuels, 2.7% renewables, 12% hydro)	Coal	Oil	Gas	Renewables
Residential and commercial	34	2	14	32	18
Industry	30.6	13.9	22.2	27.8	5.6
Transportation	2	–	92	–	6

Sources: Gas in Focus/Observatoire du Gaz (2013) for consumption by sector; Réseau de transport d'eléctricité (2011) for France's electricity generation sources

TABLE 0.3 India, final energy consumption by sector by energy source, 2010 (%)

	Electricity (generation sources: 57% coal; 19% hydro; 12% biomass and other renewables; 9% gas; 2% nuclear; 1% diesel)	Coal and lignite	Oil	Gas
Agriculture	44.4	–	55	0.65
Residential & commercial	39.8	–	59.8	0.5
Industry	15.5	63.4	20.9	0.3
Transportation	1.9	–	98.1	–

Source: TERI Energy Data Directory and Yearbook 2012/13 for consumption by sector; US Energy Information Agency for electricity generation sources

grow their economies. They do not tell us whether the country's energy usage and sources jibe with its energy policy. What the tables do tell us, for example, is that about one third of the energy that homes and businesses in France use is in the form of electricity. Two-thirds of the energy they use presumably goes to heating and cooling. The tables also tell us that France gets most of its electricity from nuclear power, while India gets most of its electricity from coal, followed by hydropower. Are these 'good' energy profiles? It is hard to answer that question without knowing France and India's energy goals, or the benefits and limitations of the various energy sources. In the chapters that follow you will learn about these and other energy sources, their benefits and drawbacks, and in what ways they have been used in a variety of countries. At that point you should be able to make an informed decision about what a good energy mix for your country looks like.

Consensus in science and the climate change debate

In the US popular press, there has been considerable debate about the existence of manmade global warming and its linkage to climate change. However, there is no such debate among climate scientists or in the scholarly literature. What explains this disconnect? Much of it has to do with the way scientists communicate their work to the public, a public that does not

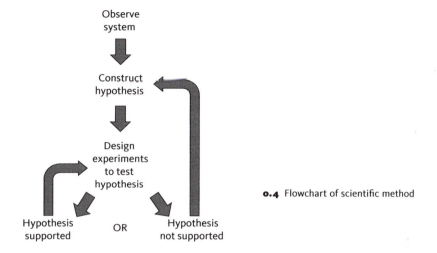

0.4 Flowchart of scientific method

understand how science progresses, journalists who believe every story has two sides, and outright propaganda for political gain.

Ideally all scientists follow the scientific method. The scientific method is a way to empirically figure out how natural systems work. A system is observed, a hypothesis is developed as to how the system behaves and then experiments are designed to test how well the hypothesis predicts the behavior of the system. Figure 0.4 shows a common flowchart of the scientific method.

Notice that there is no endpoint to the flowchart. Once you have tested a hypothesis and found it to be predictive – that is, it explains how the system functions – it does not mean that you stop testing it. At a fundamental level, everything in science is mutable, or subject to revision, if new data comes to light. A popular saying goes: 'Science is not a democracy, it is a dictatorship; data is the dictator.' In other words, whatever the data says must be explained, regardless of what we humans may feel about it. Many of us who work in science education seek to remove the idea of scientific 'laws.' No hypothesis, no matter how well tested, is above challenge.

One outcome of this type of thinking for scientists is that we come to view the world as a soup of probabilities. There is some finite chance of almost anything occurring at any given time, even if that probability is vanishingly low. There is no absolute certainty, with the exception of the mathematical certainty of an equation. Also, nothing is ever proven beyond doubt, a very different situation from most modern legal systems. This view of the world seems to be rather unsettling for many non-scientists to deal with and leads to misunderstanding and mistrust. Why can they not give us a straight answer? What do they mean by 'not absolutely sure'? One can get used to it – the average scientist has four to ten years of training after secondary school – but it is not the way most people communicate.

While awkward communication can be part of the problem, another issue is that most people do not understand how scientists come to a consensus. Most scientific communication happens in the scientific literature. A lot of communication also happens at professional meetings as well, and increasingly on the internet, but it is usually not considered official until it is published. Journals in the sciences are peer-reviewed. That is, to get a publication into a science journal you must be able to convince other scientists that your methods and results are valid. Generally a scientific paper is submitted to a journal and then sent out to several other scientists considered knowledgeable in the relevant area. These scientists review the study and report back to the journal their opinion as to whether the methods are sound and the results reasonable. In contentious cases they will try to replicate the results; reproducibility of results is considered a foundation of science. Only if all the reviewers feel that the study is sound and reasonable will it be published. Consider how different this is from newspaper, magazine, and television stories, where there is only editorial oversight, and the editor often has little or no specific expertise in the subject of the article.

Once an article is published the testing of the ideas in the paper often continues. Any scientist is now free to use the methods described in the paper to try to reproduce the results. So even in cases where reviewer oversight fails, there is a mechanism to catch faulty results. Generally this probing will also reveal new aspects of the original work and provide new avenues of inquiry. As more papers on a subject accumulate in the literature, the system becomes better understood and more scientists come to feel that the weight of evidence supports a particular hypothesis or explanation.

Scientists are not a monolithic group, however; there will always be some scientists who disagree with a particular hypothesis. This is actually good for science as a whole, as it ensures that someone will keep testing a hypothesis long after most other scientists have moved on. Occasionally they are proved right. However, these contrarians are vulnerable to misrepresentation. Special interest groups can highlight the few scientists who still disagree with a particular hypothesis to obscure the fact that the vast majority of scientists accept it.

Such a tactic is often called 'creating the appearance of doubt' and can be quite successful. This tactic was used for decades by the tobacco industry to avoid cigarette regulation and more recently has been used against the notion of human-caused global warming – for a fascinating but disquieting overview see Oreskes and Conway (2010). As an example, a recent study has looked at all scientific journal articles about anthropogenic (human-caused) climate change, a so-called meta-data study because it combines many separate studies into one. The study found that 97 percent of articles in peer-reviewed journals, amounting to several thousand articles published over the past twenty years, support the idea that climate change is occurring and is influenced by human activities (Cook et al. 2013). Most scientists would say that this shows that the weight of evidence supports human-influenced climate change, but those same scientists would also agree that the issue is not completely settled. It is this seemingly schizophrenic attitude that helps support the 'creating the appearance of doubt' strategy.

Organization of this book

Energy policy discourse is full of terms like feasibility, potential, states of technology, and crisis. How well are we able to judge the veracity of those terms? What do they mean in terms of acting today or waiting for tomorrow? The following chapters provide you with the tools to understand common energy sources and current technologies for electricity generation. We begin in Chapter 1 with some basic science and policy background that will be necessary for the chapters that follow. There are several terms defined in Chapter 1 that you may want to return to for later reference. The rest of the chapters in this book are devoted to particular energy sources, and include a few case studies that illustrate different policies and challenges. For each country case study we briefly present the country's energy policy, before discussing the specific energy source focused on in the chapter.

Chapter 2 addresses fossil fuels and explains why they are so attractive as an energy source, despite drawbacks and non-renewability. Chapter 3 explains nuclear power, the challenges of nuclear waste, and the effects nuclear accidents have had on various countries' energy policies. Chapter 4 looks at liquid fuel production (biofuels) and electricity generation from biomass. Chapter 5 looks at hydropower and tidal power as energy sources. Using water as an energy source presents some challenges for global politics, because rivers that are dammed often flow through more than one country. Chapter 6 focuses on harvesting energy from the wind, and discusses the environmental and aesthetic concerns about turbine placement. Chapter 7 examines how geothermal energy can be extracted from below ground and used for heating and cooling purposes. Chapter 8 delves into how we use power from the sun. Photovoltaic and thermal solar systems are discussed both at the large generating-station level and at the smaller community/home-based level. The concluding chapter asks: where do we go from here? We ask that question of you, the reader, because we want to bring home the point that energy policy is not just for government policymakers to decide. We face some significant challenges, and in order to face those challenges we need to have dialogue, deliberation, and an informed, engaged, citizenry.

1 | BASIC ENERGY AND POLICY CONCEPTS

When asked to think about energy, most people imagine a light going on in a house or driving a car. Certainly both of these activities require energy. But where does that energy come from? What source(s) was it derived from? How was it transported to the consumer? How does our energy usage affect the world around us? These are all important questions that require some knowledge about energy systems and sources to answer. As citizens, we have a responsibility to be able to rationally discuss energy-related topics. This chapter will provide an overview of terminology and concepts that will help our discussions of energy in the rest of the book.

Sustainable energy systems

Before we dive into energy-related terminology, let us take a look at where we, as a species, should be heading in terms of energy systems. We need more sustainable energy systems. Sustainability – to borrow Thiele's working definition, which draws on science and ethics – 'satisfies meeting current needs without sacrificing future well-being through the balanced pursuit of ecological health, economic welfare, social empowerment, and cultural creativity' (2013: 4–5). We currently get most of our energy by mining solar energy captured eons ago by photosynthesis and stored as coal, oil, and natural gas in rock formations. It will take millions of years to produce new resources of this type, although we will not run out of oil or natural gas anytime soon, as we discuss in the chapter on fossil fuels. The carbon stored in these 'fossil' fuels is being released into the atmosphere, which is driving climate change. Climate change in turn will increasingly disrupt human activities, requiring us to expend more and more energy and resources just to maintain our current lifestyle. It would be preferable, and cheaper in the long run, to reduce carbon emissions gradually over the next several decades. The various ways that this reduction might be accomplished will be a main focus of the policy analysis of this text.

As an example of a sustainable energy system let us consider the Amazon rainforest. The rainforest is fueled entirely by solar power, sunlight absorbed by plants. This occurs at a fairly low total efficiency of around 1 percent, but encompasses a vast surface area. The concept of low efficiency but ubiquitous solar energy capture is a lesson for humanity and an idea we will return to in the chapter on solar power. Solar energy captured by plants is converted to sugars and other bio-molecules, which are, in turn, food for the teeming animal biodiversity of the rainforest. Dead animals and plant matter fall to the floor of the forest, where bacteria and fungi rapidly break them down, releasing nutrients needed for new plant growth, beginning the cycle anew.

The solar energy first absorbed by plants is lost from the rainforest system as waste heat of metabolism at every energy transaction – for example, when an insect eats a plant and digests its tissues or when a bird eats that same insect. Nearly every usable bit of energy is extracted and nutrients are recycled in the rainforest; almost nothing stays in the soil. This is a truly sustainable system, and barring major climate change or being cut down by humans, it can continue to run indefinitely. As an aside, this is also why clearing the rainforest for agriculture requires so much additional energy input once the forest is cleared. Considerable amounts of manmade fertilizer, the making of which is an energy-intensive process, are required to make the land suitable for modern agriculture. This lack of nutrients stored in the soil also explains the use of slash-and-burn agriculture by the native peoples of the Amazon, and by those who have colonized the Amazon basin. Burning plants rapidly concentrates nutrients in ash that then improves the soil. However, this is a very inefficient process, and most nutrients are lost as escaping gases during burning. As a result, after a year or two, the soil is depleted, at which point the people move to another patch of forest.[1]

Compare the Amazon rainforest to human systems. Many of our heating, cooling, and manufacturing systems are woefully inefficient when compared to natural systems. Large amounts of waste material are generated at every level of our society; much of this material ends up in landfills, where it sits taking up space, representing yet more wasted energy. Natural systems have had eons to evolve to their current states. We cannot wait so long, nor do we need to. We have the advantage of being able to change much more rapidly than natural systems can. Going forward, the societies or countries with the most sustainable energy systems are the ones most likely to endure. We have incentive to improve.

Let us start our discussion of energy with some basics of how we describe the movement of energy.

Thermodynamics Thermodynamics is classically defined as the study of heat flow. Thermodynamics led to improvements in the steam and internal combustion engines that helped to drive the Industrial Revolution forward. Today we generally think of thermodynamics in the wider context of energy flow, not just heat. Thermodynamics places constraints on what energy systems can and cannot do.

First Rule of Thermodynamics: Energy can neither be created nor destroyed; it can only be converted from one form into another There is a set amount of energy in the universe and you cannot make more. You cannot generate energy, for instance, you can only harness or convert energy that already exists. You can generate electricity, but this requires extracting energy from something else to cause a flow of current, which is electricity. Another way to state this law is that there are no free lunches. Energy must be extracted from a source, usually with consequences such as destruction or alteration of the energy source. There are a number of ways to state the first law, but the above version is among the most straightforward.

Second Rule of Thermodynamics: An isolated system, if not already in its state of thermodynamic equilibrium, spontaneously evolves towards it In thermodynamic equilibrium, there is no energy flow between parts of the system, because all parts of the system have exactly the same amount of energy. This rule also means that disorder tends to increase until all parts of the system are equally disordered. This rule makes more sense if we think of it in conjunction with the third rule.

Third Rule of Thermodynamics: The entropy of a perfect crystal at absolute zero is exactly equal to zero The third law also speaks to disorder, stating the only condition under which there is no disorder, implying that for other systems there must be disorder. The second and third laws together invoke the concept of entropy, which is variously described as 'disorder' or 'energy not available to do work.' According to the second law, disorder, or entropy, almost always increases in any energy transformation. This has practical applications; no energy transformation is 100 percent efficient; energy will always be lost to increase entropy. Often this lost energy is in the form of waste heat, which is diffuse energy that is difficult or impossible to capture to do useful work. So the more times you try to convert energy from one form into another, the less useful energy you have remaining.

An example of the utility of basic thermodynamics is the gas modifier scam. When automobile gas prices go up there is often an explosion of ads on the internet for gas modification systems that supposedly increase your gas mileage by 10, 20, 30 percent, or more. Often these systems also claim to never need replacing or recharging. Such claims should arouse considerable suspicion from a thermodynamic perspective. While it is possible to try to squeeze more energy out of gas combustion in an automobile engine, and carmakers have been trying to improve efficiency with limited success in various ways for decades, these systems invariably claim to modify the fuel. Consider carefully, though; if you are really modifying the fuel, then this is an energy transformation and entropy should have to increase. Furthermore the extra energy you get out of the fuel has to come from somewhere. Where is it coming from? Not the gas modifier, because that supposedly never needs replacing or recharging. Yet if it is adding energy to the system the gas modifier should get used up. Such claims fall under the umbrella of perpetual motion machines, machines that claim to need no input of energy to do work. Such machines are thermodynamically impossible.

Another way to state the three rules of thermodynamics is the poker analogy.

1st Rule: You cannot win. (You cannot take home more energy than you started with.)

2nd Rule: You cannot break even. (Entropy always increases, so you can only minimize your losses.)

3rd Rule: You have to play the game. (Entropy is positive for any temperature above absolute zero, so you lose energy whether you play or not.)

The poker analogy is pretty depressing and it makes one wonder how life is possible if you can never win in the energy game. If it keeps you from wasting money in casinos, then it is a good thing; a truism in both gambling and thermodynamics is that the house, entropy, always wins in the end. However, thermodynamics mainly talks about closed systems, where all the energy stays in a box and there is no net exchange with the outside environment. While this assumption may seem artificial, it is more applicable than you might think. Many human-engineered systems are essentially closed in a thermodynamic sense, thus the theory's utility.

Just by existing you are performing energy transformations and increasing entropy. In fact living organisms are sometimes referred to as entropy engines. We extract energy from the environment, giving off waste heat to entropy and using the rest of the captured energy to create order in our structured bodies. Evolution shapes living systems over time to be more and more efficient through competition, which results, for instance, in the rainforest example above. Human-made systems are not subject to natural evolution, but they are subject to market forces, where real markets are allowed to exist, and by public policy. We need to increase the efficiency of our human-made systems; this is the holy grail of engineered system sustainability, maximum thermodynamic efficiency. Increases in efficiency are likely to be as important as switching to truly sustainable energy sources to create a sustainable society.

The Earth itself is not a closed system. Energy from sunlight and heat from the radioactive decay of naturally occurring radioactive elements in the Earth's crust warm the Earth, and energy leaves as infrared, or heat, radiation to space. In fact it is a lowering of this output end of Earth's energy balance sheet that is behind global warming; more energy stays on Earth instead of being radiated away. As mentioned above, systems designed by humans are distinctly unnatural and we are just beginning to realize the full range of unintended consequences that we have unleashed on the Earth by changing the amount of heat that the Earth can radiate away to space by pumping greenhouse gases (GHGs) such as CO_2 into the atmosphere. The Earth will find a new thermodynamic balance; we humans, along with myriad other species, will likely not be able to live as we currently do in the climatic conditions of Earth's new equilibrium.

Types of energy There are different types of energy. A few concepts that will help our understanding of energy are: kinetic and potential energy, and energy density. Kinetic energy is the energy of moving objects and is described by the equation:

$$F= \tfrac{1}{2}M \star V^2$$

where F is the force the object can apply on striking another body, M is the mass of the body, which is equal to its weight on the Earth's surface (but weight is a product of gravity and will be different in space or on other planets), and V is the velocity of the object – that is, the speed at which it is traveling. Notice that the V term is squared, so velocity is much more important than mass. This is what makes a bullet so damaging. A bullet does not weigh much, but it is traveling at a high rate of speed, which, when squared, equals a large amount of energy released on impact. This is also what makes wind energy work. Air does not weigh much, but it can still carry a reasonable amount of energy when it starts to move.

Kinetic energy is not often directly applicable to energy systems; the exceptions are wind and hydropower. The kinetic energy of the wind can be converted into electricity or used directly to run equipment, such as an old-fashioned wind-powered grindstone for milling grains. Likewise hydropower harnesses the force of moving water.

What about water in a reservoir? Certainly it can be used to do work, but only once it is sent moving downhill under the force of gravity. How about before it starts to move? When the water is still in the reservoir it is said to have potential energy, it can be made to do work, but is not currently being used. Most energy systems rely on potential energy in one form or another. The water in the reservoir example is pretty easy to understand, but what about gasoline? It too has potential energy, but that extractable energy is locked in its very molecular structure, stored as chemical bonding patterns. When gasoline reacts with oxygen in a flame, the carbon compounds of gasoline are joined with oxygen from the air to create CO_2 and energy is released. It is the portability of compounds storing chemical potential energy that underlies much of modern life and is the one reason human societies have become dependent on fossil fuels.

Energy density An additional reason that human societies use so much oil and gas, both fossil fuels, is because of their high energy densities. Energy density is usually defined as the amount of energy stored per unit of volume; however, some people also use it to mean energy per unit of mass. This ambiguity in the definition is unfortunate. The density of a fluid has a single definition, mass per unit volume – no ambiguity there. Unfortunately you will see energy density used to mean measured as either mass or volume. For some compounds this makes little difference. Gasoline, a liquid, has a high energy density whether you measure it in volume (liters or gallons) or mass (kilograms or pounds).

For gases such as methane or hydrogen, however, it matters a lot whether you are talking about mass or volume. For instance, hydrogen is a very good transportation fuel from a mass standpoint, assuming it is a liquid, which for hydrogen is quite an assumption because it takes tremendous pressure or very low temperature to liquefy hydrogen. Hydrogen is a very bad transportation fuel from a volume standpoint, assuming it is in its normal gaseous state, which occupies a large volume. So energy density is a useful term, but we must remember to compare apples to apples and make sure that the way the term is defined for a particular comparison is consistent.

Humankind's dependence on fossil fuels makes sense from an energy density perspective. Fossil fuels have a very high energy density. While it may have been possible to develop our current standard of living without relying on the remarkable energy density of fossil fuels, development would have proceeded at a much slower pace. The thorniest technological and regulatory hurdles ahead involve weaning humanity off our addiction to the high energy density of fossil fuels. We are not likely to find alternatives to fossil fuels that have as favorable an energy density; this is partly why advances in efficiency are so vital. We will need to learn to do more with less energy input.

Electricity generation In the developed world the most ubiquitous form of energy is electric current. Electricity is useful for some of the same reasons that gasoline is useful as a transportation fuel. Electricity can be moved long distances relatively easily and it can power a wide variety of devices. However, electric current is not just found or mined, it must be made. The term 'capacity factor' is used to measure how much electricity can be produced by a particular generating source. The capacity factor is the total theoretical generating capacity, often called 'nameplate' capacity, divided by the amount of time the system is actually generating electricity, basically the percentage of time a generating station is running at full power. For instance, most nuclear stations can achieve a 90 percent capacity factor, whereas wind turbines tend to be between about 25–40 percent of full capacity because the wind is not always blowing.

In the 1830s, English physicist Michael Faraday discovered that a magnet rotating inside a copper coil would induce a flow of electric current. Today's high-speed electric-generating turbines still run on the same basic principle. The energy input in making electric current flow is rotating the magnet. Wind and water turbines harvest naturally flowing material, air or water, respectively, to turn the turbine, which makes electricity. Combustion plants burn fuel to heat water into high-pressure steam that is then used to turn the turbines.

The burning fuel in a combustion electric plant is an energy transformation. Chemical potential energy is being extracted from the fuel and used to heat water into steam, which is then used to rotate the turbine. Notice that there are really two energy transformations here. First energy is extracted from the fuel to heat the water into steam, and then energy is extracted from the steam to drive rotation of the turbine and produce electric current. Think back to our discussion of thermodynamics. Usable energy should be lost to entropy at every conversion, so electric generation plants cannot be anywhere near 100 percent efficient. In fact, their efficiency is a lot less than that. A modern coal-fired electric plant is at best about 40 percent efficient, and older ones much less.

The primary loss of efficiency in combustion plants is cooling the steam used to rotate the turbines back into liquid water. The steam must be cooled to allow it to expand upon reheating to once again generate enough pressure to drive turbine rotation. Considerable energy was required to heat the water to boiling in the first place, and taking it back to a liquid likewise requires giving up a lot of energy. The rub is that there is not a good way to capture the energy given up in turning the low-temperature steam back into water. The energy removed from the steam to condense it back into water is referred to as waste heat. When you see large masses of vapor rising from an electric power plant, you are likely seeing the water vapor released by the cooling systems that are cooling steam back into liquid water to be sent back to the boiler to be heated again. The water vapor is harmless; what is less harmless are the harder-to-see combustion by-products coming out of smaller, often higher, smokestacks near by. The combustion smokestacks are higher to release the smoke high enough above the ground to give it time to mix with normal air and become less immediately toxic.

A way to increase the efficiency of combustion electric plants is to use the waste heat from steam cooling to heat nearby buildings. This arrangement is known as combined heat and power (CHP) or co-generation (co-gen). Because the waste heat is being utilized rather than released directly into the atmosphere, the efficiency of co-gen plants can be much higher, approaching 60 percent for traditional combustion plants.

To achieve even higher efficiencies one has to move away from uncontrolled combustion to direct chemical oxidization of fuels, which can be accomplished with fuel cells. A fuel cell does not use flame to extract energy from the fuel but instead uses a series of separate chemical reactions to break the fuel down in a more controlled fashion to extract energy. This process is more efficient; some fuel cells approach 60 percent efficiency and running in a co-gen configuration may be able to achieve nearly 80 percent efficiency. The simplest fuel cells run on hydrogen. More complicated fuel cells can run on methane (natural gas) or more complex hydrocarbons, including biofuels.

Fuel cells are very scalable, meaning that they can be used to power a car or an entire town. The Achilles heels of fuel cells are the chemical catalysts that are needed to make them work. The catalysts can be expensive and have been prone to fouling or breaking down. Lastly fuel cells tend to operate at considerable temperatures, often several hundred degrees Celsius, making them non-ideal for some applications, although the waste heat can be used for co-gen applications, as noted above. For a good but somewhat technical review of solid oxide fuel cell technology, sec Wachsman and Kang (2011).

A number of companies now offer fuel cells in various configurations. Currently these fuel cells are around 45 percent efficient; better than an internal combustion engine, but not as good as a modern natural-gas-fired power plant or even a coal-fired co-gen facility. Their primary advantage is their scalability and relatively small size. Hyundai, for instance, is planning to introduce a hydrogen fuel-cell-powered car in 2014 (Lindberg 2013). Additional advances in efficiency, reliability, and lowering cost will be needed to make fuel cells more generally useful.

Comparing electricity generation sources Each of the following chapters describes how we get energy from various energy sources. In the final chapter we weigh the costs and benefits of the energy sources. In this section we describe two of the measures we will often use, called Energy Return On energy Investment (EROeI), and Levelized Cost of Electricity (LCOE).

EROeI is the amount of usable energy that is extracted from an energy resource divided by the amount of energy it takes to access the energy resource.

EROeI = Total energy extracted/Energy expended to achieve production

EROeI is a ratio. So an EROeI of 1.0 is break-even; you are just recovering the amount of energy you invested. If EROeI is above 1.0 you yield more energy than is put in and are a source of net energy to drive other processes. However, because EROeI is a ratio, as you increase in value from 1 you at first produce only a little net energy. Until you reach an EROeI of about 3 there is not much net energy available for other processes, which is the point of obtaining an energy source. This observation is often referred to as the 'net energy cliff,' to describe the rapid fall-off in net energy for EROeI values below five. So, for instance, it would be basically impossible to run a society on corn-based ethanol with an EROeI of 1.3. Even though the EROeI is above 1, there would be almost no net energy left from the production of the ethanol for other applications.

The inverse is also true. As you achieve EROeIs above 20, the actual incremental net energy yield grows progressively smaller. This means that the difference between an EROeI of 25 and 50 is only about 4 percent more net energy for the EROeI of 50. So beware of comparing large EROeIs as well. A list of a few EROeIs for various energy sources is shown in Table 1.1.

As with any complicated analysis, you have to be careful with EROeI values. Calculating EROeI requires knowing a lot about the system and defining the boundaries of the system, what to include or not include is not always

TABLE 1.1 Energy sources and their EROeIs

Energy source	EROeI
Hydropower	100
Oil (early 1900s)	100+
Coal	80
Nuclear (current)	10
Nuclear (thorium cycle)	50
Wind (onshore)	18
US domestic oil 2005	14.5
US imported oil 2005	12
Natural gas (conventional)	10
Photovoltaic	6.8
Ethanol (sugar cane)	5.0
Ethanol (corn)	1.3

Source: Murphy and Hall (2010)

agreed upon. It is also easy to cherry-pick conditions to make a point. Be careful with EROeI numbers from sources without review (websites, blogs, or popular press articles). EROeI should not be taken as the only arbiter of the appropriateness of a particular energy source. Externalities, most notably greenhouse gas emissions, environmental degradation, public health impacts, military spending to guarantee access, and pollution are not generally included in EROeI calculations.

A related way to look at the economics of energy decisions is to look at Return On Investment (ROI), which is measured in currency. For instance, in the USA it costs about $5 million to drill and hydraulic-fracture a natural gas well in shale that will produce around $8 million of natural gas over its producing lifetime. In this case the well has an ROI value of about $3 million, likely less after maintenance and cost of shipment of the natural gas through pipelines. This is why wells are being drilled; you can make money on them. This is also why drilling has backed off so much over the past few years; as natural gas prices bottomed out in the USA, it was hard to make a profit on a well with natural gas prices below $5 per thousand cubic feet of gas.

Another common measure for comparing different electricity generating systems is levelized cost. With levelized cost, or more specifically Levelized Cost of Electricity (LCOE), the output number is usually in terms of cost per kWh or MWh. The levelized cost should include all land acquisition, construction, financing, operation, maintenance, and fuel costs of a generating station over a set span of time, usually twenty, thirty, or forty years. The estimate is also modified by the assumed capacity factor. This total cost is then divided by the total average electricity output of the station over the declared time span. Some levelized costs are listed in Table 1.2.

TABLE 1.2 Levelized cost of selected energy sources

Generation type	Levelized cost in 2011 USD/MWh
Conventional coal	100.10
Coal with Carbon Capture and Sequestration (CCS)	135.50
Conventional natural gas	67.10
Natural gas with CCS	93.40
Nuclear	108.40
Wind (onshore)	86.60
Wind (offshore)	221.50
Solar PV	144.30
Solar thermal	261.50

Source: US Energy Information Administration (2013a)

Levelized cost comes in two flavors, real and marginal. Real levelized cost is what was explained above and is generally preferred by policymakers. Marginal levelized cost includes an estimate of future inflation, which raises the cost. Investment banks and others in the financial services industry often prefer marginal levelized cost. Marginal levelized cost is more justified when working in rapidly developing countries such as China and India, where inflation rates can be quite high.

As with EROeI, you have to be careful with levelized cost, as a lot is hidden behind the calculation and it is easy to modify numbers. Be careful of where your levelized cost estimate is coming from. Preferably you should be able to review the inputs to the calculation. Levelized cost will vary more than EROeI for a particular energy system in different countries as it takes into account inputs like connection to the distribution grid, fuel costs, and municipal taxes that legitimately vary from country to country. Like EROeI, levelized cost often does not account for externalities like greenhouse gas production, environmental degradation, pollution, public health impacts, or military spending.

Electricity distribution systems Electricity behaves in some interesting ways. Like water it flows and follows the path of least resistance; unlike water it does not flow under the force of gravity. Electricity can be carried through various metals, which allows it to be produced in one place and then used in another. Electric current does not involve the flow of a stream of actual electrons through a wire, but rather is the passage or propagation of an electromagnetic wave through a material. This wave interacts with the atoms of the material through which it passes. The interaction is very fast, but does take a finite amount of time. Electricity flowing through a copper wire, for instance, will be traveling at a high percentage of the speed of light, generally 95–97 percent of the speed of light in a vacuum. Thus we have the unique problem with electricity that, for most distances on Earth at any rate, there is very little time elapsed from when an electric current is generated to when it arrives at wherever it is to be used. This presents some real problems in terms of distributing electricity, discussed below.

Conductors are materials that allow an electric current to flow through them; other substances actively resist the propagation of electromagnetic waves and are called insulators. In reality all conventional conductors have some resistance to current flow, and even the best insulators allow some current to pass through them. Conductor and insulator are terms assigned to opposite ends of a spectrum of ability to pass electric current. Conventional copper wire, which is nearly ubiquitous in electric distribution systems, is a good but not perfect conductor, with a resistance sufficient to cause the loss of about 1 percent of the energy carried by the current per 100 kilometers of transmission. The energy is lost as heat from the wire. High-voltage transmission lines use an aluminum alloy instead of copper wire, but have similar losses. Transmitting electric current over large distances can result in substantial loss of energy. For instance, distance losses in the USA run to about 7 percent of total power generated (US Energy Information Administration 2012).

Amps = # of wave fronts

Measuring electricity Electric current 'flow' is measured in amperes (amps, or A). This is the number of electromagnetic wave fronts (often incorrectly expressed as electrons) passing a point per unit of time. Think of it as the amount of current flow. The ability of the electric current to do work requires another value, voltage (V), which is the potential energy difference between two points on a conductor. Think of voltage as the pressure behind the electric current. Together amperage and voltage determine how much work electric current can do. Typical electric service in US residences is 100A at 120V (this varies from country to country).

Electric power is measured in watts and watt-hours. Watts are an instantaneous measure of electric power. A 75-watt bulb, for instance, will use 75 watts of electricity over the course of one hour. We measure electric power plant output in watts. Power plants generate so much electric power that we use a unit of 1 million watts, or a megawatt (MW), to measure their output. An average-sized coal-burning power plant's output will be around 500 MW. A megawatt will power about 750–1,000 average-consumption American homes. We can put a unit of time into the measure, which makes it more useful. We measure electricity usage in kilowatt-hours (kWh), or 1,000 watt-hours. For the example of the 75-watt light bulb above, if it is on for three hours it will consume 0.225 kWh of electricity (75 x 3 = 225 divided by 1,000 to convert to kilowatt hours is 0.225 kWh). American homes use between 25 and 100 kWh of electricity per day. Time of year, swimming pools, number of appliances, central air conditioning, the amount of insulation, and electric heat will dramatically affect the amount of electricity a house consumes per day. It should be noted that Americans have among the highest per capita electricity usage in the world, owing to large houses and a plethora of electronic devices.

Types of electric current Other important terms for electrical power distribution are direct current (DC) and alternating current (AC). Direct current uses a constant voltage, whereas alternating current alternates the value of the voltage over time, oscillating between positive and negative maximum voltages. Direct current is pretty simple to understand, and was the first type of electric current generated and used in electrical distribution systems. The concept of AC was developed only a little later. You can design an electrical distribution system around either current type.

An interesting piece of history surrounds our contemporary system of large electric generating plants that mostly burn fossil fuels, and the thousands of miles of cable used to carry electric current to where it is needed. At the beginning of the twentieth century electric power was just starting to take off, even though a basic understanding of electricity had been in existence for about eighty years. Thomas Edison had developed an economical light bulb to turn electric current into light, and heating elements existed to cook or to heat a house with electricity. Edison preferred direct current produced in small plants where the waste heat could be used to heat local buildings (co-gen). Smaller electricity generating plants were also required because low-voltage DC current does not travel far from where it is generated, necessitating multiple, small generating stations.

DC power's initial rival was natural gas, a source of power for heating, cooking, and even lighting. You may recall seeing gaslights in movies set in London in the 1860s or 1870s, for instance; they were also common in the upper Midwest of the United States. However, electricity is easier to move than natural gas; gas requires underground pipelines, which are relatively expensive to build. Also, natural gas can create unpleasant odors when used for interior lighting. By the turn of the twentieth century it was clear that electricity would be the primary power source for residential and commercial lighting. However, AC current was developed at about this time and a new economic battle began.

On one side was Thomas Edison and his model of smaller distributed co-gen electric plants with a DC distribution system, and on the other side was George Westinghouse, an industrialist who envisioned centralized electricity generation at fewer large electric plants and an AC distribution grid.[2] AC and DC current can be interconverted and a distribution system can be designed around either type of current. So why did Westinghouse's AC system win out?

Westinghouse certainly had the advantage of better access to capital and an established company to push his interests forward. He also benefited from the fact that his generating stations could be sited well outside of cities, where land was cheaper and fewer people would complain of the noise and smoke, because AC current can travel farther than low-voltage DC current.

There are two take-home messages to this story. One is that in the absence of regulation these types of systems tend to grow organically and once established are hard to change. There was no central planning or government regulation that shaped the formation of the electric grid in the USA. The second is that if Edison had won out, energy usage would be different, at least in the USA. AC was developed in Europe and there was never much doubt as to which type of distribution system would become established in Europe. Edison's co-gen systems were more efficient, which would have reduced the consumption of coal, natural gas, and heating oil, and as they must be located near cities and towns there would likely have been more pressure to reduce pollution.

The electric distribution system in any given country develops over time, as was the case in the USA, and there tend to be differences in the distribution system among countries. This is, of course, why you have to be careful about plugging in a hairdryer purchased in the USA in France; the line voltage and type of AC used will be different enough to cause problems and quite possibly destroy your device. As a traveler it pays to carry a selection of small plug-in transformers to convert the local current into a form more compatible with the devices purchased in your country of origin.

The grid The system of electricity generating stations and transmission lines used to carry electricity to where it needs to go is often referred to as the grid. In the USA there are really three electrical grids: the Eastern interconnect, the Western interconnect, and the Texas interconnect (see Figure 1.1). Each regulates current flow within its boundaries. There are limited connections between the three systems, so limited power sharing is possible, especially near the borders of each interconnect, but transcontinental electricity sharing does not really occur. The grid in European Union (EU) countries is largely unified. As noted above, copper is not a perfect conductor and losses to the electrical resistance of copper wire tend to run to about 10 percent per thousand kilometers. So sending current across the USA would cause a loss of about 40 percent of the electricity just by having it go through thousands of kilometers of wire. The transmission loss problem can be partially offset by using very high-voltage DC transmission (HVDC), and a few of these lines have been built. Remember that conversion from DC to AC is pretty efficient so the lower loss of the high-voltage DC line more than offsets the efficiency cost of converting back to AC power.

The primary problem with running any one of these interconnects is that

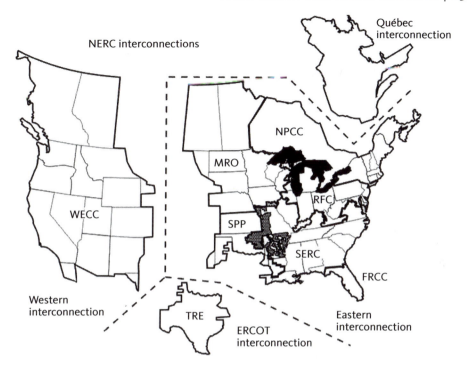

1.1 The North American power grid – interconnects in the United States and Canada (*source:* Courtesy of the North American Energy Reliability Corporation)

the grid is an on-demand system. Electricity flows through a wire at nearly the speed of light, essentially instantaneous travel from point of generation to point of usage. There is no significant storage capacity built into the grid. There is more generating capacity built into the system than is needed, with some electrical generating plants, called 'peaking plants,' running only when demand is very high. The frequent brownouts, temporary losses of power due to insufficient supply, affecting many developing nations are caused by insufficient transmission lines or generating capacity.

An electricity generation source that is able to quickly change the amount of electricity produced is referred to as dispatchable. Not all forms of electricity generation are equally dispatchable. For instance, existing nuclear plants and most older coal-fired power plants can change their levels of output electricity only slowly, much too slowly to make much difference to the grid, which cares about fractions of a second. Hydropower is often considered the most dispatchable electricity source, as it can usually rapidly increase or decrease electricity production by regulating the amount of water released from a reservoir. However, this can vary seasonally; in low water conditions a hydropower dam may be unable to increase electricity production. Natural-gas-fired turbine generators are also highly dispatchable. A related concern for maintaining grid balance is energy sources that are intermittent. An intermittent electric generating source is one that does not always produce electricity. Wind and solar power are the prototypical intermittent power sources as the sun does not always shine and the wind does not always blow, which we discuss in greater detail in Chapters 6 and 8.

Issues of energy storage We cannot store enough electricity to matter to the grid because of resistance and speed of conduction. Remember that copper is a good but imperfect conductor. Theoretically, you could build a large bundle of copper wires in a circle a mile in diameter and have electric current run around the loop of wire until needed. Practically, however, because of the speed of electromagnetic wave propagation, this would mean the electricity would run around the one-mile loop about 175,000 times a second and travel about 175,000 miles. Remember that the loss of transmitting current across North America, a distance of just 3,000–4,000 miles, would amount to a loss of 30–40 percent of the energy in the current. Thus you can see that the copper loop idea is doomed as a storage device for electric current for any realistically useful amount of time. All the energy in the current would be lost to resistance in a fraction of a second. There would actually be another problem with the copper loop idea. The energy in the current would be converted into heat by resistance in the copper wire, likely resulting in melting the wire.

Existing batteries cannot be used for storage of enough energy to matter to the grid. First, a common misconception, batteries do not store electricity. They store energy, but not as electric current. A battery stores energy as chemical potential energy that can be converted back into electricity when connected to an electric circuit. Some battery chemistries are reversible, thus enabling rechargeable batteries. Conventional solid-state batteries are great for small energy requirements because they are so portable. However, batteries have some real problems. First, because batteries are converting chemical potential energy into electric current they are subject to the rules of thermodynamics, meaning that they must lose at least some energy with each energy conversion. This makes rechargeable batteries less efficient as they must go through two conversions, charging and discharging. As a practical matter most batteries are pretty efficient at energy conversion, with a typical efficiency of at least 80 percent, so not a lot of energy is lost there.

The second problem with rechargeable batteries, and more of a concern for applications such as storing electricity for the grid or for use in electric cars, is that as solid-state batteries go through charge and discharge cycles the physical integrity of the battery slowly breaks down. This is because chemicals must move through the battery to create current flow, eroding material at one terminal and depositing it at the other. As this process goes back and forth with charge and discharge cycles the chemicals are not deposited evenly, eventually resulting in material building up and bridging both poles of the battery, destroying it. Most lithium ion batteries in cell phones and computers can sustain about a thousand charge/discharge (duty) cycles. As most people do not keep a phone or laptop for more than a few years this is not too much of a problem. For batteries large enough to provide grid support, longevity is a must as they will be quite expensive.

Expense and energy density are the last issues with batteries. Electricity provided by a lithium ion battery is about twenty times more expensive than that provided by the grid. Electricity from a lithium ion battery costs roughly $24/kW while electricity from the grid costs about $0.12/kWh in the USA. The higher cost of the electricity from the battery reflects the limited lifespan of the battery and the cost of materials and production. Lithium ion batteries also have a low energy density, about one eighth that of gasoline. A considerable mass of battery is required for something like an electric car, which, combined with concerns over the lifespan of batteries, is the main impediment to electric cars at present. The sheer mass of lithium ion battery required for grid support is completely uneconomical. There are liquid sulfur batteries that are being used in some locations for grid support, with up to about fifty MW of capacity, but these systems are quite expensive and unlikely to become cheap enough for large-scale deployment.

There is a battery technology that might work for grid support, but not electric cars. Liquid metal batteries are an interesting technology that allows batteries to be scaled up to the sizes that would be useful for grid support, possibly at a reasonable cost. As the name implies, the batteries store energy in two different liquid metals separated by an insulating material through which chemical compounds can move to carry current. As you might imagine, these batteries must be kept quite hot, typically 400–600°C (750–1,100°F). Also, as it contains liquids, the battery cannot be moved or jostled suddenly; the liquid metal sloshing around inside the battery could breach the insulator and short-circuit the battery, destroying it. The liquid nature of the metals storing the chemical potential energy has the advantage that recharging should not lead to degradation of the battery, as liquids do not have a defined structure that could breach the insulator separating the two liquid metals, as happens with solid-state batteries over time. This means that liquid metal batteries could have very long lifetimes, with a very high number of duty cycles, possibly measured in decades rather than years. For grid support you would build huge batteries, the size of large buildings, that do not need to move, so both the heating problem and the sloshing around problem are controllable. Furthermore the materials in these batteries can be quite inexpensive. Aluminum-tin liquid metal batteries are one promising combination (Kim et al. 2013). There is a start-up company producing liquid metal batteries for grid applications; the next few years will determine whether they can truly be made economical or not (LaMonica 2013).

There are two non-battery technologies for storing energy to rapidly produce electric current to support the grid during high demand that are currently in use. These are hydrogravitic and pressurized air energy storage. Hydrogravitic, or pumped, storage involves pumping water uphill when you have extra electricity and then allowing the water to flow back downhill to drive turbines and produce electricity again when needed. The system has a very rapid response time, and can generate current quickly. Unfortunately this system requires building an additional reservoir near, but at a higher point than, an existing hydropower station. The pumped storage system is used only for peaking purposes, making it quite expensive. Compressed air energy storage, as its name implies, uses compressors to pressurize air into holding tanks or underground chambers; when electricity is needed the air is released to drive turbines. Compressed air energy storage takes up less space than hydrogravitic and is more easily scalable, can be built to different sizes, but is still more expensive than building extra generating capacity, at least capacity fueled by coal or natural gas.

If we are ever going to use renewable energy sources for a significant portion, more than about 25 percent, of our electricity generation, we will have to have some economically priced method of storing energy. The simple reason is that the most abundant renewables are wind and solar, both of which are intermittent energy sources – that is, they do not produce power all the time. The sun is up for only about half the day and the wind does not always blow, even in relatively windy areas. We return to the problem of intermittency in the chapter on wind power. The other solution to intermittency is to back up the intermittent renewable source with a more conventional power source, such as nuclear to avoid CO_2 emission, or fossil-fueled, which will increase CO_2 emissions.

Knowing how electricity generation is being measured is important when it comes to intermittent sources like solar and wind. This comes back to one of the recurring science messages of this book: understand what is being measured! One can quite easily find news stories about the high percentage of electricity met in some countries, notably Denmark, Scotland, and Spain, by intermittent sources of wind and solar. The key to understanding the data is the time period associated with the percentage. It often refers to a monthly or annual percentage. In other words, it is all the electricity generated within the borders of the country over the time period divided by the total amount of electricity consumed in the period. We must remember the way electrical grids actually work. That is, they are on-demand systems constantly shifting electricity from one area to another. On any given day a sizable percentage of wind- and solar-generated electricity does not stay within the borders of the country but is likely transferred to other countries. As we will see with Denmark, discussed in Chapter 6, on other days, when wind and solar are not producing sufficient power, electricity is imported. This is the advantage of distributed renewable energy generation.

In summary, the electrical grid distributes electric current to where it is needed. The system must be able to rapidly increase production of electricity to meet rising demand. Significant storage is not currently built into the system, requiring the use of peaking plants to provide more electricity to meet periods of higher demand. Grid distribution systems can be configured in many ways; there is no one perfect configuration. Thus national electrical grids tend to evolve differently in each country over time owing to the particular histories of industrial development and governmental regulation in each country. The cost of installing the infrastructure for an electric grid is high. This is one of the reasons why it is challenging to build an electricity distribution system in developing countries. It is also important to note that developed countries face similar challenges. The grids in countries of the global North are often old and outdated. For example, although one consistently hears President Obama speak of the need for a smart grid, and some funding from the 2009 American Reinvestment and Recovery Act went towards smart grid improvements (White House 2009), there is little political will to invest in fully updating the USA's electricity infrastructure.

Policymaking

There have been many books written about policymaking and the environmental policymaking process in particular. Our purpose here is not to provide an extensive overview of the environmental policymaking process; others have done so quite well (see especially Smith 2012; Axelrod et al. 2011; and Rosenbaum 2013). We do, however, want to highlight the challenges to crafting energy policy, describe some basic policymaking instruments, and briefly explain the international and domestic factors that shape the policymaking environment. As Smith (2012: ix) points out, 'we often understand what the best short- and long-term solutions to environmental problems are, yet the task of implementing these solutions is either left undone or completed too late.' In this section of the chapter we discuss the reasons why this shortfall occurs at the international and the domestic levels.

Environmental policy and energy policy are not synonymous. Environmental policy is designed proactively or reactively to deal with environmental issues. In keeping with the systemic definition of sustainability, environmental issues are rarely solely domestic. Environmental problems cross borders, and what happens in one region can have impacts far away. Environmental policy is crafted domestically, but it also shapes and is shaped by political and environmental events in other parts of the world.

Energy policy guides how a country uses energy and from what sources it gets energy. It can be crafted proactively to achieve certain outcomes or reactively to address the already existing problematic issues. The government writes laws, issues orders, or crafts incentives and disincentives to implement and enforce the policy. Energy policy affects transportation, heating, business, households, the military, and imports and exports – in other words, all sectors of the country's economy. Political and environmental issues impact energy policy, and energy policy will also have an impact on the environment.

Climate change presents ecological, economic, political, and technological challenges. Acknowledging the challenges and changing behavior to meet those challenges are not one and the same thing. Many have noted the paradox that we are aware of the threats of climate change and other environmental issues, yet we do not change our behavior to address those challenges (Giddens 2011; Smith 2012). There are several explanations for the paradox, including uncertainty, a longer time horizon, and structural impediments. Human beings do not like to make decisions in the face of uncertainty (Marx and Weber 2012). Psychologically speaking, it is difficult for us to assess risk in the face of uncertainty (Wakker 2004; Hastie and Dawes 2010). Economically speaking, the assumptions that underlie our decision-making weaken in the face of uncertainty. Economists routinely discount the future in order to carry out a cost–benefit analysis in the present. Politically speaking, an uncertain future will influence actors' behaviors today. For example, the US Congress has intermittently offered a wind power tax credit to spur development of wind power and technology, but that discontinuity decreases the likelihood of investment in wind (Barradale, quoted in Logan and Kaplan 2008: 6).

Uncertainty increases the longer the time horizon. It is not that we are incapable of thinking about what will happen thirty or forty years in the future, but we generally consider what is happening today to be of more pressing concern than what might happen in the future. Politicians generally focus their attention on the next election, shortening the time horizon even further. Finally, it is disingenuous to lay all the blame on individuals and argue that we are not changing our behavior today in the face of information about climate change, when the industrialized world is one structured by decades and centuries of decision-making privileging fossil fuels. This is where energy policy comes in; it can decrease uncertainty, and potentially bring about structural change. An example of structural change would be investing in public transportation infrastructure, so that the option of public transportation becomes a realistic alternative to driving.

Policymaking tools Policymakers implement policy in a number of ways. One of the most common is to pass legislation. A law might mandate an outcome, or set regulations to achieve a desired outcome. In terms of energy policy, a country might mandate that a certain percentage of its energy portfolio come from a particular energy source. A common regulatory mandate is a Renewable Portfolio Standard (RPS), defining the portion of a state's energy that must come from renewable energy sources. It is sometimes called a Renewable Electricity Standard.

A country might also put in place incentives to encourage power generation from an energy source. Incentives range from subsidies such as direct payments, tax breaks, or tax credits, to some less direct benefit. A direct incentive example from the United Kingdom would be the 2010 feed-in tariff that pays communities, individuals, or businesses for the electricity they produce using small-scale low-carbon electricity generation systems (DECC and Department of Transport 2013). Feed-in tariffs require electric utilities to purchase a set amount of renewable energy at a higher-than-market price from those producing it. See the Appendix for a table of policy tools to promote renewable energy by country.

An indirect incentive example addressing the uncertainty issue is a provision in the UK's Energy Act of 2013 – the section on Electricity Market Reform calling for 'long-term contracts to provide stable and predictable incentives for companies to address low-carbon generation' (ibid.). A country can legislate disincentives, or negative incentives, as a way to change behavior, such as imposing a carbon tax on goods or services that emit CO_2. Incentives are meant to be a short-term tool to promote or protect an infant industry or to encourage investment in a particular sector. However, once they are in place they can be politically difficult to remove.

One often hears arguments that regulations are unnecessary, and that a market will achieve the most efficient outcome. US president Ronald Reagan's energy policy of the 1980s, discussed in Chapter 2 on fossil fuels, is a good example of such arguments. When it comes to energy policy, however, there are several reasons why regulations are needed. First, the most efficient outcome may not be in the national interest. A country's energy policy may be influenced by its broader foreign policy goals, which would not be taken into account by a market price. Secondly, markets fail when it comes to dealing with free goods. For example, a hydroelectric power plant generates electricity from water, which is a public good. The cost of the water, or the cost of decreased supply to downstream users, is not accounted for in the price of hydropower. Fossil-fuel-based plants pollute the air freely; there are real costs associated with air pollution, but those costs are not included in the price of electricity or fuel. Thirdly, market efficiency assumes consumers have full information and real choices available to them. As we demonstrate in Chapter 2, past energy policies structure the present, strongly weighting the viability of some choices over others.

Energy policy will have international, national, and sub-national drivers. It is not just a one-way street where the international impacts the domestic or vice versa. Since ideas cross boundaries, we should not think of the international and the domestic as discrete units with the international sphere affecting the domestic sphere. A dynamic relationship exists with lots of influences between the two.

International policy drivers International drivers of a country's policy include multilateral and bilateral agreements or treaties, intergovernmental organizations, and the exchange of ideas. Multilateral agreements are those that include several countries, who potentially become signatories to a treaty or convention. Some examples of multilateral conventions that may affect a country's energy policy are the United Nations Framework Convention on Climate Change (UNFCCC) (1994), and the resultant Kyoto Protocol (1997) and Marrakesh Accords (2001), the goals of which are to limit the impact of climate change and the release of GHGs, and the Protocol on Environmental Protection to the Antarctic Treaty (1991), which prohibits mining in Antarctica. Being a signatory to agreements such as these implies that a country will act to conform to the agreement, although non-compliance does not necessarily bring sanctions or have legal repercussions.

Bilateral agreements are between two countries, such as when Canada and the United States signed the Air Quality Agreement (1991) to reduce the amount of acid rain falling in Canada because of sulfur dioxide emissions from the United States. China and the United States recently signed the Strategy for Clean Air and Energy Cooperation between the Environmental Protection Agency of the United States of America and the State Environmental Protection Administration of the People's Republic of China (PA 2013). As with multilateral agreements, the degree to which bilateral agreements are legally binding depends on the agreement itself, but even without the threat of legal sanction, these kinds of agreements can shape a country's energy policy.

Intergovernmental organizations can also impact a country's energy policy. Two prominent examples are the Organization of the Petroleum Exporting Countries (OPEC) and the Intergovernmental Panel on Climate Change (IPCC). OPEC was formed in 1960 'to coordinate and unify the petroleum policies of its Member Countries and ensure the stabilization of oil markets in order to secure an efficient, economic and regular supply of petroleum to consumers, a steady income to producers and a fair return on capital for those investing in the petroleum industry' (OPEC 2013). Even though not all oil-producing countries are members of OPEC, OPEC's decisions impact the world oil price. In recent years reports issued by the IPCC have been influential on policy both because of the perception of veracity of the data and analysis, and the fact that mainstream media publicize a report's release, thus drawing the public's attention. Although many have noted the paradox that even in the face of scientific consensus and growing concern about climate, countries' policies are not sufficiently addressing the challenges presented by climate change. The IPCC directs reports to policymakers (IPCC 2007a, 2007b, 2014).

Current events, as well as the actions of non-governmental organizations, political parties, activists, and ideas in one country, can also impact what people in another country think, which can shape a country's energy policy.

As illustrated in several of the case studies, the 1973 oil crisis had a strong impact on oil-importing countries, and was indeed when those countries began to look to renewable energy sourses for their energy policies. Public opinion is discussed in more detail in the domestic policy driver section below.

For EU member countries, an additional policy driver is Agreements from the European Parliament. The EU is a supranational institution; it sits above member governments, and requires member states to harmonize their policies. Concerted environmental policy in Europe actually pre-dates the European Union, dating back to the establishment of the European Economic Community, which passed environmental action plans beginning in 1973 (Axelrod et al. 2011: 215). The EU case study in the biofuels chapter provides an example.

Domestic policy drivers Policymaking processes differ across political systems. Even if we compare democratic systems, we find that how policy is made and who influences and makes policy differ by country, the structure of governance and electoral systems, and political culture. Generally, a country's public policy will address a problem, or will work to achieve a recognized goal. Problems might be identified because of current events, public opinion, lawmakers' interests, or the actions of an interest group or non-governmental organization.

The USA has a federal system of government where power is shared between the central, or federal, government and state governments. In addition to the national energy policy, states and municipalities might also have energy policies. California tends to have higher environmental standards than other states, so national policy is often influenced by California's policies. At a more local level, when the USA failed to sign the Kyoto Protocol, many municipalities set policies that would meet Kyoto's targets, even in the absence of a federal mandate to do so.

We will address some of the broad differences in terms of government structure here. The following chapters provide case studies that will illustrate some of those differences in greater detail. The remainder of this section focuses on the roles that energy security, public opinion, scientific literacy, and displaced hardships associated with climate change play in energy policy formation.

Democratic versus authoritarian political systems In democratic political systems, citizens should have a voice in government. In what ways their voices are heard depends on the government's structure. In a republic like the United States, citizens have a voice through their elected representatives, and they will elect representatives from their local to the national government. Without going into too much detail, the US electoral system is set up such that the candidate who gets the most votes – that is, a plurality of the votes – wins, even if that candidate does not have a majority of the votes. The legislative branch is set up such that there are single-member districts, meaning only one person can represent the district. In practice, this has led to the norm of having two political parties – currently Democrats and Republicans. Occasionally a third-party candidate will garner support, but what tends to happen is that the aspects of their platform polling strongly will be co-opted by one of the major parties in an effort to keep its dominance.

Democracies that use a system of proportional representation with multi-member districts tend to have larger numbers of political parties. There are a number of different ways representation in proportional systems can be organized. In those systems, seats in the legislature will be allocated based on the percentage of the vote a political party receives, which generally leads to strong political parties with coherent platforms. This structural difference is one of the main reasons why Green parties have been much more successful in Europe than in the United States and Latin America.

Most democratic systems consist of three branches of government – the executive, the legislature, and the judiciary. In the USA, policies can be initiated in the executive or the legislative branch; their legality is tested in the judicial branch. They can be killed or greatly slowed down in any branch. In 1975, for example, President Gerald Ford proposed the Energy Policy and Conservation Act that for months was ignored by the US Congress. Ford addressed the American people directly, a people that had recently experienced gas rationing and shortages, and basically called out the Congress for obstructing the Act (Ford 1975a). In all democratic systems, public opinion matters to the extent that politicians care about being reelected. However, because energy policy is so closely connected to a country's energy security and national interest, the extent to which it can be shaped by grassroots efforts is limited.

In authoritarian political systems, even those that might have some kind of consultation with citizens, leaders can craft policy without concern for how it will affect their reelection bids. Leaders also do not have to be concerned with another branch of government changing, not funding, or not approving the proposed policy.

Public opinion Public opinion is an important factor in policymaking. Politicians cite public opinion polls in support of their agenda, and democratic governments are based on citizens' input. It is important to recognize that there are several limitations to public opinion and to the deliberative process whereby people form their opinions. Looking at energy policy in the USA draws attention to the fact that the public's focus on an issue can be short lived. When President Obama introduced his energy policy blueprint in 2011, he noted, '[w]e cannot keep going from shock to trance on the issue of energy security, rushing to propose action when gas prices rise, then hitting the snooze button when they fall again' (White House 2011). US energy policy usually falls into the reactive category of policymaking. James S. Fishkin identifies four limitations on public opinion and deliberation – people have low levels of information, people will give an opinion on something they know very little about, people do not often expose themselves to diverse opinions, and public opinion is vulnerable to manipulation (Fishkin 2009: 2–3). In the case of energy policy, we can add two important limitations – people are not scientifically literate enough to understand the information they do have, and climate change will likely have a greater impact on those in the South than those in industrialized countries responsible for decades and centuries of GHG emissions (displaced hardship).

In 2009, a public opinion poll conducted in nineteen countries comprising about 60 percent of the world's population found that a majority of respondents thought their country should place a higher priority on climate change (World Public Opinion 2009). Publics in both the North and South wanted their governments to place a higher priority on climate change. Climate negotiations often break along a North/South divide, usually with the USA as an outlier among the industrialized countries. The 2009 poll, and another conducted in 2011, suggests that there is more agreement among the public than among politicians about energy policies to address climate change (Patrick 2011). In the USA, the world's highest emitter of CO_2 per capita, energy policy has moved at a glacial pace to address climate change. In the 2009 World Public Opinion poll, only a little more than half of Americans polled thought that climate change should have a higher priority. Germany was the only industrialized country to score lower, but that was because the German public thinks that the government is doing enough to address climate change. In a 2013 Pew Research Center poll only 28 percent of Americans thought the government dealing with climate change should be a top priority for the year; dealing with climate change placed last in a list of twenty-one other priorities (Pew Research Center 2013a). That same year 59 percent of Canadians thought climate change should be a top priority for their government (McCarthy and Blackwell 2013). More than two-thirds of the people polled in Argentina, Bolivia, Brazil, and Chile, and more than half of those polled in El Salvador, Mexico, and Venezuela, thought that climate change is a major threat (Pew Research Center 2013b).

Debates about US energy policy demonstrate well the limitations on deliberation and public opinion. People often confuse weather – the short-term atmospheric changes – with climate – long-term atmospheric trends (NASA 2005). Detractors of alternative energy point to failed companies that received clean energy government-backed loans (Washington Post n.d.), without recognizing that it took more than eighty years to get the electric light bulb to work (Koerth-Baker 2012). Many people get their information from sources with views similar to theirs; therefore they never question their assumptions, or look at alternative evidence. Television commercials and billboards promote clean coal, as if it exists and is in widespread use. Research on climate change is presented as inconclusive or contradictory, often without consulting research by climate scientists. Partisanship also plays a large role in terms of what one thinks about climate change and what should be done to address it, and there is very little trust of differing perspectives.

Concern about climate change is not the only driver of public opinion on energy policy. Energy policy shapes the cost of transportation and heating fuel. The University of Texas at Austin's Energy Poll, conducted biannually, showed in 2012, after a year of steadily rising gasoline prices, that the public's attitudes shifted toward more concern on several energy issues (Brooks 2012). Publics around the world show high levels of concern about energy security (Council on Foreign Relations 2012).

Energy independence A country that is energy independent would be able to meet its energy needs using domestic energy sources. Calls for energy independence date back at least to the 1973 oil embargo, and are often repeated by politicians and those who lean toward isolationism. The reality of energy independence for a fossil-fuel-dependent country is unlikely in the absence of a state-owned energy sector. As we discuss in Chapter 2, oil is a global commodity. In a market-based system with a global market, there is no assurance that increased oil production in the USA, for example, would solely supply the US market.

Energy independence is often a part of energy security, discussed below. Japan, a country without fossil fuel resources, has looked to alternative energies for energy sources. Its Strategic Energy Plan, revised in 2010, seeks 70 percent energy independence, or self-sufficiency, for the country by 2030 (METI 2010). It includes plans for construction of a new coal-burning power plant, but also looks to nuclear and renewable energy sources. We discuss Japan in greater detail in Chapter 3 on nuclear energy.

A final point to consider regarding energy independence is that if countries like the USA were able to achieve energy independence, it would hugely impact geopolitics. Energy politics shape decision-making, alliances, and international relations. Energy independence would not likely mean that the USA would no longer be involved in international politics.

Energy security Energy security is the most pressing energy issue for most countries. Energy security is 'the uninterrupted availability of energy sources at an affordable price' (OECD/IEA 2013c). Seeking energy security may result in an attempt to be self-sufficient in energy production, to reduce reliance on foreign-owned energy sources, or to secure energy sources from 'friendly' countries. Increasingly, countries also look to renewable or alternative energy sources to meet energy demand. Global demand for energy is rising, and future projections show no decrease. The US Energy Information Administration projects that demand will increase by 56 percent between 2010 and 2040 (US Energy Information Administration 2013c). Much of that rise is due to increasing demand accompanying economic growth in the global South, while demand in the global North continues its upward trend.

Energy security has several facets. At the personal level, our modern notion of standard of living rests on the availability of technologies that make our lives comfortable.[3] Using many different measures, there are not enough resources for everyone on the planet to live the way most people in the industrialized world live. If everyone on Earth were to live 'as an American' does, we would quickly run out of resources to fuel that lifestyle (De Chant 2012; Princen et al. 2002). Energy security is about more than just maintaining a decadent lifestyle; it also involves maintaining basic needs: heating and cooling, health-care, education, and a healthy economy.

At the national level, energy security is tied to the economy, and to business's ability to operate and innovate. Industrialization has long been seen as the key to economic development; hence energy security is an issue for both developing and developed countries. Owing to the connection between energy usage and economic growth, energy security is viewed not only as a matter of personal comfort, but of national security. A country's energy policy can strongly influence its foreign policy, how, and with whom, it allies internationally; to this end energy policy may contradict foreign policy. The business-as-usual approach to energy issues has been to find the least expensive energy source possible that packs the biggest energy punch. For reasons that will be explained in the next chapter, fossil fuels fit the bill quite well.

Conclusion

Energy policy can play a decisive role given the environmental and other challenges we face. As illustrated in this chapter and in the case studies you will read throughout this book, energy policy can be reactive, proactive, or ad hoc. As citizens, we have important roles to play in shaping energy policy, questioning the claims of politicians and policymakers regarding energy, and advocating for better policies. In order to be able to do that, we need to understand some basic science and policy concepts. This chapter presented a great deal of information. We will draw on these concepts and refer to the terms in the following chapters.

2 | FOSSIL FUELS

Fossil fuels dominate the world energy market. In 2012 coal, oil, and natural gas comprised 87 percent of the world's energy consumption (Gonzalez and Lucky 2013), down from 91 percent in 1997.[1] Fossil fuels power the modern world. In industrialized countries they are in large part what power our vehicles and machinery, and warm and cool our buildings, homes and workplaces. In the course of a day, most of us will drink or eat from a plastic container made from fossil fuels, wear clothing such as fleece or polyester made from fossil fuels, and eat food grown with energy input from fossil fuels.

Fossil fuels' dominance can be explained in terms of science and policy. We begin this chapter by examining fossil fuels through the lens of science and why it is that they make such a great energy source. Unfortunately, all of that energy comes with the byproduct of CO_2 production, one of the GHGs responsible for climate change. In the case studies we demonstrate how policy choices shaped fossil fuel dependence, and how they continue to structure political interactions.

Carbon compounds are good energy storage molecules. CO_2 is an oxidized carbon molecule, in which there is little useful energy left. Energy from sunlight can be used to pull oxygen atoms off the carbon, storing some of the solar energy as increased potential energy in the carbon atom. This is photosynthesis; plants take in CO_2, H_2O, and solar energy and produce molecular oxygen (O_2) and carbon compounds, such as sugars (carbohydrates). Carbohydrates store chemical potential energy. Carbohydrates have many carbon-to-carbon atom linkages; each carbon atom must have four bonding, or electron-sharing, interactions with other atoms to be stable. One or two of these bonds will usually be with other carbon atoms, most of the remainder with hydrogen and oxygen atoms, with an occasional bond to other elements (nitrogen, sulfur, phosphorus, etc.). Figure 2.1 shows the structure of octane, a component of gasoline which is structurally similar to carbohydrates.

Carbohydrate molecules are then used as raw material for the wide array of other bio-molecules: proteins, amino acids, fats, etc. These bio-molecules in

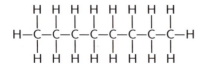

2.1 Hydrocarbon molecule, octane – each C is a carbon atom, each H is a hydrogen atom

turn were used to build the bodies of ancient plants and microorganisms. It was these plants and microorganisms which were buried, compressed, heated, and transformed over millions of years, changing their chemical structures to solid (coal), liquid (crude oil), and gaseous hydrocarbons (natural gas) – fossil fuels. When we use fossil fuels we release stored solar energy captured millions of years ago. Combustion of fossil fuels accesses the hydrocarbon's potential energy and converts the carbon atoms in it back into CO_2.

The primary attraction of fossil fuels is their high energy density, as discussed in Chapter 1. The ease of accessing material through mining or drilling also makes fossil fuels attractive, although access is getting increasingly difficult for petroleum and natural gas. Simply put, the current standard of living enjoyed by citizens of the developed world would not be possible without fossil fuels. As other countries aspire to and achieve such standards of living, the use of fossil fuels is rising and will continue to rise unless we are able to both reduce energy usage through increased efficiency and find alternative sources of energy.

There are several downsides to the use of fossil fuels. The most publicized currently is the production of CO_2, which as a GHG contributes to global warming and climate change. Just as important, though, are several other issues, including social costs and environmental degradation caused by exploration, extraction, transport, and processing of fossil fuels. Economists use the term 'externality' to refer to these costs, because they are external to, not included in, the market price of the product. However, we still pay for these other costs, for instance in taxes to support military spending to guarantee access to oil. In many cases these costs are borne by society as a whole, not by those who profit most from the product. Ecological economists argue that one should include externalities and other costs in the market price of an energy source. This is not commonly done today (but see Kammen and Pacca 2004 for an accessible explanation of assessing the full cost of energy sources).

We will discuss each of the fossil fuels in turn, starting with coal.

Coal

Coal is presently the least 'sexy' of the fossil fuels; few wars have been fought over it in the last hundred years and very few people today dream of striking it rich by finding coal in their backyard. Nevertheless, it has been, and continues to be, very important globally. Coal was the predominant fuel for the eighteenth and nineteenth centuries, for much of the Industrial Revolution, and continues to fuel nearly half of global electricity production. Coal is also the easiest of the fossil fuels to obtain and transport, and unfortunately is the dirtiest, in terms of pollution, to use.

Coal comes in three different types: anthracite, bituminous, and lignite, in decreasing order of carbon and energy density. They are differentiated by the extent of chemical modification, based on the temperature and pressure they were exposed to underground. Anthracite is the least abundant and most desirable form of coal, but most anthracite deposits are exhausted, uneconomical to mine, or physically inaccessible under towns, parks, or other protected areas. Much of the world's current coal use is met by bituminous and increasingly lignite. Use of lignite is particularly worrisome because it emits much more CO_2 than bituminous for the same energy release.

Coal is a solid material with a complex chemical make-up. Coal is formed by the compression and chemical modification of organic material by geologic burial. That is, the organic material is covered by thousands of feet of additional deposition and/or the material is moved deeper underground by faulting or folding of the Earth's surface. Coal's starting material is plant life, so coal is found in regions that were covered by extensive swamps in past geologic eras. Composed primarily of carbon and hydrogen, coal also contains significant quantities of sulfur, phosphorus, nitrogen, mercury, arsenic, and small amounts of naturally occurring radioactive elements. Of most concern, beside the carbon which is converted to CO_2 upon combustion, are sulfur, mercury, and arsenic, which are released into the atmosphere by coal burning.

Coal is extracted by mining. At first coal was mined primarily by shaft or deep mining. In traditional deep mining some rock must be left to support the mine's ceiling, so not all the coal can be removed; typically about 40 percent is left behind. In recent decades there has been a resurgence in deep mining owing to so-called 'long wall' mining, where a long line of machinery removes all the coal, letting the ceiling collapse behind it as it moves forward. In western Virginia and southern West Virginia (USA) more tons of coal are now being deep-mined by 'long wall' mining than strip-mined because it is high-quality, low-sulfur coal more than 150 meters (about 500 feet) underground.

Where coal layers or seams are closer to the ground surface, the rock above the coal, called overburden, can be removed to expose the coal in a strip or open pit mine. This type of mining has become the predominant form of coal extraction in most coal regions. In some areas, such as the Powder River basin of Wyoming in the USA and several regions in China, huge strip mines march across the land. Some have working faces that are hundreds of feet high and miles long. In West Virginia and a few other places in the USA, mountains are leveled to expose coal in a process known as 'mountain top removal' or mountain topping, where the mountain above the coal is removed and dumped in adjacent valleys. Strip mines can be reclaimed to near their original landform contour and a vegetative cover planted that will mature over a few decades. However, it will be hundreds of years before they return to mature forest and full ecological function. The long-term problem with even the best current reclamation is that the buried broken rock leaches large amounts of acid and heavy metals into the ground and surface waters for hundreds to thousands of years, so-called 'acid mine drainage.' In the USA, strict government regulation has been necessary since the 1970s to force the coal industry to properly undertake strip mine reclamation.

China, the USA, Russia, India, and Australia are currently the world's major coal producers. The largest coal consumers are China, the USA, India, and the EU. Only about 5–7 percent of coal mined in the USA is exported, although this is rising as natural gas displaces coal in domestic electricity production. It is estimated that the USA, with the world's largest coal reserves, has sufficient coal for continued extraction at the current rate for about another 250 years. China, on the other hand, may be near the peak of its coal production. Estimates range from thirty to forty years of supply at 2012 use rates. China will need to either import more coal or switch to alternative sources in the years to come; India is in a similar position. Of course, this will still entail China and India burning many billions of tons of coal with the concomitant release of vast quantities of CO_2. In fact, most of the growth in CO_2 production over the coming decades will come from China and India, not the USA and Europe, meaning that the developed world has a large stake in helping these countries find alternative sources of energy.

One of the driving factors behind coal use is its high EROeI. The EROeI of coal varies between 60 and 80, meaning the net energy yield is sixty to eighty times the energy input needed to obtain the coal. This EROeI is for coal as an energy source, irrespective of how it is used. The EROeI for uses such as electricity generation will be lower, as it must take into account the energy invested in transportation to, and the efficiency of, a coal-burning power plant. Again, EROeI does not take into consideration externalities. This is particularly problematic with an energy source as dirty as coal.

Burning converts the carbon in coal to CO_2, and also releases sulfur, mercury, arsenic, and other compounds into the air. Sulfur oxides formed in the burning process are converted to sulfuric acid in the atmosphere, which markedly increases the acidity of natural rain, called acid rain. In the USA there are currently requirements in place on coal-fired electric power plants to capture a significant amount of the emitted sulfur, which has helped to reduce acid rain in the USA. The history of reducing sulfur emissions at coal-burning power plants in the USA is a revealing cautionary tale.

Prior to the passage of the 1970 Clean Air Act and its amendments in 1977 and 1984, the coal and utility industries claimed that the Act was 'too stringent' (Congressional Digest 1985: 36). President Reagan 'noted that there is not enough scientific evidence about the effects of acid rain to justify the billions of tax dollars a control program would cost' (ibid.: 38). Interestingly, Republicans in Congress argued for a cap-and-trade system for sulfur oxides, so that the utility industry would have sufficient incentives to innovate and curb emissions, an option that ten years later they rejected for reducing CO_2 emissions. Putting scrubbers on coal-fired power plants to lower sulfur emission, according to 1974 ads placed in the *New York Times* by the American Electric Power system, was 'unreliable and impractical for a major electric utility' (7 May 1974), would create 'galloping unemployment' (26 March

1974), and 'provide part-time electricity' (9 July 1974) (cited in Baxter 2012). None of these dire predictions came true, and the Clean Air Act has been successful in reducing air pollution and curbing, although not eliminating, acid rain in the USA, as well as improving air quality and human health. It is always wise to question estimates produced by special interest groups. The US Environmental Protection Agency (EPA) determined in 2000 that regulation of mercury emission was warranted (EPA 2000), and issued national standards for mercury emission from power plants in December 2011 (EPA 2011). Arsenic emissions remain under study.

In the near term coal use is likely to decrease in the USA, but increase in China and India. The decrease in coal use in generating electricity has led to a modest drop in CO_2 emissions in the USA, which is more than offset by increases in the developing world. In the future it may be possible to capture CO_2 and other pollutants released by coal burning and store them deep underground, a process known as Carbon Capture and Sequestration (CCS). This technology has been misleadingly referred to as 'clean coal' by interest groups in the USA. However, at present the technology is not economical and has so far been deployed only at pilot-plant scale. The technology would have to improve significantly and/or the price of energy would have to increase to make CCS a reality.

A final challenge for predicting future coal use is coal conversion to liquid fuels. While coal cannot be used directly as a fuel for cars, it is a hydrocarbon material and can be converted into a liquid fuel via the Fischer-Tropsch chemical process. This conversion process is inefficient, consumes large quantities of water, and produces more CO_2 than burning straight gasoline or diesel fuels. It has only ever been used at a large scale by Nazi Germany when it was cut off from imported oil during World War II. If the price of oil were to stay above \$100 a barrel for long enough there will be pressure in the USA to build coal conversion plants. Such plants, if not built in a CCS configuration, would increase CO_2 output considerably.

Crude oil

Crude oil as it comes out of a well is a mixture of three components: liquid hydrocarbons, gaseous hydrocarbons, and salt water or brine. At the well-head the three components must be separated. The brine is placed in surface holding ponds or injected back underground. The gas is separated and often just burned or flared at the well if there is not enough to justify a pipeline. The oil, the highest-value part, is either trucked or pumped through a pipeline to a refinery. Gaseous hydrocarbons are short carbon chains that have a low boiling point and tend to be gases at room temperature. Methane (CH_4), for instance, is a primary component of natural gas, but is also produced in crude oil extraction and refining. Liquid hydrocarbons are longer carbon chains that have a higher boiling point and remain liquids at room temperature, such as octane (C_8H_{18}), a component in automobile gasoline. Very long chain hydrocarbons are solids at room temperature and are used in products such as waxes, tar, and asphalt. Crude oil itself is not particularly useful, and in fact was at first discarded as waste when obtained from early wells drilled to find lighter hydrocarbons such as naptha and natural gas. The development of refining allowed for the separation of crude oil components and conversion of one component into another, depending on what final products were needed. For example, if you want more gasoline, you would break longer carbon chains into medium-length chains in a refining process called cracking.

Crude oil is formed by heating and compressing organic matter over long periods of time, similar to the way coal is formed. Most oil deposits are thought to have originated from shallow seas where dead microorganisms that grew in the water column fell to the bottom and slowly accumulated over millions of years. Once buried by additional deposition and heated, the organic material recombined into longer molecules, creating what we know today as crude oil. Crude oil often moved from where it was created and became trapped against impermeable rock layers, creating underground 'pools' of porous rock saturated with oil under pressure. It is this pressure which creates the iconic gusher when the pool is first tapped, although not all such reservoirs are under enough pressure to create a gusher. It is also worth noting that in most oil fields standard drilling and pumping can remove only a modest percentage of the oil. Often upwards of 60–70 percent of the oil is left in the ground. More oil can be recovered by successively more energetic removal techniques, such as pumping water or CO_2 down the well under pressure to force the oil out, but this raises the cost of extracting the oil. The crude oil in porous and permeable rock that can be simply pumped out is called 'conventional oil.'

The EROeI for oil is an instructive case in declining returns. Initially oil was probably the best energy source in the world. Well-head estimates of EROeI for early oil wells (pre-1925) range from 100 to several hundred. Over time, as the easy-to-get oil was pumped out, it has taken progressively more and more energy to extract the same amount of oil, and well-head EROeI has likewise fallen. By 2005 well-head EROeI for US domestically produced oil had fallen to about 15.

Like coal, not all oil is created equal. Crude oil from different regions has different properties based on the exact mix of starting materials and the geologic evolution of the area. Light sweet crudes, which can be found in Nigeria, the North Sea, some oil fields in Saudi Arabia, and the USA, are rich in short chain hydrocarbons and low in sulfur, and are easier to refine. Heavy, sour crudes, which can be found in much of the Middle East and South America, contain a higher percentage of longer hydrocarbon chains, more sulfur, and are harder to refine into usable products.

The top global producers of oil are Russia, Saudi Arabia, the USA, and China. The top five consumers are the USA, China, Japan, and India. Even though the USA is a top producer, as the number-one consumer it uses considerably more oil than can be produced domestically. The USA imported about 40 percent of its oil in 2012 (US Energy Information Administration 2013b). US oil imports have fallen slightly since 2005 owing to the recession of 2008 and domestically produced oil from hydraulic fracturing of oil containing rock, so called 'unconventional oil.' China currently imports about half of its oil, but that will grow as demand rises rapidly. India, another populous developing country where CO_2 emissions are poised to grow dramatically in the future, imports most of its oil.

Peak oil Peak oil is a common yet misunderstood term. Peak oil refers to the tendency of the supply of any finite resource to plateau before production inevitably trends downward towards zero. This does not mean, however, that we will run out of oil anytime soon. There is still a lot of oil left to recover. What is happening is that the price of extracting a given barrel of oil is increasing and will continue to increase if we indeed have reached peak oil. Higher demand and less supply drives up prices. Supporting the idea of peak oil is the fact that no new large conventional oil fields have been found in the past twenty years. Many of the large Middle East oil fields were found and brought into production fifty years ago, and their remaining recoverable oil is dwindling. Also supporting the peak oil hypothesis is the fact that oil prices have stayed high for the last several years. Oil is a volatile commodity, subject to wild price swings, particularly when there is little excess supply to meet demand. Historically, at such times additional production would have been brought online to meet demand, but that has not happened, suggesting that there is little additional oil that can be easily put into world markets.

Here it is worth noting two terms commonly encountered in reference to measuring oil and gas deposits. 'Resource' is a term applied to a hydrocarbon or mineral deposit soon after it is discovered. Geologists have determined that at least some material exists in a particular area and make estimates as to its extent based on available evidence, and expertise. As they develop a better idea of the deposit's extent and how much can be economically recovered, new numbers are calculated and designated as 'unproven reserves.' With further exploration and when wells or mines start functioning, yet another round of estimates are made, and referred to as 'proven reserves.' Resource numbers by their very nature should be viewed with caution; large errors may be present in the estimate owing to insufficient information. Reserve values should be much more closely predictive of how much material can actually be recovered for a particular extraction price. This does not mean that reserve numbers are absolute. There is the potential for purposeful reserve value distortion, and transparency can be an issue where there are monopolies, either state or privately controlled.

Debates about when we reach(ed) peak oil rage on, but we argue it is a distraction. In the absence of alternative energy sources, there are good reasons to be concerned about the supply of oil when demand is high and so much of the way we live our lives depends on it. As Leggett (2014) argues, there are systemic risks if we continue to rely on fossil fuels, and human beings are largely ignoring those risks. We should not be misled by debates over peak oil. If we are mired with questions like when will peak oil happen, or has peak oil happened, we are asking the wrong questions, and wasting our time on finding answers that in the end do not matter. We need to reduce our usage of fossil fuels to stem climate change, not because we are running out of fossil fuels.

The structural effects of cheap oil The petroleum industry got its start in Pennsylvania in 1859. From that time through the 1950s the United States was the world's leading oil producer, and since then the USA has remained in the top three global oil producers. Today, when people think about oil cartels, they often think of the Organization of the Petroleum Exporting Countries (OPEC) and the oil crises of the 1970s. The first oil cartel pre-dates OPEC by about three decades and was controlled by European and US companies. In 1928 representatives from Royal Dutch Shell, Standard Oil (later Exxon-Mobil), and the Anglo-Persian Oil Company (later BP) met in Scotland to work out a way to share the world's oil (Sampson 1980; Al Jazeera 2013). Four other oil companies joined with them, and they became known as the Seven Sisters. The Seven Sisters controlled the world oil industry until the end of the 1960s, when the oil-producing countries demanded a greater share of oil profits, and there was a power shift from oil-consuming countries to oil-producing countries (Department of State 2011).

Oil and politics are inextricably linked.[2] Oil shapes domestic politics and policies. Oil politics played a formative role in shaping overt and covert foreign policy. The power shift described in the preceding paragraph was not a genial handing over of power. Examples include the Arabian American Oil Company's (Aramco) financing Abd al-Aziz Ibn Saud in 1930 as he approached the end of his three-decade-long fight for control of the Arabian Peninsula, which in 1932 became the Kingdom of Saudi Arabia (Mitchell 2002: 4), and the 1953 coup in Iran (National Security Archive 2000). Those two examples help to explain the USA's close relationship to Saudi Arabia and poor relationship with Iran in 2013. The USA put the Shah of Iran into power after the 1953 coup; he was overthrown in the 1979 Iranian Revolution.

Our interest for the purposes of this book is to discuss the ways in which the availability of oil, cheap because the consuming nations set the prices, influenced domestic policies and decision-making. Cheap oil shaped political, physical, and cultural structures in the USA. We will discuss some of the political effects in the Saudi Arabia case study in this chapter. One needs only look at the 1950s planning of suburbs, the number of gas/petrol stations, huge, gas-guzzling cars, the shift of stores from downtown areas to strip malls in sidewalk-less suburbia, to acknowledge that the availability and cost of oil were not a consideration in physical infrastructure and planning. In terms of cultural structures, 'the good life' came to be defined as an ever-larger home away from the city, a car, and later an SUV, in every driveway, many electric appliances, and disposable goods to make life and work easier.

Cheap oil essentially came to an end with the oil shocks of the 1970s, although fuel prices in the USA today remain cheap because gasoline is not as heavily taxed as it is in much of the rest of the world. In 1973, OPEC placed an embargo on the USA, the Netherlands, Rhodesia (Zimbabwe today), and South Africa, which materially supported Israel during the 1973 Arab–Israeli war. The 1973 price per barrel (in 2007 dollars) was $14.48.[3] By 1974, the price per barrel (in 2007 dollars) had risen to $51.88 (Earth Policy Institute 2007). There were profound political and economic effects as a result of the embargo, not all of which had to do specifically with energy policy. It was in the context of the 1973 Arab oil embargo that the USA began to form policies on energy efficiency and conservation, and created the Department of Energy. It was also in this period that many oil-importing countries turned to nuclear power to reduce reliance on imported oil. After the embargo many oil-exporting countries nationalized the foreign-owned oil companies operating in their countries. In the USA the embargo also marks the beginning of the pattern of high public attention to and demand for an energy policy that falls off when prices stabilize. The US public's attention lurches from crisis to crisis, or from price increase to price increase, instead of demanding a consistent energy policy. We seek alternative energy and more fuel-efficient cars in times of crisis or high gas prices, but when the crisis ends we return to business as usual. The short-term nature of crises will not lead to structural change; it takes a longer time horizon to reconstruct or reconstitute what defines 'normal.'

Unconventional oil and hydraulic fracturing As the price of oil increases, unconventional oil will increasingly be tapped. Conventional oil is the prototypical pressurized underground reservoir. Unconventional oil requires more effort to recover. There are four major types of unconventional oil: tight oil, deep sea oil, oil sand, and oil shale. The first three unconventional sources are economically viable today, if we ignore externalities, and the fourth one will be economic if oil prices continue to rise or if extraction technology improves.

Tight oil is trapped in the rock where it was formed and cannot move on its own. Technology has been developed to fracture the host rock to allow the tight oil a pathway to pipes leading to the Earth's surface; this is the process of hydraulic fracturing (HF), or 'fracking.' HF can be used to liberate either oil or natural gas, and often both. Hydraulic fracturing is not a new technology. HF has been used on vertical wells in the conventional oil and natural gas industries for decades. What is new is the combination of HF

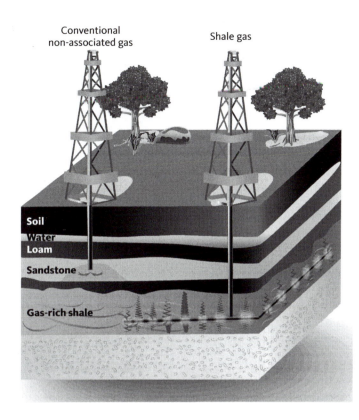

Conventional
non-associated gas

Shale gas

Soil
Water
Loam
Sandstone

Gas-rich shale

2.2 Overview of
hydraulic fracturing
(HF) (*source*: Courtesy
Shutterstock)

and horizontal drilling to allow the accessing of large volumes of host rock, making oil and natural gas sources that had not been economically viable to tap usable. This history is important in respect to the relative safety of HF. We can reference the very long history of conventional oil and natural gas drilling to get some idea of the effects and likely problems of HF as applied to these new unconventional hydrocarbon sources.

The HF technique in unconventional oil and shale gas involves drilling a single vertical well down to the host rock layer where the oil or natural gas is trapped. This single bore may then be hydraulically fractured or multiple horizontal bores can be drilled out from the primary vertical shaft in a radial pattern to access more host rock volume. Once the horizontal wells are drilled, huge pumps are brought in to push a mixture of water, chemicals, and sand down into the rock. With enough applied pressure the host rock breaks, creating small fractures that radiate out from the boreholes. The sand in the HF mixture then flows into the cracks and helps to keep them open after the pressure is released. The HF fluid is then pumped back to the surface where it can be either used again or must be safely disposed of. Oil or natural gas can then be pumped to the surface. Fluids will also continue to come to the surface along with the oil and natural gas, adding to the volume of waste material that must be safely dealt with.

The amount of water used and disposal of the large volumes of HF fluid containing a number of chemicals and salts are two of the thornier issues around HF. Horizontal drilling technology allows upwards of sixteen wells to be drilled from a single platform, accessing up to a square mile of host rock (see Figure 2.2 for an overview of HF). HF has increased the amount of oil and natural gas that can be accessed in the USA and in other countries as well. China and Russia, for instance, are likely to have significant tight oil and gas reserves, and a large potential tight oil field has recently been found in Australia (Pearlman 2013). However, recent data on the relatively rapid fall-off in production of HF wells suggests that the sometimes wild speculation about tight oil and gas production leading to US energy independence is likely overblown (Murray and Hansen 2013). There are currently no good estimates for well-head EROeI for oil from hydraulically fractured wells. The HF oil boom really only got started in the USA in 2009. However, given the extra energy invested in the fracturing process it seems unlikely that EROeI could be higher than about 10.

Hydraulic fracturing of unconventional oil deposits has faced serious opposition in some areas of the USA, and is currently banned in most of the EU. The experience with HF in the USA has so far been mostly benign. For example, only 219 of 6,466 HF wells drilled in the Marcellus shale of Pennsylvania from 2008 to March 2013 were cited for problems, a rate of 3.4 percent (Vidic et al. 2013). There have been some high-profile incidents in Pennsylvania, such as a spectacular well blowout in 2011 (Soraghan 2011) and multiple problems with HF wells around the town of Dimock in northeastern Pennsylvania (Gardner 2012). Concerns about man-made seismic activity, or induced seismicity (discussed in Chapter 7), and damage to local sources of groundwater are harder to assess. Most aquifers used for drinking water are near the Earth's surface; hydraulic fracturing usually occurs at considerable depth, often thousands of feet below surface aquifers. It is also worth pointing out that below a few hundred feet underground all groundwater is salty and as one goes deeper the water gets progressively saltier and contains more dissolved metals and even radioactive elements (salty groundwater is also called brine). So it is not only the original HF injection of water that is a problem; natural deep brines that could be released to the surface are also an issue.

In some areas there will be, and are, groundwater contamination problems, although not necessarily linked to HF. In northwestern Pennsylvania, where oil drilling got its start, there are an estimated 100,000 old oil wells whose exact locations and conditions are unknown. These old wells can serve as a conduit to deeper rock layers and pose a potential danger of releasing HF fluids to the surface in the future. There are also some areas with natural connections to deeper rock layers (Warner et al. 2012).

Degradation of surface water sources and disruption of local ecosystems are real concerns that need to be addressed through regulation of HF site placement and access road construction. Of greater concern is the disposal of spent HF fluid, which contains chemicals and salts, including radioactive elements, from deep underground. In a particularly egregious instance of special interest policymaking in the USA, the components of HF fluids were exempted from regulation and allowed as 'trade secrets' by a rider on the Energy Policy Act of 2005, often referred to as the 'Halliburton loophole' by HF detractors. Initially much of this liquid waste was sent to municipal sewer systems poorly equipped to deal with it. Currently much of the HF fluid is reused in other wells, but if well drilling slows down, as has begun owing to the drop in the price of natural gas in the USA, then reusing the fluid will be less of an option. An additional area of concern is the amount of freshwater used in HF, on average 2–5 million gallons per well, though some wells require much more.[4] Regulation is required to prevent drawing down surface water sources such as streams, negatively affecting their ecology, or drawing down groundwater resources.

Another set of concerns with HF is making sure that rapid development does not hurt the rural municipalities where most HF is occurring. HF involves considerable use of heavy trucking, often over roads not designed to handle such loads, leading to rapid road degradation. Unless local municipalities are prepared to extract additional fees from drillers, considerable damage can be done to local infrastructure. The last concern is disruption of the local social-economic structure with a large influx of workers from outside the area. Proponents of HF often tout job creation, and this is valid, but most high-paying jobs are filled by out-of-state workers who spend only a small percentage of their income in the drilling area. Local problems associated with the influx of workers from out of state include increases in petty crime, increases in cost of living, decreases in availability of housing, and magnification of local wealth disparities (Brasier et al. 2011).

The two other forms of unconventional oil that have begun to be utilized are deep sea oil and oil sands. Deep sea oil generally refers to wells drilled in more than 610 meters (2,000 feet) of water, often far from land. There are technical hurdles to bringing deep sea oil to market, but the primary impediment is simply that deep sea drilling is expensive and can be risky, as the Deepwater Horizon disaster in the Gulf of Mexico in 2010 demonstrated. Current regulation in US territorial waters for deep sea drilling has not kept up with the technical challenges and is in need of improvement. Other countries with offshore oil fields, Brazil and Norway, for example, require additional, often redundant safety features to prevent major oil spills (Gold et al. 2010).

Oil sands, also called bitumen, are basically overcooked oil mixed with sand. All of the short-length hydrocarbons are gone. The tarry goo that remains requires considerable energy and large amounts of water, with a concomitant large volume of liquid waste produced, to separate it from the sand and recover a material comparable to crude oil. Vast deposits of oil sand exist across central Canada, much of it close to the surface and easily recoverable. As a comparison, Canada's oil sands are more than equal to all the oil reserves in Saudi Arabia. Both deep sea oil and oil sands are not economical when oil is below about sixty dollars a barrel. EROeI for synthetic crude oil from oil sands has improved from about 3 in 1970 to around 5 in 2008 (Herweyer and Gupta 2008). Further improvements in the separation process are possible, so modest improvements in the future may be seen.

The USA lost the geologic lottery on oil sands, but won on oil shale. US oil shale deposits are again roughly equivalent to the amount of oil in Saudi Arabia. Oil shale is similar to oil sand, but the hydrocarbons are very long and locked up in solid rock, sometimes far below ground. The technology for extracting the oil from oil sands does not work well for oil shale. In addition, most of the US oil shale is located in the fairly arid Rocky Mountain states, where water is at a premium. Hydraulic fracturing also does not help much with oil shale; the material is too viscous to flow on its own. A number of companies are working to improve the technology for oil shale development, but it is unlikely that oil shale will be utilized on a large scale anytime soon.

Natural gas

Natural gas is related to oil formation. Areas that contain oil or natural gas are called fields or plays. In fact natural gas and oil are often recovered from the same geologic formations and are thought to develop from the same source material. Natural gas represents the shorter-chain hydrocarbons produced by the evolution of oil from organic material. Natural gas is primarily methane (CH_4) with small amounts of ethane (C_2H_8) and propane (C_3H_{12}) mixed in. It is a good fuel for cooking and heating buildings, and is the source hydrocarbon for most low-density plastics, such as polyethylene soda bottles.

Like oil, natural gas is accessed by drilling wells. Natural gas can be moved most efficiently through pipelines under pressure. Unlike oil, however, it is much more difficult to move by rail or ship. Because natural gas is a vapor at room temperature, it occupies a large volume unless chilled to a very low temperature or compressed. When chilled or compressed it is referred to as liquefied natural gas (LNG). LNG freighters ship the gas internationally, but these ships are expensive to build and maintain, to say nothing of the fact that they are basically large floating bombs. When the pressure containers are ruptured the natural gas rapidly mixes with the surrounding air, creating the conditions for a large explosion. Thus most natural gas to date has been moved only by pipeline across land and traded largely within continental boundaries. Natural gas is not a major energy import for much of the world, with the exception of Europe, owing to the difficulty of shipment across oceans.

Whereas coal is a solid and cannot be directly used as a motor vehicle fuel, natural gas can be used as a transportation fuel. However, as an unpressurized gas it occupies a large volume. To be useful as a transportation fuel, it must be pressurized. There are a number of vehicle manufacturers that offer natural-gas-powered vehicles, particularly light trucks and buses that have the space for pressure tanks. Like coal, natural gas can also be converted to a liquid transportation fuel. A natural gas conversion plant is currently planned for Port Lake Charles, Louisiana (USA), and more may be built if the price of natural gas stays low relative to gasoline (Fisher 2013). The rapid deployment of hydraulic fracturing has largely been responsible for the surge in supply of natural gas in the United States.

Hydraulic fracturing has turned a grim scenario for natural gas in the USA into an overabundance in the last decade. Natural gas from conventional sources was declining rapidly in the early 2000s, and predictions were made that by 2015 upwards of 15 percent of US natural gas would have to be brought in by LNG tanker. Several East Coast cities were looking into construction of LNG offloading terminals. Instead, the hydraulic fracturing boom caused a decline in natural gas prices from 2008 to 2012 as thousands of new wells were brought online. Now there is discussion about reviving the LNG terminals on the East Coast as LNG export centers rather than for imports. In 2012 natural gas from HF wells constituted about 60 percent of US natural gas production, HF shale gas was about 30 percent and growing (US Energy Information Administration 2013a: Figure 91). Similar scenarios are possible in other countries with significant tight oil and gas reserves.

The well-head EROeI for conventional natural gas in the USA is about 12. HF-produced natural gas should have a lower EROeI if we use the same logic as for HF oil; the extra input of energy should reduce EROeI. However, there are scenarios where HF could release dramatically more energy than it costs to undertake. Indeed, in some literature EROeI values run as high as 60 for HF natural gas, but these estimates are using production numbers that seem overly optimistic (Aucott and Melillo 2013). One real effect of HF-produced natural gas in the USA has been to shift electricity generation away from coal to natural gas since 2006. This has helped the USA to reduce total CO_2 emissions by a modest amount, a fact often touted by natural gas proponents. Methane leakage from gas wells and production facilities reduces this benefit, something that is usually not disclosed.

Case studies

China The Chinese Communist Party governs the People's Republic of China. In the 1970s, under the leadership of Deng Xiao Ping, China began a period of economic reform and opening up to the rest of the world. What followed was a period of rapid industrialization and economic growth, powered for the most part by fossil fuels. China's energy policy goals are 'giving priority to conservation, relying on domestic resources, encouraging diverse development, protecting the environment, promoting scientific and technological innovation, deepening reform, expanding international cooperation, and improving the people's livelihood' (PRC 2012). China's 2012 energy policy notes that the amount of energy it uses per unit of gross domestic product growth, or its carbon intensity, is declining, meaning China is using its energy more efficiently, but it lags far behind developed countries (ibid.).

In 2012 China used coal for 70 percent of its energy needs, burning nearly four billion tons of coal, or roughly 50 percent of all coal burned worldwide in 2012. China has the third-largest coal reserves in the world at an estimated 128 billion tons; however, with a growth rate of consumption averaging nearly 10 percent over the past decade, China must face the reality that its coal supply will last only another thirty to forty years depending on continued rate of consumption growth (US Energy Information Administration 2013d). An equally important issue is the CO_2 and other toxic emissions from burning such vast amounts of coal. Chinese cities often top lists of the cities with the world's worst air pollution.

China started importing coal in 2009 and imports have grown every year since, owing largely, it is thought, to internal problems with extraction and transportation. China has many small poorly regulated, woefully inefficient coal mines that kill thousands of workers each year (China Labor Bulletin 2013). Adding to the problem is the fact that China has been unable to build its rail network fast enough to keep up with economic growth, resulting in transport bottlenecks. In many areas of coastal China it is simply easier to import coal by ship than bring it in by rail (Tu and Johnson-Reiser 2012). Nonetheless, the rapid increase in coal imports should be a wake-up call to the Chinese leadership. The era of coal's total dominance of China's energy needs is coming to an end. China risks following the USA into the trap of becoming dependent on an imported energy source.

Considering that most of the growth in GHG emissions will come from China and India, the end of the coal era cannot come soon enough. Hopefully, seeing the approaching end of domestic coal, these two developing countries will work to more rapidly replace coal with renewable sources of energy. Indeed, China currently leads the USA in installation of wind, solar, and hydropower electricity generating capacity.

The USA Oil has shaped the USA's domestic and foreign policies. The United States first developed oil drilling and refining technology. For decades Rockefeller's Standard Oil had the monopoly on US oil production, and was one of the Seven Sisters consortium of international oil companies. More recently, the USA developed the technology behind hydraulic fracturing. For the first half of the twentieth century the USA was a net exporter of oil and petroleum products. However, by the 1960s the reality of peak US oil production arrived, and by the early 1970s the USA was importing 15 percent of its oil. Imports climbed rapidly during the 1970s to a peak of about 42 percent, despite two OPEC oil embargoes.

Every US president starting with Richard Nixon has noted the need to be less reliant on foreign oil.[5] President Richard Nixon stated in 1973, 'the capacity for self-sufficiency in energy is a great goal. It is also an essential goal, and we are going to achieve it' (Nixon 1973). President Ford, arguing for an energy bill in 1975, noted that the USA was dependent on foreign sources for 37 percent of its energy needs. His solution was to increase conservation and the development of domestic energy sources (Ford 1975b). President Jimmy Carter's energy policy focused on conservation, recognized the need for change and sacrifice, but argued that in the short and medium term the USA should 'turn to plentiful coal' to achieve the goal of reducing dependence on foreign oil and in the long term could focus on renewable sources (Carter 1977). President Reagan's energy policy plan at the start of his first term was quite short, arguing that the government's role was to make sure the Strategic Petroleum Reserve was full, but beyond that consumers could figure out how much energy they wanted and the market would take care of the rest (Reagan 1981). President George H. W. Bush's energy policy resulted in the passage of the Energy Policy Act of 1992, which was supposed to diversify energy supplies and reduce US GHG emissions (Bipartisan Policy Center 2012). President Clinton proposed to shift research and development funding from coal and nuclear to renewable and alternative fuels (ibid.). President Clinton also signed the Kyoto Protocol, but did not submit it to the Senate for ratification.

President Clinton was the last president required to present his energy program to Congress. Presidents could use that presentation or the annual State of the Union address to attempt to set the congressional agenda, but Congress does not have to act on the president's agenda. As of the time of writing, none of the proposals in President Obama's *Blueprint for a Secure Energy Future*, published in 2011 and described in greater detail in Chapter 3's US case study, has been proposed as legislation.

Oil imports peaked in 2005 at 60 percent of total oil consumption and have since trended downward to 40 percent in 2012, owing largely to lowering of demand by the 2008 recession, increases in efficiency, and increased domestic production due to hydraulic fracturing. Even at 40 percent of consumption, oil imports represent a strong drag on the economy. In 2011 the USA spent $327 billion dollars importing oil. Forecasts are for the USA to remain an oil importer for the foreseeable future.

A curious outcome of hydraulic fracturing increasing supply of both oil and natural gas has been to keep American gasoline prices high. This would seem to be counterintuitive; increasing supply of both the source of gasoline and a competing energy source would generally be thought to drive down prices. The reverse has happened, for several reasons. First, the USA has the lowest gasoline prices in the developed world, so gasoline produced here will command a higher price just about anywhere else in the developed world. Secondly, cheap natural gas has lowered the cost of refining crude oil into gasoline. Lastly, gas demand has been flat in the USA for at least four years now and many refineries are looking for a way to stay profitable. This perfect storm of conditions has led to a rapid increase in gasoline and diesel fuel exports from the USA, creating artificial scarcity and higher domestic prices. In this light, business interests pushing for the construction of the Keystone XL pipeline, which would carry Canadian oil-sands-derived oil to the Gulf coast, to reduce US gas prices is disingenuous. Increasing the amount of oil sent to the Gulf Coast, where much of US oil refining capacity is located, will not necessarily reduce US gas prices. It will likely increase exports of distillates (refined oil products such as gasoline) and increase profits for the refining companies.

The possibility of the USA becoming energy independent based solely on increases in production appears to be a pipedream, largely due to the fall in production of many hydraulically fractured wells (Murray and Hansen 2013). The 'Drill Baby Drill' mantra of some US politicians misses the geologic reality that there is not much oil left to recover in US territory, and the economic reality that in the absence of a national oil company, oil extracted from new sources would go on the world market, not to the lower-priced domestic market. The only ways for the USA to become energy independent are to increase our use of coal, a bad idea from an emissions standpoint, renewables, and/or nuclear power, and seek continued increases in efficiency. Policy mechanisms to speed up the transition away from fossil fuels such as a carbon tax or cap-and-trade system for emission of CO_2 would also help. Of course, the surest way to energy independence is not to have so much demand in the first place, which would require, among other things, investing in public transportation, and behavioral and cultural shifts.

One prominent but poorly publicized issue in the USA is the fact that consumers of oil and gasoline pay far less than the real cost that fossil fuel use entails. Particularly in the USA, consumers effectively bear only the direct cost of extraction, transportation, and processing, but none of the indirect costs for environmental degradation, release of CO_2 and climate disruption, or the cost of maintaining a military presence in oil-producing areas and along trade routes to ensure continued supply. Saudi Arabia discounts the oil it sells to the USA, ostensibly to account for transportation costs, and in return the USA maintains a military presence in the Persian Gulf, and continues its support of the Saudi monarchy (Morse and Richard 2002: 21).

Saudi Arabia Saudi Arabia is a monarchy, which has been ruled by the Saud family since 1932, after Abd al-Aziz Ibn Saud won his thirty-year fight to unify and control the Arabian Peninsula. Saudi Arabia plays an incredibly important role in the global oil economy. Venezuela proposed the idea for OPEC, but Saudi Arabia is its most powerful member. Saudi Arabia is committed to keeping the price of oil high enough to meet its revenue targets on oil exports, but not so high that high prices spur importing countries to search for alternative fuels. Domestically, the country's energy policy includes a move toward renewable energy, in part so more of its oil can be exported. It is also because all of its electricity and water desalination are powered by fossil fuels. Research and development for alternatives is centered in the King Abdullah City for Atomic and Renewable Energy, or K A CARE, the Sustainable City.[6]

Aramco was completely nationalized in 1980 (ExxonMobil 2013). The Saudi Arabian government is represented in Saudi Aramco through the Supreme Council of Petroleum Affairs, which is also the highest authority in K A CARE. In addition to oil extraction, Aramco is involved in domestic economic development and construction (Akhonbay 2012: 2). Many policymakers in the Saudi government have been affiliated with Aramco (ibid.: 2).

Saudi Arabia is the most powerful member of OPEC because of its surplus capacity, sometimes called 'swing capacity,' because it can be raised or lowered as desired. Saudi Arabia pumps more oil than it exports, although there is some concern that as domestic oil demand rises the country will have less surplus capacity. Other contributing factors are declining production in existing fields, and aging infrastructure. Addressing those issues also drives its new focus on alternative energy. As a swing producer, Saudi Arabia can add or subtract oil from the global market, thus affecting the price of oil. The country has used the surplus capacity strategically. If OPEC members exceed production quotas, as happened in the 1990s when Venezuela announced it would triple its production, Saudi Arabia's response is to increase its oil production, greatly decreasing prices, which in the 1990s brought Venezuela back to its OPEC production target (Morse and Richard 2002: 20–1).

Saudi Arabia is a classic rentier state. The term refers to states that sell a valuable commodity on the world market, where the revenues are called rents. There are economic and political implications of being a rentier state, and of having a single-commodity export-based economy. Economically, it is completely rational to concentrate an economy on a high-profit commodity. Saudi Arabia receives 80 percent of its national budget revenue from crude oil and natural gas liquids (Akhonbay 2012: 1), and in 2013 this was as high as 92 percent of the country's budget (Mahdi 2013). This has political implications, too, as we will discuss in the next paragraph. In general, a disadvantage to being a single-commodity exporter is that the country's budget is reliant on a global commodity whose price and demand are out of the control of the exporter. For example, Venezuela wanted to take advantage of higher oil prices and announced in 1996 that it would triple production, when oil was at $28.97 (in 2007 constant dollars). However, as we saw in the preceding paragraph, when it attempted to overproduce its quota and would not respond to diplomacy, Saudi Arabia brought the world oil price down to $18.23 (in 2007 constant dollars) by 1998. A wealthy country like Saudi Arabia can take a short-term hit in its income, but for countries like Venezuela, Ecuador, and other developing nations it would mean they would not have the revenue they had estimated when they built their national budgets. Historically, because of its surplus capacity, high world oil demand, and OPEC's market share, Saudi Arabia has actually had a good deal of control over the global price of oil.

Rentier states are funded by exports. In most countries, citizens' taxes fund national budgets. That sets up a responsibility on the part of the state to its citizens. If a state gets its funding from external sources, for whose interests will it be responsible? Rentier states are often undemocratic. Those in power, in this case the ruling Saud family, which granted is quite large, are those who receive the rents, and are therefore unlikely to support the idea of political change. Rentier states often buy off domestic dissent. In Saudi Arabia, the state subsidizes electricity and desalination to the tune of about $33 billion per year, and fuel subsidies are $8 billion per year (Akhonbay 2012: 3–4). Rentier states are unlikely to diversify their economies, because the profits are so high there is little incentive for investing in economic diversification.

Saudi Arabia does face some domestic dissent. A good example of a state buying off its domestic dissent is what happened after protests in Saudi Arabia during the 2011 Arab Spring. 'King Abdallah in February and March 2011 announced a series of benefits to Saudi citizens including funds to build affordable housing, salary increases for government workers, and unemployment entitlements' (Factbook 2014). It also represses dissent, especially among the minority Shia population (Matthiesen 2012: 628). In 2013 there were also protests by Saudi women, who drove their cars in defiance of the de facto ban on women driving. Saudi Arabia does not issue drivers' licenses to women (Guardian 2013).

Saudi Arabia faces several challenges in addition to domestic dissent. The importance of its role because of surplus capacity may be on the decline owing to decreasing domestic production, the increase in North American oil production, and the growth of alternative energy technologies (Akhonbay 2012: 1; Mahdi 2013). OPEC's share of the world oil market has declined. The government recognizes the need to diversify its domestic energy sources, and to train and create jobs for its educated young people. In 2012 Saudi Arabia had 28 percent unemployment among fifteen- to twenty-four-year-olds, who represent 20 percent of the population (Factbook 2014). It is a young country, demographically. Almost two-thirds of the population is working age, between sixteen and fifty-four, but foreign workers make up about 80 percent of its workforce (ibid.). Recent funding of research and university centers aims to meet those needs, but it is going to be very difficult to get off the gravy train of oil revenues.

Russia Russia is a top fossil fuel producer. It is geographically located between two big energy markets – the EU and China. Russia's energy policy seeks 'to maximize the effective use of natural energy resources and the potential of the energy sector to sustain economic growth, improve the quality of life of the population and promote strengthening of foreign economic positions of the country' (MERF 2010: 10). Russia's energy comes primarily from fossil fuels, which generate 68 percent of the country's electricity. Large-scale hydropower provides about 20 percent, with 11 percent coming from nuclear power (US Energy Information Administration 2013e). Russia is one of the world's top oil producers, alternating with Saudi Arabia. It has the world's largest reserves of natural gas and the second-largest coal reserves, although it is fifth in world coal production. Russia's energy policy calls for research on renewable energy sources, but production is minimal if one excludes hydropower. Russia receives about half of its annual budget through energy exports. While this does not make Russia a traditional rentier state, it does put it in the uncomfortable position of being quite dependent on oil and gas commodities for budgetary planning.

The Soviet Union began liberalizing its energy sector under Premier Gorbachev in 1985, and this continued after the breakup of the Soviet Union under President Yeltsin. The period of liberalization came to an end under President Putin in 2000 (Goodrich and Lanthemann 2013). Oil oligarchies that arose in the 1990s during liberalization were broken up. For President Putin, energy security and national security are intricately related. Russia's actions under President Putin, and later under President Dmitry Medvedev, centered on securing pipeline and transit points for Russian gas, even beyond Russia's borders. Prior to becoming Russia's president, Medvedev served as Gazprom's chair of the board of directors. Much of Russia's energy sector is monopolistic. The Russian government is the majority stakeholder in Gazprom, which produces 90 percent of Russia's gas (Shaffer 2009: 119; Smith Stegan 2011: 6506). The state also owns the gas pipelines.

Pipelines are required to transport natural gas. The pipelines carry natural gas, but a pipeline itself is infused with political and economic power. Which route the pipeline takes, what countries it passes through, who will get paid transit fees, who owns the tanker terminals where it will be shipped off the continent are all questions of political power. Pipeline politics exist worldwide. Keith C. Smith, former ambassador to Lithuania, uses the term 'pipeline imperialism' (Smith 2006: 5) to refer to Russia's engagement of what others have called the 'energy weapon.' Smith, who, after leaving the US State Department was a consultant to energy companies, provides this timeline of the engagement of pipeline imperialism in his testimony to a US House of Representatives subcommittee on energy:

- In 1990 Russia cut off energy supplies to the Baltic states of Lithuania,

Latvia, and Estonia, as they moved toward independence from the Soviet Union.

- In 1992 Russia again cut off supplies to Baltic states when they demanded Russia remove its military forces.
- In 1993 and 1994 Russia lowered gas supplies to Ukraine for late payments and to gain control over domestic energy infrastructure.
- Between 1998 and 2000 Russia stopped the flow of crude oil via a pipeline to Lithuania nine times to try to stop the sale of its pipeline, refinery, and port to a US-owned company.
- In 2004 Russia interrupted supply to Belarus in an attempt to take over that country's gas pipeline system.
- In 2006 and 2009 Russia cut off natural gas to Ukraine, through which the pipeline continues on to Europe, because it said Ukraine was skimming gas off.

In addition to the stick, however, Russia also uses the carrot. Former Soviet republics friendly with Russia pay lower prices for natural gas than those who look more to the West (Smith Stegan 2011: 6509–10). In December 2013 Ukraine agreed to suspend an EU association agreement and instead received an aid deal from Russia, whereby Russia bought $17 billion of Ukrainian government bonds, and cut gas prices to Ukraine by 40 percent (BBC News 2013). In this case, the carrot was not sufficient, and Ukrainian citizens protested Prime Minister Yanukovych's decision, ultimately removing him from power. Russia then annexed the Crimean Peninsula, and raised gas prices to Ukraine by 80 percent (Burmistrova and Zinets 2014).

Ukraine's new government is working closely with the EU, the USA and the International Monetary Fund to keep the country solvent. Smith Stegan (2011) argues that the 'energy weapon' concern for Europe is overblown. She argues that Russia is not always successful in its use of natural gas supply as a political weapon, measured by whether the country in question acquiesced on the policy in question (ibid.: 6511). I would argue that use of the 'energy weapon' should still be a matter for concern because energy security includes both reliable and affordable energy. Even if they did not give in to a demand, the country affected had its supply disrupted and its economy damaged.

Russia faces several challenges going forward. Domestic energy prices are 'at a fraction of world market price' (Smith 2006: 5). There is no incentive for Russians to conserve electricity, which leaves less electricity available for export, an important source of Russia's revenue. The majority of its exports currently go to Europe and Central Asia, but Russia expects the demand for hydrocarbons from Europe to decrease. Russia intends to diversify its energy exports and shift eastward to Asia, where demand is growing. Russia also wants to decrease its reliance on energy exports (MERF 2010: 22), but it is generally difficult for countries to diversify exports, especially when the revenues flow directly to the state. Those in power tend to have difficulty making decisions that will harm their self-interest.

Conclusion

It has become apparent that there are considerable unconventional oil and natural gas reserves worldwide. This raises an uncomfortable possibility for those of us who would like to see humanity weaned off fossil fuels (see Princen 2014 for an argument for a faster transition). It may well be possible to continue our fossil fuel addiction for the foreseeable future, through the end of the century. This has been made possible partly by advances in extraction technology, but paradoxically just as much by advances in energy efficiency that those who care about sustainability want to see. For instance, it has been hypothesized that when oil prices stay above $150 a barrel, renewable energy sources will be attractive enough to displace oil. It is unlikely that oil will go that high and stay there for the next several decades. Various geopolitical scenarios – war with Iran, for instance – could transiently send oil above $150 a barrel, but it is unlikely to stay there.

What may happen instead is that the price of oil will slowly rise, slowly enough to be largely offset by gains in efficiency that will essentially keep oil and natural gas competitive with other more renewable energy sources. In other words, the 'cold turkey' scenario where a rapid rise in oil prices causes economic shocks that drive a switch to renewables that some have looked for in peak oil seems unlikely to occur. A paradigm shift away from using fossil fuels will not likely happen because of that kind of crisis. Increased efficiency arguments to curb our use of fossil fuels play similar mitigating roles and just stave off the need to make changes. Rather, if we wish to avoid serious climate disruption from global warming, we will have to take the harder route of choosing nuclear power or renewables over fossil fuels. Given the economic and political clout held by the entrenched industries involved in fossil fuels, this will not be an easy road.

3 | NUCLEAR POWER

There is no source of energy more misunderstood and feared for the wrong reasons than nuclear power. People tend to have very passionate opinions for or against nuclear power, often based on assumptions, not facts. Part of the misunderstanding comes from the fact that the energy liberated in nuclear power is unlike that obtained from fossil fuels. Fossil fuels represent stored solar energy captured long ago by living organisms and involve chemical reactions not unlike those that occur in our own bodies. Nuclear energy comes from within the atom and represents a fundamentally different power source, one that hails back to before the formation of our planet and solar system. Nuclear power involves the conversion of mass into energy, a process that is disturbing to some, and is associated with technology for nuclear weapons.

There are currently 439 operating nuclear reactors in thirty-one countries worldwide (McDonald 2008). Another seventy-two reactors are under construction, five in the USA, most of the rest in China, Russia, South Korea, and India. The top nuclear-powered country is France, with a staggering 75 percent of its electricity coming from nuclear power, supplied by fifty-eight nuclear reactors (World Nuclear Association 2013a). Several smaller eastern European countries such as Hungary and Slovenia also get large proportions of their electricity from nuclear power, but this tends to be from just a few reactors. The USA has 100 operating nuclear reactors – two are in the process of decommissioning as of 2013 – and obtains about 19 percent of its electrical power from nuclear energy. China currently gets only 2.1 percent of its electricity from nuclear energy, with twenty-one operating reactors, but has twenty-eight reactors under construction (IAEA-PRIS 2014). China is committed to increasing nuclear to 6 percent of total electricity production by 2020.

China is new to large-scale nuclear power and rapidly investing in new commercial nuclear reactors. In the case of France, the UK and the USA, far more reactors will near their maximum operating lifetimes over the next fifteen years than are being built. These countries will soon have to decide whether to build new reactors to replace those approaching decommissioning, or to generate the missing electricity with other power sources. It takes four to six years to build a nuclear power station, placing a time pressure on deciding which path to take.

Nuclear energy has several benefits. It is a nearly carbon-neutral technology, because nuclear plants emit little CO_2 into the atmosphere. Building the plant and producing nuclear fuel from uranium ore do produce CO_2. New nuclear power plants, but not most older designs, can quickly increase or decrease the amount of electricity supplied to the grid, known as load following. Lastly, uranium-rich countries can use domestic fuel sources. The drawbacks of nuclear energy include the potential proliferation of nuclear weapons technology and materials, questions of what to do with spent nuclear fuel, and the dangers of potential nuclear accidents.

To make informed decisions about nuclear power we will need some background. Nuclear power is complex, and there are several building blocks that must be explained before we can get to how a nuclear power plant works. First we review basic atomic structure. We then explain how and why uranium is used to fuel nuclear power plants and how they work, give a primer on radiation and its effect on living organisms, and discuss the challenges presented by nuclear waste. After that we focus briefly on three famous nuclear accidents influencing views of nuclear power. We conclude the chapter with three case studies – France, the United States, and Japan.

Atoms

An atom is the smallest unit of chemical identity. An atom consists of three smaller subatomic particles: protons, neutrons, and electrons. Protons (positive charge) and neutrons (charge neutral) together make up the nucleus, or center, of the atom with a 'cloud' of electrons (negative charge) around it. The masses of each particle are shown below:

Neutron = 1.6749286 x 10–27 kg
Proton = 1.6726231 x 10–27 kg
Electron = 9.1093897 x 10–31 kg

All three particles are vanishingly small. Put another way, if we set the mass of a neutron equal to 1.0 then:

Neutron = 1
Proton = 0.99862349 of a neutron
Electron = 0.00054386734 of a neutron

Notice that an electron plus a proton is approximately equal to a neutron. A neutron is basically a proton that captures an electron and becomes charge neutral. This process is reversible in certain circumstances, including nuclear fission. Fission is the breaking apart of an atomic nucleus. Electrons carry a formal negative charge and spin around the nucleus in vaguely defined regions called orbitals. Orbitals are defined by energy, rather than position. Electrons can change orbitals as they gain or lose energy. Atoms can also gain or lose whole electrons. Electrons are about 1/10,000th the mass of a proton, so gaining or losing them does not appreciably affect the total mass

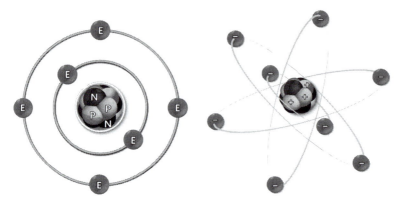

3.1 Atomic diagram of carbon (*source*: Courtesy Shutterstock)

of the atom. It is the gain, loss, or sharing of electrons between atoms which governs the discipline of chemistry.

In nuclear power we are primarily concerned with the atomic nucleus. Electrons carry little mass and matter only in terms of chemical properties; the rest of the atom, about 99 percent of it, is empty space. The number of protons in the nucleus determines the number of electrons that orbit the nucleus, one electron per proton. Thus elements are usually ranked by the number of protons they have, as seen in a periodic table. Hydrogen, the lightest element with just one proton and one neutron, is element number one; carbon, with twelve protons, is element number twelve, and so on. Figure 3.1 is a depiction of a carbon atom. Note that the subatomic particles and nucleus are not drawn to scale.

The number of protons in an element's nucleus is constant. What is less constant is the number of neutrons. Neutron number can vary because neutrons do not carry a charge and do not affect how many electrons can be held in stable orbits. However, an atom whose nucleus has more neutrons than protons is more likely to be unstable. Atoms with the same number of protons, but varying numbers of neutrons, are called isotopes. Two isotopes of the same element have almost exactly the same chemical reactivity, but different masses. Heavier isotopes of the same element do react slightly more slowly than lighter ones, known as the isotopic effect. Isotopes can be separated, with difficulty, based solely on their mass difference. The larger the mass difference, the easier it is to separate them. Uranium enrichment is possible because we can exploit the mass difference of uranium isotopes.

Radioactive atoms Not all nuclei are stable; some tend to spontaneous fission, a process known as radioactivity. Radioactivity is governed by the interplay of atomic-scale forces, but generally speaking a high neutron/proton ratio or a high atomic number can lead to nuclear instability. The stability threshold for a nucleus is eighty-two protons. Lead, element eighty-two, is the last stable element. Nuclei with more than eighty-two protons, elements heavier than lead, are unstable and all are radioactive. Elements with a lower mass than lead could be, but are not necessarily, radioactive if they have more neutrons than protons. For example, deuterium is an isotope of hydrogen with one proton and two neutrons, but is not radioactive. Tritium, a heavier isotope of hydrogen with one proton and three neutrons, is radioactive. *>82 = radioactive & unstable*

Uranium Uranium, with ninety-two protons, occupies a special place in nuclear lore because it has some special properties. There are three naturally occurring isotopes of uranium, U238 (99.3 percent abundance[1]), U235 (0.7 percent abundance), and U234 (0.0025 percent abundance). Several other uranium isotopes can also be created by neutron capture or fission of heavier elements but generally do not occur naturally. Uranium isotopes are named for their respective masses, as they all have the same ninety-two protons. Because all three naturally occurring isotopes have more than eighty-two protons their nuclei are unstable, and all three isotopes are radioactive. U238, though, is unusually stable for a nucleus with this many protons. Its nuclear fissions are so rare that if you started watching one ounce of U238 you would have to wait 4.47 billion years for the atoms in half of that ounce to fission. This is called half-life, the amount of time it takes for half of a radioisotope to decay away. Importantly, the entire atom does not go away. Rather, it loses mass by spitting out a range of subatomic particles, smaller nuclei, and/or electromagnetic energy, to become another lighter element, which itself may be radioactive and go through further fission events until a stable nucleus with no more than eighty-two protons is produced.

This type of nuclear disintegration is also the basis for radioisotopic dating. If you know the half-life and can measure the amount of isotope remaining in an object, you can figure out how long the object has been around. This scenario assumes that there is no loss of isotope through pathways other than nuclear disintegration, so the properties of the sample must be well understood. Radiocarbon dating, for instance, relies on the decay of C14, an isotope of carbon formed in the upper atmosphere by cosmic ray bombardment. The abundance of C12 is about 98.9 percent, C14's abundance is 1.1 percent, and C13's is even less. C14-carrying CO_2 molecules can be incorporated into plants by photosynthesis and we can pick them up by eating plants or other animals that eat plants. As long as you are alive you are always picking up more C14, and the amount in your body stays fairly constant. When you die acquisition of C14 stops and the radioisotope clock begins to tick. C14 has a half-life of about 5,700 years. While we can detect very small amounts of radioactivity, C14 dating is limited to about 60,000 years, a bit more than ten half-lives. Other radioisotopes can be used for dating over much longer time spans. Uranium 238 dating goes back billions of years, because the half-life of U238 is 4.47 billion years, allowing dating of ancient rocks and meteorites.

The process of fission and mass-loss for radioactive nuclei continues until a stable, non-radioactive, nucleus is created; this is called a decay chain. The most common decay chain for U235, for instance, eventually leads to lead 208 with ten other elements, all radioactive, along the way. Those ten intermediate decay elements have half-lives ranging from a few seconds to several thousand years. Remember that lead, with eighty-two protons, has the heaviest stable nuclei, so many decay series end with a lead isotope. Some decay chains end in elements lighter than lead. Note that U235's whole decay chain to lead 208 involves losing only ten protons and eighteen neutrons over ten steps, but it takes thousands of years to complete. This is the most difficult problem with both spent nuclear fuel from power plants and fallout from nuclear weapons. It can take thousands of years for radioactive elements created by atomic fission to run through their respective decay chains and become non-radioactive elements.

The ancient alchemists would be jealous of our knowledge of one element transforming into another. Alchemists struggled to turn lead and other heavy elements into gold in the Middle Ages, and during their struggles helped to found the science of chemistry. Today it is actually possible to turn lead into gold in an atom collider, but the quantities of material produced are vanishingly small and are created only with a huge, and costly, energy input. Small amounts of precious metals, mainly silver but also some platinum and other valuable elements, are actually produced by nuclear fission and decay chains in nuclear reactors, but the prospect of dealing with all the radioactive isotopes in the spent fuel has so far quelled any interest in purifying precious metals from spent reactor fuel.

U235 is less stable than U238, with a half-life of 704 million years. Note that the half-life of U238 is roughly equal to the age of the Earth, so we have lost just about half of the U238 the Earth started with, but nearly all of the U235. All of the U238 on Earth was forged in the hearts of collapsing stars and colliding neutron stars. Fission is the splitting of atoms, as described earlier; fusion is the joining of atomic nuclei, which can also release energy. The heavier the two nuclei you are joining, the lower the fusion yield until you reach iron, where the fusion yield becomes almost zero. All elements heavier than iron actually require energy input to form through fusion. There is only one natural source known for elements heavier than iron; it is worth a brief side trip to take a look at the process of stellar nucleosynthesis. We will return to fusion later in the chapter when we talk about the potential of fusion reactors.

The Big Bang 13.7 billion years ago created only the three lightest elements: hydrogen, helium, and traces of beryllium, element number three. Luckily the hydrogen and helium were not perfectly dispersed and began to aggregate into clumps that then collapsed under the force of gravity to create stars. The high gravity of a star crushes elements together to drive fusion reactions. The energy released by fusion, in turn, helps prop the star up against gravity, called stellar inflation, and produces the light we see coming from our sun and other stars. As a star ages it fuses hydrogen into heavier elements. Fusion slowly produces all the elements up to iron, element number twenty-six. Almost all of the energy a star produces comes from hydrogen fusion. Heavier element creation is incidental, but important to us, as we would not exist without them. When hydrogen runs out, large stars collapse under their mass; our sun is small enough to avoid this fate. When stars collapse tremendous amounts of energy are released. Some of the iron in the stellar core is converted to heavier elements when the star collapses. When the shock wave from the star's collapse rebounds from the center of the star, it blows apart, creating a supernova, which distributes the heavier elements into space. Uranium and other heavy elements were created in the cores of generations of stars that were born, lived, and died as supernovae. We really are all made out of stardust.

Eventually these heavy elements were incorporated into the cloud of gas and dust that would coalesce into our solar system. It is good that we have uranium and other long-lived radioisotopes on Earth, for it is the heat from ongoing radioactive decay which helps keep Earth's core molten and thus enables the formation of Earth's magnetic field, which in turn shields us from charged particles shot out of the sun that would, over time, strip away our atmosphere and oceans. This is partly why Mars is barren today; it is smaller than the Earth and its core is no longer molten enough to generate a protective magnetic field. Having some uranium around can be a good thing.

Nuclear chain reactions An intriguing aspect of uranium is that the more abundant isotopes U235 and U238 react in opposite ways when struck by a neutron. U238 can capture the neutron and convert to plutonium 239 when one neutron splits into a proton and an electron to convert the uranium (element 92) into plutonium, element 93. When a neutron collides with U235, however, its nucleus is likely to undergo fission. The fission event releases two or three more neutrons and creates one of several possible new elements. U235 to thorium 232 is common and starts the decay chain mentioned earlier that ends with lead 208. An even larger mass split creates both krypton 89 and barium 144. The neutrons released from a fission event may then collide with other nearby U235 nuclei, causing them to undergo fission as well, releasing more neutrons that can also induce fission events. This is what is known as a nuclear chain reaction.

Chain reactions can occur at different rates. If just one other U235 nucleus is split by the neutrons released from a U235 fission event, then the process is said to be a sustained or critical chain reaction; each atomic fission produces one additional fission, and so on. This is the type of nuclear chain reaction that is used in nuclear power plants, as it releases a steady amount of energy, mostly as heat. The other possibility is that more than one U235 nucleus is struck by the neutrons produced from a fission event, inducing fission in those nuclei and producing more neutrons. In this case more and more nuclei are struck and fission occurs at every step or generation of the chain reaction. This is a supercritical or exponential nuclear chain reaction and is what happens in a nuclear bomb explosion. As the neutrons travel at near the speed of light and the neutron–nuclei interactions are very fast, a large number of generations in a nuclear chain reaction can occur in a fraction of a second.

A number of factors govern which type of chain reaction occurs. The first factor is the density of packing of fissile material such as U235. The more U235 in a given volume, the more likely released neutrons will strike additional nuclei. It is worthwhile to return here to the natural abundance of uranium isotopes. U238 is the more abundant isotope at 99.3 percent abundance, so a solid block of uranium without additional processing would be 99.3 percent non-fissionable U238 and only 0.7 percent fissionable U235. Under normal circumstances it would not be possible to achieve a sustaining nuclear chain reaction with this density of U235, to say nothing of the more dangerous exponential chain reaction.

The other factor governing nuclear chain reactions is the neutrons produced in nuclear fission. Fission releases neutrons carrying varying amounts of energy at nearly the speed of light. The terminology here is confusing but has logic to it – slow neutrons have less energy than fast neutrons, although both move at nearly the same speed. Because atoms are mostly empty space the neutrons can often pass through considerable volumes of solid material without interacting with anything. This is one reason why the density of fissionable material matters. A neutron has a greater chance of hitting other fissionable nuclei if more of them are around. In addition, if you have a material around the fission site that tends to cause neutrons to bounce around and lose energy, then they are more likely to hit another U235 nucleus. These types of materials are called moderators, because they affect the probability of neutron collisions with atomic nuclei.

With the proper moderator it is possible to use natural-abundance U235 in a nuclear reactor. The most common moderator of this sort is deuterium oxide (D_2O or heavy water). Heavy water reactor technology was pioneered in Canada; the design is often referred to as CANDU. Canada and a number of other countries use heavy water reactors for nuclear power precisely because no enrichment of uranium is needed and production of weapons-grade uranium is not possible. Heavy water reactors are only marginally more expensive to build than light water (H_2O) reactors. Fuel is much cheaper, but the initial investment in D_2O increases initial construction cost. The decision to go with light water (H_2O) reactors is at least partially a political one. Pursuit of light water reactors means uranium enrichment technology is necessary, but the enrichment technology can also be used to develop nuclear weapons.

Uranium enrichment It is possible to separate U235 from U238 by exploiting the mass difference between the two isotopes. This process is called enrichment, because it is altering the natural ratio of the two isotopes of uranium in favor of U235. Low-grade enriched uranium is 3.5–5 percent U235 and is suitable for nuclear reactors. Highly enriched uranium is 75 percent or more U235. It is weapons grade for the simple reason that it can now support an exponential nuclear chain reaction. Unfortunately, given enough time the same technology that creates low-grade enriched uranium can also produce weapons-grade uranium.

Most modern enrichment utilizes centrifuges, machines that spin material at very high speeds. The uranium is converted into a hexafluoride gas and fed into the centrifuges, where, because it is slightly heavier, U238 tends to move toward the outer edge of the centrifuge. Material can be transferred from the center of one centrifuge to another centrifuge to slowly increase the enrichment of U235. Centrifuges can be made small enough these days to fit several hundred of them in a modest-sized warehouse, making the technology relatively easy to conceal. This dual use of enrichment technology is at the heart of the conflict over Iran's nuclear program. Iran claims that it wants only a civilian nuclear program to produce electricity, thus has been developing technology for uranium enrichment, which could also be used for nuclear weapons development. It should be noted that Iran has substantial uranium reserves so wanting to utilize them is understandable.

To this point we have mainly discussed how radioactive atoms disintegrate and factors that govern their fission rate. We have not looked too closely at what leaves the fission site. Some fission events produce neutrons, most notably U235 and plutonium 239; other possible products are gamma rays, positrons (antimatter electrons with a positive charge) and even whole nuclei. Ejection of a helium nucleus (two protons and two neutrons) is common enough to have its own term, alpha radiation. However, if you go back and add up all the mass of particles coming out of a fission event and compare it to the starting mass you notice that some mass has been lost. This is usually a small percentage, 1–2 percent or less of the total starting mass. The lost mass was converted into electromagnetic energy of various wavelengths. You can calculate the energy conversion using Einstein's famous equation:

$$E = Mc^2$$

where E is energy, M is the mass converted into energy, and c is the speed of light (about 300 million meters per second or 187,000 miles per second), squared. The energy result is a factor of 349,600,000,000 or about 350 trillion.

Einstein's equation tells us that even small amounts of mass convert into huge amounts of energy. This is the allure of nuclear power. A single fuel pellet in a nuclear reactor weighs about 7 grams, less than one ounce, but can release the energy equivalent to that stored in 1,700 pounds of coal or 150 gallons of oil (Nuclear Energy Institute 2013). If all that energy is released at once in an exponential nuclear chain reaction, then you have a thermonuclear explosion and a horribly destructive weapon.

As you may already have surmised, highly enriched U235 can support an exponential nuclear chain reaction and be used for nuclear weapons. About 440 pounds of U235 must be brought together to support an exponential chain reaction. This amount of material is called the critical mass. However, it is possible to reflect some of the neutrons emitted by fission back on the U235, thereby reducing the critical mass needed to around fifty pounds. During World War II, Germany largely gave up on nuclear weapons because German scientists failed to see, or purposely failed to follow, the neutron reflection idea and determined that 440 pounds of U235 was too much to enrich with the technology available in a reasonable amount of time.

Plutonium 239 is also fissionable, and with neutron reflection has an even smaller critical mass of about thirteen pounds. However, there is no significant natural source for plutonium 239. It is formed by neutron capture from U238, but is a rare event. While neutron capture can and does happen in natural uranium ores, the half-life of plutonium 239 (24,000 years) is too short for it to accumulate in nature. Instead plutonium is purified from spent nuclear reactor fuel. Remember that we said that for light water reactors low-grade enriched uranium is used at about 3.5–5 percent U235. The remaining 95–96.5 percent is U238 and is available to capture neutrons, some of which will be transformed into plutonium.[2]

Light water → 3.5-5% U235
heavy water → 3-5% U235
heavy water 0.7%

Nuclear fission reactors

First and foremost it should be evident by this point that a conventional nuclear power plant cannot produce an exponential nuclear chain reaction and thermonuclear explosion. Most nuclear power plants use 3.5–5 percent U235 in their fuel, which cannot support an exponential chain reaction; it simply is not possible. Steam and hydrogen explosions, which can damage containment structures and potentially allow radioactive material to escape into the surrounding area, are possible, but a truly devastating thermonuclear explosion is not. This is not to say that there are not concerns and dangers associated with conventional nuclear power, but thermonuclear explosions are not one of them.

At first glance a nuclear-powered electricity generating station looks similar to a fossil-fuel-powered station. Both use an energy source to heat water to steam, which drives turbines that produce electric current. Both stations must cool the steam back into liquid water to start the processes again. The primary difference is in where the waste goes. For a fossil fuel plant, combustion products go up the smokestack, hopefully with some attempt to capture the worst pollutants, to be released into the surrounding air. In a nuclear power station the idea is to keep all the fission products and radioactivity inside a containment structure in the plant, and nothing but water vapor from the cooling system is released. The spent fuel is then the major problem, as it will remain radioactive for many thousands of years; we will come back to the thorny issue of spent fuel in a bit.   *Problem of spent fuel*

In the most common current nuclear power plant design, the pressurized water reactor (PWR), the water used to cool and moderate the reactor core does not leave the containment structure, nor does it come into direct contact with the water heated to drive the turbines. A series of steel pipes carries the reactor vessel water into a heat exchanger, where water from outside the reactor is heated to steam. This design helps keep the radioactivity inside the containment structure.   *PWR → Water doesn't leave containment*

Boiling water reactors (BWR) are an alternate reactor design, using steam directly from the reactor to drive turbines without using a heat exchanger. Once used in older reactors, the concept returned in some new designs because it allowed for easier changing of a reactor's power output to load-follow the demand for electricity. Not using a heat exchanger works as long as the fuel pellets are intact, as most radioisotopes created directly in water by neutron bombardment, primarily nitrogen-16, are short lived, with a half-life of seven seconds, and do not accumulate. Where BWR designs have problems is in the case of accidents. A containment breach is harder to avoid because of the large mass of water-carrying piping, which can become contaminated by radioisotopes from damaged fuel pellets.   *BWR → Steam from reactor to drive turbine*

The reactor core sits inside a sealed metal structure called a pressure vessel, which in most reactor designs itself sits inside a reinforced concrete outer containment structure. Inside the reactor core are long metal tubes that hold the uranium fuel pellets, called fuel rods, and a second type of metal tube filled with a neutron-absorbing material, called control rods. The water surrounding the fuel and control rods serves to moderate or slow down neutrons released in fission events so they are more likely to collide with another U235 nucleus before escaping the reactor. The water in the reactor core also serves to carry heat away from the core to cool it and generate electricity.

The purpose of the control rods is to regulate the number of neutrons available to produce additional nuclear fissions. When a reactor is shut down, the control rods are dropped into the core and the sustained nuclear chain reaction is short-circuited in less than a second. As most neutrons are absorbed, there are not sufficient free neutrons to cause additional U235 fission events. However, this does not mean the reactor is not still producing heat. Remember that each U235 fission can start a decay chain that produces additional radioactive material. Neutron capture by U238 also produces plutonium, which is radioactive. These radioactive elements accumulate while the reactor is running and are not affected by the control rods; their fissions are not governed primarily by neutron collision but instead by their own instability.

Thus dropping the control rods into a reactor core is not the end of the story. The circulation pumps need power to move cooling water through the reactor for at least several days after the control rods are dropped in to avoid dangerous overheating. A reactor pressure vessel is basically a giant pressure cooker. If you leave a pressure cooker heating on a stove too long without venting off steam, it will eventually build up enough pressure to rupture the metal wall of the cooker. The same thing will happen to a nuclear reactor that loses power immediately after shutdown.

Once the control rods are inserted into the reactor core the reactor is not generating enough heat to produce electricity. The amount of heat released by radioactive decay falls off fairly rapidly because many of the isotopes involved have short half-lives. Still, the heat represents a few percent of full power operation for the first several days after reactor shutdown. This is sufficient heat to cause a steam explosion that can rupture the reactor vessel, produce hydrogen that is explosive when mixed with oxygen in the air, and melt the fuel pellets. Melting of the fuel pellets, a meltdown, releases considerable amounts of radioisotopes into the reactor core water, which if it escapes the pressure vessel can produce significant contamination of surrounding areas. It was a failure to cool shutdown reactor cores that led to the 2011 Fukushima Daiichi nuclear disaster in Japan, which we will return to in the 'Nuclear disasters' section of the chapter.

Once the amount of U235 in the fuel pellets falls below about 0.5 percent it becomes difficult to control a sustained nuclear chain reaction and the fuel must be replaced. As already mentioned, however, the fuel cannot simply be dumped somewhere, as it will remain dangerous for thousands of years. It is first kept in pools of water referred to as cooling ponds for at least three years. In a cooling pond the spent fuel rods are submerged in sufficient water to absorb the heat generated by radioisotope decay. The pool water is generally not physically contaminated; radiation comes not from radioisotopes dissolved in the water, but rather directly from the decaying isotopes in the spent fuel carried by energetic photons that heat the water. After at least three years, most of the short-lived radioactive isotopes have decayed away and the spent fuel no longer poses a melt danger. Current protocols in the USA call for transfer after ten years from cooling ponds to large metal casks for indefinite onsite dry storage. The USA lacks a long-term repository for spent fuel, as discussed in the case study at the end of the chapter. The longer-lived radio-isotopes in the spent fuel will remain a problem for many thousands of years.

Radiation and nuclear waste To discuss the future of nuclear power we need to address spent nuclear fuel and nuclear safety issues. To adequately address those issues, we first need to tackle radiation and its effects on living creatures.

Radiation carries energy though space. Sunlight is radiation; the light coming out of your household lamp is radiation. Radiation comes in a dizzying array of types, only some of which are harmful. What is frightening to many people is that radiation is invisible and not easily detected without the proper equipment. You cannot see radiation traveling through the air, and while its effects, such as sunburns caused by the sun's UV radiation, are sometimes visible, other radiation effects such as cancer may not be seen for many years after exposure. Fear of the unknown is one of the stronger instinctive fears in humans. It is natural to be afraid of radiation until you understand how it works, how it can be detected, and how to manage exposure.

What we need to keep in mind with radiation is how much energy the particular type of radiation carries. Sunlight is only modestly harmful because UV rays do not carry a large amount of energy, and some UV exposure is actually necessary to produce vitamin D in the skin. On the other hand, gamma rays carry a large amount of energy and are always damaging if they strike molecules in your body. Unfortunately, different radioactive isotopes produce different types of radiation when they fission, so a mixture of radioisotopes will produce a witch's brew of different types of radiation. It would be unnecessarily confusing to address all the different radiation types, so we will stick to aggregate measures and radiation's effects on living organisms.

Measuring radiation exposure Radiation can be measured as either the amount of energy released into space, the amount of energy that hits an object or person (exposure), the amount of energy actually absorbed (dose), or as the biological effect of that dose on a living organism (effective dose). Unfortunately, the different types of radiation measurements are not directly comparable. This is because atoms are mostly empty space, so some energy from radiation will simply pass right through your body without hitting anything. The radiation-measuring units are listed in Table 3.1. We list two measures for each category – one metric (SI) and one imperial system unit (still used in the USA).

TABLE 3.1 Measuring radiation

Measurement	SI unit	Abbreviation	Imperial unit	Abbreviation
Total energy released	Bequerels	Bq	Curie	Ci
Radiation exposure	Coulombs/kilogram	C/kg	Roentgen	R
Absorbed dose	Gray	Gy	Radiation absorbed dose	Rad
Dose equivalent (biological effect)	Sievert	Sv	Roentgen equivalent man	Rem

Becquerels (Bq) and curies (Ci) measure the total amount of energy released by radioisotope decay. Radiation traveling through air, often called radiation exposure, is usually measured in coulomb/kilogram (C/kg) or Roentgen (R).

The amount of radiation that actually hits atoms in your body, as opposed to harmlessly passing through, is called the absorbed dose and is measured in Grays (Gy) or radiation absorbed dose (rad). However, even if the radiation hits an atom in your body, it does not necessarily mean that there will be a negative consequence. The biological effects of absorbed doses, called dose equivalents or effective dose, are measured in Sievert (Sv) or Roentgen equivalent man (rem) units (US Nuclear Regulatory Commission 2013a). We will try to keep radiation measures in effective doses, Sv or rem. For reference a Sievert is equal to 100 rem.

As you can see from the list above, which measurement of radiation is used matters a lot, so be aware when you see two different types of measurement being used to compare effects. Listing huge numbers in becquerels is easy to do, but not very helpful in figuring out the health risk of that radiation. It should also be noted that effective dose, rem or Sievert, is calibrated to radiation damage effects in humans and may not be accurate for other organisms; some bacteria, for instance, are amazingly radiation resistant.

Radiation sources and effects Depending on location, the average yearly radiation dose from natural sources for most people living at sea level is about 1–3 milliSieverts, mSv, thousandths of a Sievert, or 100–300 millirem (mrem). Nearby naturally occurring uranium-bearing rocks will have a substantial effect on radiation exposure. This is called background radiation and is largely unavoidable; you can move somewhere with lower background radiation but cannot completely avoid radiation exposure. The US Nuclear Regulatory Commission (NRC) has a nice calculator for figuring out your yearly background radiation dose.[3] One interesting tidbit the calculator shows is that owing to naturally occurring radioisotopes in coal, coal-burning power plants actually release more radiation than nuclear power plants. *Release*, not *contain* – there is far more radioactivity in the nuclear reactor's fuel than is released by a coal-fired power plant.

Another natural source of radiation is cosmic rays produced by supernovae and other energetic cosmic events, where exposure depends on elevation. The higher the elevation, the thinner the Earth's atmosphere and the less shielding it supplies. Elevation is also why the amount of air travel matters for radiation exposure. Most long-distance flights travel at altitudes above 30,000 feet, above most of the atmosphere. Radon gas produced by radioisotope decay in rock formations is also a significant background radiation source and varies depending on the geology of the area. In some areas radon gas seeping up into a house from beneath can provide radiation exposure whose negative health equivalent is smoking a pack of cigarettes a day. For most of the USA, local county governments can tell you whether you live in a radon risk zone. Remediation for radon in buildings is fairly simple; extra ventilation can be installed in a basement to vent the radon and prevent it from building up in the house.

For most people medical procedures are the primary non-natural sources of radiation exposure. For point of reference, a chest X-ray involves about 0.1 mSv (10 mrem), depending on the machine used, whereas a dental X-ray involves only about 0.05 mSv. A whole-body CAT, CT, or PET scan, however, ranges from 6 to 20 mSv, owing to the need for multiple X-rays to build a composite image. A person should limit their number of CT scans. It is worth keeping in mind that CT scans and MRI scans use radically different technology; MRI systems do not produce significant radiation exposure.

The biological effects of absorbed radiation doses depend on the magnitude of the dose. At high dosages, several thousand mSv or several hundred rem, proteins and DNA within cells suffer enough immediate molecular damage that cellular function is impaired or blocked, leading to cell death. If enough cells die, eventually organ failure and death of the affected individual follow, usually within a few weeks of exposure. Cellular damage of this magnitude is not treatable; medical support can be provided to alleviate pain but death cannot be avoided. This type of response is referred to as acute radiation poisoning. These high doses are, thankfully, rare and usually only seen in people at the site of a severe reactor incident, people who survive the immediate effects of an atomic bomb, i.e. the shock wave and heat flash, and severe accidents in nuclear weapons production plants.

Some radioisotopes have been used as assassination weapons. Radioactive polonium 210 was used on former Russian security services agent Alexander Litvinenko in Great Britain in 2006 to lethal effect (Jordan and Finn 2006). The polonium 210 was given to Litvinenko in a cup of tea; he died three weeks later. Polonium 210 makes a good weapon, as it is tasteless and difficult to detect. It emits only alpha radiation, which is not detected by a Geiger counter, the standard radiation detection instrument. It can be produced only in a nuclear reactor or particle accelerator owing to its short half-life, 138 days, meaning polonium 210 is hard to obtain.

At moderate radiation doses, between about 100 and 1,000 mSv, there is evidence for a roughly linear (i.e. 1:1) relationship between increasing radiation dose and increasing lifetime cancer risk. In this case cellular damage is not sufficient to cause cell death, but the DNA in a person's cells may be damaged, leading to mutation and increased future cancer risk. This data comes mostly from studies on the atomic bomb survivors from Japan.

The effect of lower-dose radiation exposure, below 100 mSv (10 rem), is much harder to quantify. There is no directly observable biological effect at this level of irradiation. Lifetime cancer risk may increase, but for low doses it is not possible to disentangle cancers caused by radiation exposure from other sources of cancer risk. Anything that modifies the DNA sequence of certain genes will increase cancer risk, including inherited mutations and environmental exposure to chemical mutagens. Thyroid cancer is the only cancer with a good link back to radioisotope exposure. Nuclear fission produces radioactive iodine and when ingested in food or water it concentrates in the thyroid gland, greatly magnifying potential damage to that gland and increasing thyroid cancer risk. For other types of cancer the actual cause of a particular cancer cannot usually be determined.

The conservative approach to radiation doses under 100 mSv is to assume that the roughly linear relationship seen at higher doses continues down to zero exposure. This is called the linear no-threshold (LNT) model of cancer risk from radiation exposure, and is the basis for current public risk assessment in radiation exposure in most countries. The LNT model has its detractors; cells have mechanisms to repair DNA damage and it is not unreasonable that low doses of radiation exposure can be tolerated without inducing mutation. Indeed, DNA mutation is a fact of life; copying DNA for cell replication and even basic metabolism can lead to mutation, so cells have to be able to repair some DNA damage. The idea that low doses of radiation, below about 50 mSv, have no permanent biological effect is referred to as the threshold model. In this model, exposure to radiation doses below 50 mSv results in no long-term cancer risk increase.

Still others think that low doses of radiation might even be beneficial, called the hormesis model. This model draws on the observation that precancerous cells, cells with some mutations that have not yet become fully cancerous, are generally less healthy than cells with no mutations and so may be more susceptible to killing by radiation than are healthy cells. The hormesis model is more speculative than either the LNT or threshold models, but is not biologically implausible. There is no conclusive evidence for or directly against any of the three models, summarized in Figure 3.2. What evidence exists seems to support a compromise between the threshold and no-threshold models, where radiation doses below 100 mSv produce a less than 1:1 increase in lifetime cancer risk.

International groups and many national governments, including that of the USA, generally use the LNT to define the amount of allowable non-natural radiation that a person should be exposed to as no more than an additional 1.0 mSv (100 mrem) per year above natural background. This is quite a low dose of radiation if you think back to our discussion above about the biological effects of radiation, where less than 100 mSv has no immediately measurable effect on a person. This is considered justified by the assumption of the LNT that *any* radiation exposure, no matter how small, increases future health risk.

Why does it matter which model of radiation dose effect is correct? Let us take as an example the recent 2011 Fukushima Daiichi nuclear accident. During the emergency a 20-kilometer (12-mile) swath of land around and downwind of the plant was evacuated, forcing about 156,000 people to relocate. Estimated total radiation doses more than two kilometers (1.2 miles) from the

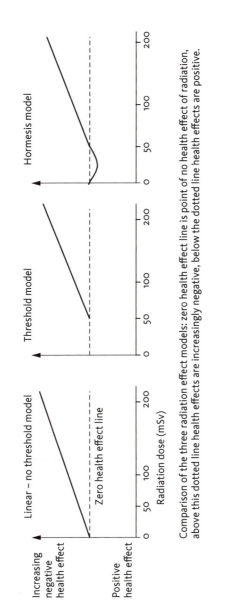

Comparison of the three radiation effect models: zero health effect line is point of no health effect of radiation, above this dotted line health effects are increasingly negative, below the dotted line health effects are positive.

3.2 Radiation effect models

plant varied but ranged from less than 5 µSv/hour (micro Sievert, equal to 0.005 mSv/hour, about 44 mSv/year) to 20 µSv/hour (175 mSv/year), or more had the people stayed there. Was the evacuation justified? Note that the lower end of the dose range is within the area where radiation effects are estimated by LNT. If a threshold effect to radiation exposure exists, then there would have been no need to evacuate all of those 156,000 people.

An area directly adjacent to the plant, generally within 3 kilometers, did become more contaminated and clearly some areas directly under the plume of airborne contamination coming from the reactors in the larger 20-kilometer area received contamination sufficient to warrant evacuation.[4] However, a significant proportion of those evacuated may not have had to leave based solely on radiation levels in their area. In defense of the local officials, part of the problem was poor communication between the plant operators, government, and local officials. In that sense, whether the LNT or any other model sets the formal guidelines, no one was consulting those models as one crisis was giving way to another. There was a considerable fear early on that a Chernobyl-style disaster was beginning; thus some officials wanted the evacuation order expanded to 30 kilometers.

Using the LNT model, calculations have shown that excess cancer deaths over the evacuees' lifespans, excess meaning caused by radiation exposure as opposed to other causes of cancer such as smoking or air pollution, would be about 130 (Normile 2012). Other estimates, most recently from the World Health Organization (WHO 2013), suggest that the effect of radiation released by the Fukushima nuclear accident will be undetectable in the affected population. Actually these estimates may be one and the same considering that the excess cancer deaths would amount to 0.08 percent, so small a number it would be difficult to quantify as 'excess.'

Spent nuclear fuel Models like the LNT also impact how we handle the spent fuel accumulating at nuclear power plants in the USA and in most countries with nuclear reactors. Generally the spent fuel must be stored onsite in a cooling pond for at least three years, as it is highly radioactive over this period and radioactive decay produces appreciable heat that could melt the fuel rods if not absorbed by the surrounding water. The spent fuel will remain more radioactive than the ore from which the fuel was made for about another 10,000 years. So we will take 10,000 years as a reasonable secure storage period. There is considerable argument over whether or not this is a 'reasonable' storage period; we'll return to this argument in the US case study at the end of the chapter.

Long-term waste storage Long-term storage is generally envisioned underground, although in some ways above-ground storage in steel casks may be better owing to lower costs, and ease of inspection and repair. Storage sites should be away from rivers and underground aquifers to minimize the chances of water contamination, which can spread radioisotopes. Ideally closed basins, valleys with no exit drainage, in arid regions are best, although such placement raises the equally problematic issue of transportation of spent fuel to what is usually a remote site.

Countries with nuclear reactors have investigated many sites for long-term storage but most sites have been abandoned owing to political pressure. Sweden is currently the only country with nuclear reactors that has approved intermediate and long-term storage plans for high-level waste (spent fuel), including deep geologic long-term storage at its Forsmark site. Several other EU countries are in various stages of approving storage sites, but it is less than clear whether they will all succeed.

A further interesting aspect of long-term waste storage is that considerable energy remains in spent nuclear fuel. Alternate fission reactors such as the CANDU heavy water reactor and thorium cycle reactors (see 'Future reactor designs' below) can actually use spent fuel from current nuclear plants as reactor fuel, and such use reduces the amount of radioactivity remaining. It may also be possible in the future to destroy spent fuel by bombardment in a particle accelerator; this is currently nowhere near cost effective. These possibilities raise the issue of potential retrieval and reuse of spent fuel in the future, which should be incorporated into design of long-term storage facilities.

Currently the assumption is that the LNT is correct and any radiation exposure above background must be minimized. This leads to expensive additional requirements for nuclear waste storage and transport of spent fuel. If the threshold or hormesis models are closer to reality then we can be less stringent about waste storage because of the lower risk associated with the release of small amounts of radioisotopes.

Reprocessing spent nuclear fuel Over time, enough of the U235 in the reactor fuel fissions and drops the concentration of U235 below the threshold for a sustained nuclear chain reaction, and the fuel must be replaced. This spent fuel still contains around 0.5 percent U235, a lot of U238, other radioactive fission products along the U235 decay chain, and about 1 percent by mass plutonium 239 and plutonium 240. Chemical processes can separate the plutonium from the spent fuel. The oldest and most common reprocessing technology is called PUREX, for Plutonium and Uranium Recovery by EXtraction. Plutonium can be used as fissionable material in specially designed reactors, but most countries have avoided this route because of the specter of potential diversion of plutonium to weapons programs. Several more modern versions of the chemical process have also been developed that can recover uranium but not plutonium.[5]

Reprocessing spent nuclear reactor fuel is, like uranium enrichment, a dual-use technology. Reprocessing spent fuel recovers usable U235 that can be put into new fuel pellets. Reprocessing can also be used to extract plutonium from the spent fuel for use in nuclear weapons. Currently only France, the UK, Japan, and Russia reprocess most of their spent fuel. The USA chooses not to reprocess its spent fuel. At first it was illegal for nuclear non-proliferation reasons to reprocess spent nuclear fuel in the USA. That law was overturned, but today it is cheaper to make fuel directly from uranium ore. Reprocessing can help reduce the volume of high-level radioactive waste, mostly spent nuclear fuel, but is much less effective with lower-level radioactive waste also produced by nuclear reactors. Reprocessing does not reduce the total radioactivity; the radioactive isotopes are still present, they have just been separated from the rest of the spent fuel and condensed into a smaller volume.

Nuclear accidents There have been a number of nuclear incidents around the world. Many occurring in the 1940s and 1950s during the Cold War between the USA and the USSR were under-reported or completely covered up, because they happened in nuclear weapon production plants or on nuclear-powered military vessels. There have been fewer incidents at civilian nuclear plants, and these are more likely to be reported. We will cover only the most significant commercial cases: Three Mile Island in the United States in 1979, Chernobyl in Ukraine in 1986, and the recent Fukushima Daiichi incident in Japan in 2011. We chose these cases because they are the most emblematic of people's concerns about nuclear power.

Three Mile Island, 1979 The Three Mile Island nuclear station is located on an island in the Susquehanna river about ten miles south of Harrisburg, Pennsylvania (USA). There are two PWRs onsite. On 28 March 1979 a series of mechanical and human failures led to a partial meltdown in the number two reactor. The pressure vessel was not breached, but some radioactive steam was vented into the outer containment structure to relieve pressure build-up and prevent a more damaging steam explosion. Exactly how much radioactive material was released will never be known. No workers in the plant were harmed and there is no credible evidence of adverse health effects in the surrounding area (US Nuclear Regulatory Commission 2013b). The remaining reactor at Three Mile Island continues to function. The spent fuel and other wastes from the partial meltdown at reactor two have been removed to secure storage. Final cleanup will be done when reactor one is decommissioned and the plant is shut down in 2034.

The take-home message from Three Mile Island, admittedly with the advantage of three decades of hindsight, is that many of the safety features of the plant worked and prevented the accident from becoming worse. The incident also revealed a need for better: training of nuclear plant operators, communication between nuclear plants and local government, and monitoring equipment at nuclear plants to more accurately measure any releases of radioactive material that might occur. The incident also spurred closer government oversight under the Nuclear Regulatory Commission.

Chernobyl, 1986 The Chernobyl nuclear station is a four reactor complex located about 130 kilometers (78 miles) north of Kiev, Ukraine, then part of the USSR. Just after midnight on 26 April 1986, a poorly planned experiment at the reactor went horribly wrong, resulting in a steam explosion that blew the top off the pressure vessel. The reactor did not have a concrete outer containment structure around it, which was typical of reactors of this vintage in the former USSR. Unfortunately the moderator in this type of reactor is graphite, which is a good moderator for slowing down neutrons, but burns in the presence of oxygen and heat, which was available after the pressure vessel blew apart. The burning graphite in the shattered reactor core sent up a plume of radioisotope-tainted smoke thousands of feet into the air, spreading radioactive material across millions of square miles of present-day Ukraine, Belarus, Russia, and northern Europe, and was detectable worldwide.

About fifty plant workers and firefighters died of acute radiation poisoning (>1,000 mSv exposure) trying to quench the graphite fire. Some 350,000 people were relocated away from the worst contamination and an exclusion zone still surrounds the plant and will for thousands of years. Somewhat surprisingly, only a few hundred thyroid cancer cases resulting in a dozen or so deaths – thyroid cancer is among the more treatable forms of cancer – can so far unambiguously be tied to Chernobyl. LNT calculations show upwards of nine thousand possible deaths over about eighty years in the most affected population – those who worked cleaning up at the plant or lived in the most contaminated regions around the plant, which is about 750,000 people (Cardis et al. 1996). Approaching thirty years since the accident it is hard to detect those predicted cancer deaths; this is one reason why some scientists are starting to question the validity of LNT. Although again it would be surprisingly difficult to detect 9,000 unusual deaths, about 1 percent of all deaths, in 750,000 people over eighty years.

Chernobyl was about as bad as a nuclear reactor accident can get. It once again proved that strict overseeing is necessary and that reactor designs need to be thoroughly investigated before they are built. Some designs are simply not a good idea – graphite moderator in a water-cooled reactor with no outer containment structure, for instance. The three other reactors at Chernobyl were shut down by 1999, but there are still about twelve reactors of the same design operating in present-day Russia or former Soviet bloc countries. Many of these countries would like to decommission the plants but cannot afford to build the replacement generating capacity.

Fukushima Daiichi, 2011 The Fukushima Daiichi nuclear station is located on the coast of Japan about 240 kilometers (144 miles) northeast of Tokyo.

The plant consists of six boiling water reactors (BWRs) brought into service in 1971; it is one of the larger nuclear plants worldwide. On 11 March 2011 a magnitude 9.0 earthquake struck about 30 kilometers (19 miles) off Japan's eastern coast, generating a powerful tsunami that washed inland for up to a mile in some locations, as some waves were 10 meters (30 feet) high. An estimated 16,000 people were killed and 340,000 displaced by the tsunami.

On that day reactors four, five, and six were in cold shutdown for refueling or repair. Reactors one, two, and three, which had been in full operation, shut down when the earthquake struck by inserting control rods into the reactor cores, as they were designed to do. Roughly fifty minutes after the earthquake the first tsunami wave washed over the seawalls, which had not been built to accommodate a 10-meter wave, and flooded the lower-lying parts of reactor buildings one, two, three, and four. Two plant workers died in one of the building basements as it flooded; they are, so far, the only fatalities from any source at the plant.

As noted earlier, inserting the control rods into a reactor core will stop the sustained nuclear chain reaction, but does not stop secondary fission of other radioisotopes in the decay chains leading from $U235$. Therefore the reactors still produced significant heat for several days after shutdown. The affected reactors still needed cooling water. Battery packs to power the pumps circulating cooling water came on automatically; however, the batteries were designed to last only a few hours, as backup diesel generators were intended to relieve them. The diesel generators, however, were destroyed in the now-flooded basements of the reactor buildings. The tsunami completely destroyed the local electricity grid and roads leading to the plant. The plant was on its own and there was no easy way to cool the reactors. Reactors one, two and three began to overheat within a few hours.

No appreciable airborne radioactivity had been released beyond the plant yet; radioactive water leaks inside the plant boundary likely existed. Early the next morning, reactor one was in partial meltdown owing to loss of cooling water, and workers vented steam from the pressure vessel into the outer containment building to relieve pressure. The steam contained radioactive isotopes that the wind carried, resulting in the first large-scale release of radioactivity beyond the plant boundary. This steam release also allowed hydrogen formed in the reactor core as it began to melt down to begin accumulating inside the outer containment building of reactor one.

Officials enlarged the evacuation zone around the plant from 3 to 10 kilometers, owing to reactor one's steam releases. That afternoon a large hydrogen explosion badly damaged the outer containment building of reactor one. The rate of radioisotope release increased dramatically after the explosion, as the outer containment structure no longer protected released material from wind. Steam venting and hydrogen explosions also occurred at reactors two and three over the next several days as those reactors also suffered partial meltdowns.

Some damage to the pressure vessel of reactor two occurred either during the hydrogen explosions or from heat-induced warping during the meltdown, as heavily contaminated water began draining into the basement of reactor two.

Until late March 2011, atmospheric releases of radioactive material continued with steadily lowering magnitudes as the reactors were cooled down both by applied water and through exhaustion of short-lived radioisotopes. Considerable volumes of radioisotope-contaminated water leaked into the ocean from both the reactor basements, and one or more cooling ponds that may also have been damaged. Normally the water in cooling ponds is not heavily contaminated with dissolved radioisotopes, but the tsunami may have slammed together and damaged spent fuel rods in the pools when it swamped them. Large volumes of radioisotope-contaminated cooling water are stored onsite. It is this water which led to the publicized 2013 problems at the plant as some of these storage containers, intended to be temporary, began to leak. Cleanup at Fukushima will take a decade or more and run to several billion dollars. Contaminated groundwater around the plant will be one of the enduring legacies of Fukushima, one that is extremely difficult, if not impossible, to remediate.

Much has been made of both Fukushima and Chernobyl being rated as Level 7 International Nuclear Emergency Scale (INES) incidents, but there is really no comparing the two accidents. Chernobyl released far more total radioactivity and much more was airborne and spread over a tremendous geographical region. We will cover lessons from Fukushima in the Japan case study at the end of the chapter.

Future reactor designs

The early research reactors built during WWII and later into the 1950s are considered generation I reactors. Currently operating PWRs and BWRs built between 1960 and 1989 are considered generation II reactors. Reactors built since about 1990 through 2010 are considered generation III reactors and have additional built-in safety features to help prevent meltdowns. In the USA the AP1000 reactor design by Westinghouse is considered a generation III+ design and Georgia (USA) intends to build two such reactors starting in 2014. China is also building at least four AP1000-style reactors. The AP1000 is designed with a passive cooling system that should keep the core below melting temperature for at least seventy-two hours after shutdown, giving time to restore outside power links or make repairs; the passive cooling system requires no human input. Roughly equivalent generation III+ reactor designs have been developed in Europe, Japan, and South Korea.

Advanced designs are considered generation IV reactors and probably will not be built until after 2020. These newer designs generally have features that further reduce the meltdown risk due to power loss or mechanical failure. Some Gen IV designs, such as the so-called pebble bed reactors, are also designed to reduce the risk of nuclear weapons proliferation by making it harder to extract plutonium from the spent fuel.

Another interesting Gen IV technology is the liquid fluoride–thorium cycle reactor (LIFTR) (Hargraves and Moir 2010; Biello 2010). This technology was initially designed in the United States, and Oak Ridge National Labs in Tennessee ran a research reactor for about three years before the project was abandoned in the early 1970s. Currently India is most aggressively pursuing LIFTR technology. India has little uranium but considerable thorium reserves. Thorium is not itself fissile; neutron collision does not induce fission, but it can capture neutrons like U238, converting thorium 232 into uranium 233, which is fissile. Thorium reactors need either a fissile 'seed' material (U233, U235, or plutonium) to produce neutrons to convert the thorium into U233 or neutron bombardment by a particle accelerator.

Accelerator-driven LIFTR is probably the most interesting idea for the future as it provides both another level of control over reactor dynamics, and control of the rate of production of fissile material. Also particle accelerators may enable more completely 'burning' of spent nuclear fuel from uranium reactors. There have been some exciting recent advances in particle accelerators that may make these types of reactors more economical.

The thorium fuel cycle has a number of advantages over U235-driven fission. It is easier to control as thorium is not itself fissile. In fact most LIFTR designs have the thorium and fissile material circulating in liquid fluoride salts. An added advantage of this configuration is that the reactor cannot melt down because the core is already liquid and can be designed in a two-chambered system with separation provided by a solid fluoride salt plug, which is kept solid by a cooling system. If power is lost, the cooling system in the plug fails and melts, dropping the liquid reactor material into a chamber designed to absorb neutrons and heat, quenching the reactor, thus making the design inherently resistant to overheating accidents that could release radioactive material. LIFTRs do not produce appreciable amounts of plutonium. They do produce U233, which is fissile and could conceivably be used in a nuclear weapon, although the technology for such weapons is not well developed and was abandoned by the USA early in the Cold War as unworkable.

LIFTRs produce more short-lived radioactive byproducts, meaning the spent fuel is dangerous for a somewhat shorter time. Spent fuel from a conventional U235 nuclear plant can also be reused in a LIFTR, which extracts more energy from the fuel and reduces the amount of radioactivity remaining in the fuel; CANDU-style heavy water reactors also have this advantage. LIFTRs can also be run in a breeder configuration, producing more U233 than they consume. Lastly there is far more thorium on Earth than uranium. Currently the price of uranium is quite low, so there is no real economic driver for development of the thorium fuel cycle in developed countries. Uranium-based nuclear power is also a mature technology and would be hard to displace.

The last comment on reactor design leads into the future of nuclear power. Unlike fossil fuels, which will eventually run out completely in a few hundred years and which will grow progressively more expensive to extract until then, the breeder reactor concept raises the possibility of greatly extending the lifespan of nuclear power by producing more fuel than is consumed. Uranium breeder reactors produce plutonium, and because they are producing more fissile material than they consume, can conceivably produce a thermonuclear explosion. Reactor designs would try to avoid this, but it would be physically possible. Most experts agree that the combined threat of proliferation from plutonium and thermonuclear explosion risk associated with uranium breeder reactors is an almost insurmountable impediment to deployment of the technology in the near future. LIFTR breeder reactors would not have the plutonium proliferation risk and U233 is less able to support an exponential nuclear chain reaction. A useful overview of reactor designs being pursued worldwide is available at the World Nuclear Association website.[6]

The future of nuclear power

Until the 2011 Fukushima Daiichi accident the future of nuclear power looked increasingly bright. There had been no serious incidents since Chernobyl and people were starting to realize nuclear power was a stable, low-CO_2-generating, source of power. A number of countries were moving forward with plans to build new nuclear plants. After Fukushima several countries scrapped plans to build new nuclear plants and a few countries, including Germany, committed to going non-nuclear. Interest in nuclear power is muted for now. How long interest remains low will likely depend on whether there is another nuclear incident somewhere in the world in the near future and how serious we get about removing carbon-emitting sources from our energy portfolios.

The expense of new nuclear plants is also often cited as a barrier to increasing nuclear power in the developed world. Owing to increased safety requirements the cost of most new nuclear plants (such as the AP1000, generally a two-reactor plant generating about 1,100 MW) has risen to $10–12 billion. The plant would make an estimated $25 billion of electricity over its lifetime (assuming an output of about 7 TWhr/year at $0.1/kWh and 90 percent capacity factor over forty years). Operating and fuel expenses run at around $300 million/year, or $12 billion over the same lifetime. So the plants should be at least breakeven over the long run, although this is far from a resounding financial endorsement of new-built nuclear power.

How the uranium fuel is enriched makes a substantial difference to EROeI calculations. Diffusion enrichment has an EROeI of 10–20, and centrifuge enrichment EROeI is upwards of 50 (World Nuclear Association 2013c). Spent fuel storage's EROeI cost is not included in the above estimates, but would certainly lower the values if included. There is little agreement on where, how, or duration of storage, so it is nearly impossible to estimate the energy expenditures with any accuracy. Some estimates of EROeI for new nuclear construction are as low as 5 (Lenzen 2008), a reasonable estimate is probably around 10. Levelized costs for new nuclear plants likewise vary widely depending on the assumptions made, but a reasonable number in 2011 dollars is $108/MWh compared to advanced combined-cycle natural gas plants at $65/MWh (US Energy Information Administration 2013a: Table 1.). Of course, the natural gas value does not include a range of externalities, such as CO_2 emissions.

Nuclear fusion reactors We cover the idea of fusion power after the future of nuclear fission as a tongue-in-cheek reference to the common saying in the nuclear industry that 'fusion power is only fifty years away and always will be.' Fusion is the power source of the stars, as described in the uranium sub-section, and would be highly desirable because it produces more usable energy than fission from the same mass of fuel and produces dramatically less radioactive waste. However, unlike fission, fusion occurs only at very high temperatures and/or pressures, which occur naturally in a star but are very difficult to produce here on Earth.

There are two current technologies that might be able to achieve useful fusion, fusion that produces more energy than it consumes. One is so-called 'hot' fusion, where fuel is heated into plasmas, the point where individual electrons are no longer bound to any one nucleus, and fused. These plasmas are so hot that no physical material can contain them; instead the plasmas are constrained by magnetic fields inside a torus or donut-shaped hollow container called a tokomak. Heat is transferred to the walls of the tokomak, which can be cooled with water, producing steam used to drive turbines. The International Thermonuclear Experimental Reactor (ITER) is an international consortium building a scale test fusion reactor in Cadarache, France, scheduled to begin operation in 2020. Even if ITER succeeds, it will be at least another two or three decades before we see fusion plants being built, and there are significant concerns that not all the technical hurdles of tokomak-style fusion reactors can be overcome.

The second technology is inertial confinement fusion, which takes advantage of the basic physical principle that an object at rest tends to stay at rest, that some amount of time is required to accelerate material from rest. By pouring a huge amount of energy into a tiny space, inertial confinement attempts start fusion before the input energy blasts the target material apart. This is theoretically possible and is being tested at the National Ignition Facility (NIF) in Livermore, California. To date early experiments at NIF have not been promising.

While it is worth investing in fusion research such as ITER and NIF because of the large potential rewards if they can be made to work, assuming that fusion power will come to our rescue anytime soon is overly optimistic. We will more likely have to face the harder tasks of making wind and solar power more efficient and quite possibly using nuclear fission technology to wean ourselves off fossil fuels.

Case studies

France France's energy policy seeks to ensure energy security, reduce consumption, provide competitive and equitable supply, and address climate change (IEA 2010a: 7). Between the Energy Law of 2005 and the 2007 *Grenelle de l'Environnement* (environmental program), France set efficiency and renewable energy development targets, and requirements to substantially reduce its GHG emissions by 75 percent. France also created a Ministry of Ecology, Energy, Sustainable Development, and the Sea (ibid.: 8). In order to encourage a reduction in consumption, the French government created the tool of energy savings certificates for energy providers if they meet target reductions within the set time period. The treasury will fine an energy provider if it does not meet the target (ADEME n.d.).

France is a fascinating case for studying nuclear energy. It is the home of Henri Becquerel, who discovered radioactivity, and Marie and Pierre Curie, who isolated polonium and radium. The three shared the Nobel Prize in Physics in 1903. In 1945 Charles de Gaulle created the Commissariat à l'Enérgie Atomique (CEA), a research organization to study application of nuclear technology in medicine, energy, and defense (K1 Team 2012). France embarked on a rapid nuclear power plant-building program after the 1970s oil shocks showed how vulnerable the country was to price and availability of fossil fuels. France has little coal and no conventional oil reserves of its own. Although it may have modest unconventional natural gas reserves, the parliament banned hydraulic fracturing.

Over the course of about twenty years beginning in the mid-1970s, fifty-eight nuclear reactors were brought into operation. Currently France gets 75 percent of its electricity from nuclear power. Considerable effort was made to reach out to the public to explain the rationale for relying so heavily on nuclear power, and robust governmental oversight was instituted from the beginning. To date France has had only a few minor nuclear incidents resulting in no deaths due to radiation exposure. Public opinion surveys have shown strong public support for nuclear power, although recently support has eroded (PBS 2008). In the aftermath of Fukushima, 80 percent of the French 'now object to building new nuclear plants, and nearly two-thirds support phasing out existing plants' (Moriarty 2012). Although fear of nuclear power continues to be high among the public, it is often seen as the least-worst alternative (PBS 2008).

France is one of a handful of countries that reprocesses all of its spent nuclear fuel. This is done to reduce high-level waste volume and to contribute to energy security; uranium fuel from ore is cheaper than reprocessed fuel. Like most of the rest of the world, France has had problems finding a permanent long-term storage site for spent fuel owing to local opposition. Currently waste is in interim storage at two sites awaiting a final long-term storage solution.

Over the next decade France must decide whether to start building additional reactors to replace those that are approaching the end of their working lifespans. Cost considerations for new nuclear plants, as well as opposition to long-term waste storage, have resulted in a lessening of interest in keeping nuclear as the primary electricity source in the country. France's neighbors, Germany and Italy, have started to phase out nuclear power since the 2011 Fukushima accident. The debate played out in the 2012 elections.

The presidential election of François Hollande (Socialist Party) in 2012 was seen as a referendum of sorts on nuclear power in France. The Socialists and the Greens joined to form a coalition government. The Socialists want to decrease France's reliance on nuclear power from 75 to 50 percent. The Greens want to eliminate nuclear power completely (Clark 2012). The Hollande government agreed to shut down the Fessenheim nuclear power plant in 2016 as it reaches the end of its license. The two reactors there have been in operation since 1977, and are in an area over an aquifer that is prone to flooding (Lévêque 2013). Hollande agreed to extend the licenses of some nuclear plants approaching decommissioning, but also canceled plans for several new plants; one new nuclear plant was already under construction and is going forward. Hollande wants to diversify energy sources, which will likely mean replacing nuclear electricity generating capacity with as much wind and other renewable power as possible. If France wants to meet its GHG emissions targets, it will have to turn to renewable power, probably with nuclear power as a backup to solve the intermittency problems of solar and wind.

It should be noted that France already has one of the lowest per capita CO_2 emission rates among comparable countries in the world, thanks largely to its reliance on nuclear power. Adding renewable energy sources could further lower CO_2 emissions. However, if too many nuclear plants are shut down, France will have to either turn to increased investment in grid upgrades and grid energy storage to accommodate the intermittent nature of wind and solar power or turn to fossil-fueled backup power, which would increase CO_2 emissions.

The United States The US Congress passed the Energy Policy Act of 2005, which was signed into law by then president George W. Bush. The Act's aim is 'To ensure jobs for our future with secure, affordable, and reliable energy.' The law authorizes loan guarantees for nuclear power plants. The 2011 *Blueprint for a Secure Energy Future*, put out by President Obama's White House, had three key components: develop and secure America's energy supplies, provide consumers with choices to reduce costs and save energy, and innovate our way to a clean energy future (White House 2011). Nuclear power falls under innovating our way to a clean energy future – generating 80 percent of US electricity from clean energy sources. The blueprint calls for energy credits for clean electricity supply, loan guarantees for building new nuclear power plants, and a focus on research and development to ensure that the USA is a leader in innovation.

In many ways the USA is in a similar position to France. It must soon decide whether to build new nuclear plants to replace those that are approaching decommissioning or replace them with other types of generating capacity. While five new nuclear plants are under construction in the USA, this is nowhere near replacement level. A large number of the existing fleet of about 100 operating plants are scheduled to retire around 2030.

Several plants are closing before retirement for economic reasons. These are generally aging, stand-alone reactors, with rapidly increasing maintenance costs owing to advancing age and tighter safety requirements post-Fukushima. Another factor working against nuclear power in the USA is that because of electricity market deregulation, base load generating plants are no longer paid a premium for their electricity. Most nuclear plants in the USA are prototypical base load plants with capacity factors approaching 90 percent. This puts large power plants, not just nuclear plants, built decades ago and designed to be primarily base load plants, at less of an economic advantage than before.

The other issue that remains unresolved in the USA and is a dragging concern on new plant construction is that of long-term waste storage. The USA has spent about $9 billion on testing and early phase construction of a site in the Nevada desert, Yucca Mountain. The saga is an interesting story about the balance of power in the USA. During his election campaign, President Obama promised to scuttle the project. In 2010 the Department of Energy, part of the executive branch, filed a motion to withdraw Yucca Mountain's license. Congress stopped funding Yucca Mountain in 2010, but did fund the Blue Ribbon Commission on America's Nuclear Future to evaluate and recommend alternatives. The NRC stopped its evaluation of Yucca Mountain, but still had $11 million unspent. Two US states brought a lawsuit against the NRC, and in August 2013 a US Federal Appeals court ruled in their favor. The NRC must continue to review Yucca Mountain as a waste site, because the mandate is from the Nuclear Waste Policy Act of 1982, passed by Congress, so the executive cannot set a policy counter to it.

Yucca Mountain was brought down by two main factors. First, from the beginning the site was chosen strictly by outsiders with no local participation. The people of Nevada were never given much choice in the matter, are understandably upset, and are largely against the project. Secondly, the government allowed an unreasonable time horizon to be attached to the project. In 2005 the EPA set limits on radiation exposure from the storage site that would have to be met for a million years (EPA 2012). A million-year period is an essentially impossible design challenge to ensure little or no radioisotope release. The longer the time horizon the more uncertainty is introduced.

The risks at Yucca Mountain over a 10,000-year time span seem quite manageable. The site could be built as well as possible now and a fund established to cover upkeep and repair in the future. A remaining issue would be transporting all the waste to Yucca Mountain. Detractors correctly point out that many thousands of tractor-trailer or trainloads of waste would need to be moved across the country. While considerable work has been put into making secure containers for waste transport, and they are amazing feats of engineering if you have ever seen the videos of them being smashed through concrete walls and knocked around by locomotives, nothing can be made completely safe.

A more reasonable technical plan would be to have a second repository east of the Mississippi river. Technically sound, however, is often not a solution in the highly charged debate over nuclear waste and not in my backyard (NIMBY) movements. The American public would have to be much more scientifically literate than it is at present to be likely to accept such a plan.

Nuclear power detractors in the USA who are passionate about the issue of storing nuclear waste need only point to the Hanford Nuclear Reservation in Washington State as evidence of how a badly managed waste site can become a continuing disaster. Hanford was the site of several reactors and associated reprocessing of spent nuclear fuel that produced much of the plutonium for the US nuclear arsenal in the 1950s. In the early part of the Cold War between the USA and the USSR, the race to produce nuclear weapons as fast as possible trumped safety and long-term storage was an afterthought. Large amounts of nuclear waste were stored for decades in containers meant to be temporary. A number of those containers are now leaking and groundwater contamination by radioisotopes has become a serious problem. Contamination of the Columbia river looms in the future as the plume of contaminated groundwater spreads. Dealing with the types of mixed high-level wastes that exist at Hanford is a technical nightmare and the cleanup process there is lagging more than a decade behind schedule and billions over budget. There is a policy angle here as well, in terms of design, regulation, and oversight. Hanford is an example of what you get with no regulatory oversight and no long-term planning.

Yucca Mountain could work as a waste repository, if evaluated solely on its merits over a reasonable time period, such as the 10,000-year period we have raised. However, that would also mean transporting large amounts of spent fuel across the country to Yucca Mountain, which seems both politically distasteful and quite possibly unnecessary. For the near future spent fuel will continue to be stored at each US reactor site, first in cooling ponds and then in above-ground steel casks. As mentioned above, this is actually not too bad a solution to waste storage in terms of most considerations except security, for which a single, preferably below-ground, site would be better.

Japan Like France, Japan turned to nuclear power because it lacks fossil fuel reserves. Japan imports 84 percent of its energy requirements (World Nuclear Association 2013b). Japan built up its reactor fleet to fifty-four reactors supplying 30 percent of its electricity by 2010 and was planning to continue to ramp up nuclear to 40 percent of total electricity generation. However, even before the Fukushima incident there were signs that Japan's nuclear industry was in trouble. Through the 1990s there were several significant accidents at reactors, fuel processing plants, and waste handling plants, some of which were minimized or ignored by the governmental agencies tasked with nuclear review in Japan, the Ministry of Economy, Trade, and Industry (METI) and its sub-agency the Nuclear and Industrial Safety Agency (NISA).

METI, as it turns out, is a dual-purpose government entity; not only was it responsible for watching over nuclear power in Japan, it was also responsible for promoting nuclear power. This schizophrenic purpose is not unlike the situation in the USA with the Minerals Management Service (MMS) prior to the Gulf oil spill in 2010. The MMS was tasked with both overseeing and promoting offshore oil drilling in the Gulf of Mexico. The Deepwater Horizon disaster revealed how lax oversight was. In both cases it is clear in hindsight that such organizations cannot be effective. The conflicts of interest within such an arrangement are simply too easy for industry to take advantage of and corrupt, preventing meaningful oversight.

In the case of METI, not only had the agency failed to force industry to make real improvements in safety and reporting, they had spent most of their energy on promoting a tale of Japanese technical prowess and invincibility in nuclear power that was unjustified by the Japanese nuclear industry's track record. Thus, for instance, no one questioned the wisdom of locating backup diesel generators in the basements of reactor buildings built just above sea level.

In the wake of Fukushima Daiichi it has become clear that NISA and the Nuclear Safety Commission (NSC) were not effective at their regulatory tasks (Fukushima Nuclear Accident Independent Investigation Commission 2012). In essence the report of the Investigation Commission found that Fukushima Daiichi was a manmade disaster waiting to happen. Furthermore the public's trust in the government of Japan and the nuclear industry in Japan has been badly shaken. According to public opinion polls, about half of Japanese citizens are against nuclear power, yet the pro-nuclear Liberal Democratic Party easily won reelection in December 2012 (Fackler 2013). The government at first kept other nuclear reactors shut down after the 2011 earthquake and Fukushima incident and had looked at moving Japan away from nuclear power. As time has gone on, however, the government has drifted back towards nuclear energy and it now appears that elected officials will attempt to ride out the storm of public opinion and try to slowly move forward with additional nuclear capacity in Japan. Whether they can succeed will likely depend on how long and how determined public anti-nuclear sentiment remains and whether they can prevent future accidents through effective regulation.

There are real economic and technical hurdles to overcome to move Japan away from nuclear power. With little in the way of fossil fuel resources, land-based unconventional oil and natural gas will not help them. Japan is pursuing methane hydrates, a fossil fuel that is a solid mixture of ice and methane, stable only under considerable pressure and low temperatures, generally in more than a thousand feet of water on the ocean floor. Essentially methane hydrates are a form of unconventional natural gas. Whether methane hydrates can be economically tapped remains to be seen; regardless, that source of energy is at least a decade away.

Renewables will require considerable work, as Japan may not be geographically diverse enough to avoid large-scale becalming in wind energy. Their solar potential is modest, although no worse than that of Germany, which has successfully built up solar power. Most of the hydropower they are willing to build has already been built. One of Japan's best renewable bets may be geothermal energy, discussed in Chapter 7. Although geothermal would have to be undertaken carefully as Japan sits atop considerable seismic hazard, as the earthquake and tsunami of 2011 demonstrated. Moving Japan away from nuclear power will not necessarily be impossible, but it will require political will, as the nuclear infrastructure and the attendant entrenched interests are already present.

Conclusion

Nuclear power is a complicated technical process, one that is feared for a number of reasons: because it is not understood, because its inherent complexity makes it susceptible to human error or human-malfeasance-induced disasters, and because of worries about radiation. All of these fears are understandable. In some ways this is similar to the fear of flying, another complicated process. It is well documented that flying is far safer, on average, than driving, but many people still view flying as dangerous. Similarly, nuclear power's safety record is quite good. Far more people have died as a result of hydropower, a power source that is often regarded as safe, owing to dam failures and flooding. Coal-burning power plants may be responsible for millions of deaths over the last hundred years owing to air pollution, not to mention the potential economic and social disruption possible because of climate change, and yet coal is often seen as a safe source of energy. Safety is highly relative and often defined by what we are used to. The advantage of nuclear power is that it is a stable, non-CO_2-emitting source of power.

One of the primary disadvantages of nuclear power is how to deal with spent nuclear fuel. It is true that the fuel will be dangerous for many years to come and safe storage is a necessity. Here there is a significant gap in understanding and confidence between people with technical backgrounds who have worked with radioisotopes and the general public. On the technical side the challenges posed by storage of high-level radioisotope waste seem quite manageable, for finite time horizons such as the 10,000-year period already discussed. Where that manageability breaks down is for very long time periods (such as the million-year period attached to the Yucca Mountain site in the USA), where uncertainties about degradation of materials and issues such as rates of groundwater movement and geologic factors such as volcanic eruptions exist.

It certainly seems possible to store waste for 10,000 years securely with existing technology; where this assumption breaks down, and admittedly where the technical folks have a blind spot, is in regulation and continued funding of waste storage sites. As the Chernobyl and Fukushima Daiichi incidents show, there is a need for strong, independent oversight of nuclear sites. Guaranteeing such oversight over long periods is no more possible than guaranteeing structural integrity over a million-year time frame. Political institutions change over time and no one can be sure that there will be sufficient oversight in centuries to come.

Nuclear power demonstrates the absolute need for stringent, independent regulation. The unifying theme in all three nuclear disasters we discussed in this chapter is that they were either directly caused, or exacerbated, by human error. Nuclear power is complicated enough that it cannot be left to for-profit companies or monolithic bureaucracies in countries with limited transparency to decide whether to review or implement safety features.

With proper oversight nuclear power can be an important part of an energy portfolio and may be essential to de-carbonizing our energy systems, as it is currently the only low-CO_2-emitting electricity generation technology that is not under strict geographic restriction the way hydropower and geothermal are, and is not intermittent as wind and solar are. We should also take a careful look at which nuclear technologies we choose to employ in the future; the continued absolute focus on uranium fission is not warranted and the thorium cycle deserves a closer look.

4 | BIOMASS AND BIOFUELS

Biomass

Biomass refers to the use of plant material as a fuel source. Wood, straw, dried animal dung, and charcoal are examples of biomass fuels than have been used by humans for thousands of years. Often biomass is burned to release some of the stored solar energy originally captured by plants. Biomass represents humans' earliest use of stored energy, so it should not be surprising that it is still a primary energy source for cooking and heating for roughly a third of the world's population, mainly in the global South. Burning biomass indoors with inadequate ventilation is a significant health hazard. Inhalation of smoke and other fumes from burning biomass leads to lung problems and infections for large numbers of women and young children in these areas (WHO 2010).

Advanced technologies just coming on the scene may be able to convert biomass into a range of liquid and gaseous fuel stocks. Ethanol, a two-carbon alcohol, is a primary biofuel at present. The world's largest ethanol producers are the USA, Brazil, the EU, and China, with the USA producing eleven times more than the EU and Brazil producing five times more than the EU in 2012 (Renewable Fuels Association 2014). The world's largest biodiesel producers in 2011 were the European Union, the USA, Brazil, and Argentina, with the EU producing about three times more than the other leaders (IEA-ETSAP and IRENA 2013: 1).

The advantage of biofuels lies in their sustainability, minimal contribution to global warming, and local production. In theory if you are harvesting plant matter to burn, the CO_2 released is taken up by new plants to again store the carbon as plant material. Unfortunately it is often not quite that simple. To be truly sustainable the biofuel must yield more energy than was put into making it, its EROeI must be at least greater than 1 and realistically greater than 3. Often there is also some input of energy from other sources, such as fossil fuels, somewhere in the production process, which reduces the biofuel's sustainability. Currently the primary driving factors for biofuels are energy security and independence, rather than sustainability.

In more arid regions with slower plant growth, such as regions of Africa and Asia where population has increased dramatically in the last sixty years, biomass may not be sustainable. Deforestation occurs when more material is harvested than regrows each year. Deforestation in turn leads to loss of topsoil and decreased yields in agriculture, as well as increased flood risk, because plant cover slows water down and allows it to soak into the ground. Awareness of these problems has led to a number of initiatives aimed at making burning biomass more efficient and less polluting to indoor spaces, and/or getting people to use alternatives such as solar stoves. As more people in developed countries have become aware of the sustainability of biomass, there has been renewed interest in using biomass to heat homes and businesses, and even generate electricity. As mentioned above, one should ensure that biomass utilization is sustainable in an area before advocating increased use.

There are a number of technologies available for indoor heating using biomass, such as wood stoves and pellet stoves. Fireplaces are inefficient and polluting to both indoor and outdoor air and should be used for no more than occasional, aesthetic use. A number of modern wood stoves used for residential heating and cooking can achieve efficiencies above 50 percent when burning at optimal temperature and produce relatively low emissions (Jetter et al. 2012). Pellet stoves can burn material based on compressed agricultural waste, wheat chaff, straw, soybean husk, etc., rather than wood derived from trees, making them particularly well suited to plains regions with few trees. Modern biomass stoves can also be used for both space heating and hot water production. While contained biomass stoves produce dramatically less pollution than open fires, there is still some concern over indoor air quality. Particularly as standards for residential insulation and allowable heat exchange rise, as they have in Europe and should elsewhere, there will be more concerns over indoor air quality. Well-sealed houses have little air exchange with the outside, meaning that even modest sources of indoor air pollution will become more significant.

In the northeast United States, outdoor biomass furnaces, generally fueled by wood, require no chimney attached to the house. Few modifications to the house are necessary beyond running water and electric power to the freestanding furnace. Some are capable of taking logs a foot in diameter and three feet long as fuel. Unfortunately, these furnaces are capable of operating over a wide range of conditions and fuel qualities. It is quite easy to set up conditions where they will burn at very low efficiency, producing prodigious amounts of smoke and fine particulates that can blanket the surrounding area. Some local municipalities have gone so far as to ban the furnaces owing to their ability to foul the air. Biomass burning is not always a good choice, even with the technology available in developed countries, and requires regulation.

The use of biomass for electricity production has grown, particularly in the northern hemisphere, where increased urbanization and declines in small-scale agriculture have allowed the return of substantial forest cover. Of particular interest going forward are small-scale (10–50 MW) combined heat and power (CHP) plants for rural towns and individual industrial plants, where efficiencies as high as 60 percent can be achieved by using both the electricity and waste heat produced by biomass burning. An unanticipated side problem with this is that in Maine, for example, some logging operations are practically 'vacuum cleaning' up the logging slash, running entire small trees and all slash through chippers to truck it to the local CHP plant and leaving the ground almost bare. The Maine Forest Service is now more closely monitoring the local operations to make sure they leave enough slash to protect the soil and help start new growth.

As a final comment on biomass, some people have theorized that biomass burning could be used as a form of geo-engineering. Geo-engineering attempts to modify some property of the environment at a global scale. In a very real sense humanity is already unintentionally geo-engineering with our reckless release of CO_2 into the atmosphere, causing global warming. Some posit that we could begin to reverse the process by burning biomass for heat and electricity and then capturing the carbon emissions and storing them underground. This is the same Carbon Capture and Sequestration (CCS) technology that is being developed to allow continued use of coal with minimal release of CO_2. In the case of biomass with CCS, plants are pulling CO_2 out of the atmosphere, and then CCS puts that CO_2 underground when the plants are burned, effectively removing CO_2 from atmospheric circulation. Thousands of power plants would be required to work over hundreds of years to make much of a dent in the CO_2 we have already released, but it could eventually work. Of course, this assumes that we have completely de-carbonized our energy infrastructure, which means no more fossil fuel use, and that we are not still releasing CO_2, but it is one of the less wacky geo-engineering ideas going around.

There is also a way to convert biomass into methane or electricity using bacteria. These bacteria are able to break down biomass and animal wastes only in the absence of oxygen, anaerobic conditions, and so this type of conversion is called anaerobic digestion (AD). Methane produced by AD is often referred to as biogas. The interiors of landfills are naturally anaerobic environments and landfills produce considerable methane gas. As methane is thirty times more potent a greenhouse gas than CO_2, it makes sense to try to capture and burn the methane as fuel, converting it to CO_2.

Other types of anaerobic bacteria are capable of generating an electric current from their metabolic activities, and systems have been designed to harness this ability to produce electricity from manure or sewage breakdown. Conceivably all municipal sewage systems and larger farms could be outfitted with AD systems to produce either methane or electricity. AD systems that produce electricity are currently economical for larger farms, particularly dairies that produce large amounts of manure. AD systems for biogas production are more economical for smaller farms and are becoming popular in a number of developing countries.

Biofuels

Food-based biofuels: ethanol and butanol Biofuels are liquid hydrocarbon fuels derived from plant matter. The simplest and oldest biofuel is ethanol, which is an alcohol molecule with two carbon atoms (C_2H_5OH). Humans learned to ferment natural sugars into ethanol approximately eight thousand years ago to help preserve the sugars from spoilage; alcohol concentrations above about 2 percent prevent the growth of most bacteria. Today we still make most of our ethanol using yeast to ferment sugars into alcohol. More advanced biofuels are made by specialized chemical catalysis or from genetically engineered microorganisms, and are just starting to come onto the market.

In this era of dominance of gasoline and diesel as transportation fuels it is easy to overlook the fact that both fuels require refining technology to produce them from crude oil and that refining technology is just over a hundred years old. Gasoline and diesel have not always been around. Indeed, the liquid fuel Henry Ford first planned to use for his Model-T automobile was ethanol, not gasoline. In the years before World War I ethanol was considered a better fuel because it could be made locally in modest volumes by fermentation from agricultural crops, whereas gasoline required expensive refineries and transport of crude oil. Ethanol was used as a transportation fuel from the late 1890s through the early 1920s, when it was supplanted by cheaper gasoline.

The death of ethanol as a transportation fuel was due to both its relatively low energy density, about 70 percent that of gasoline, and its relatively high labor cost of production. Large crude oil refineries could be built to achieve economies of scale, but fermentation was limited by the high cost of growing and transporting crops, so most ethanol was made in relatively small volumes locally at higher cost. World War II revived some interest in ethanol as a transportation fuel in a number of countries, but interest dried up when the war was over. Interest reemerged during the oil shocks of the 1970s, but in most countries it had waned again by the early 1980s. A notable exception is Brazil, one of the case studies in this chapter, which continued its biofuel program after the oil shock.

Interest in ethanol as a transportation fuel returned in the early 2000s as peak oil and energy security concerns grew around the globe. In the USA, ethanol's resurgence was also driven by the need to replace MTBE (methyl-tertbutylether), an antiknock agent added to gasoline to make engines run more smoothly. Ironically MTBE was brought in to replace tetraethyl lead (leaded gasoline), the first antiknock agent, owing to awareness of lead's toxicity in the environment. MTBE had been classified as a carcinogen, a cancer-causing agent, and was creating significant groundwater contamination problems. Ethanol is a good replacement for MTBE in that it is not as toxic and does not persist in the environment; unlike with MTBE soil bacteria can break it down. We will address both the US- and EU-specific biofuel policies in the case studies. Here we will keep the discussion to basics that apply to most countries.

The real test of a biofuel should be how sustainable it is. If a biofuel requires large inputs of energy obtained from fossil fuels or causes more CO_2

emissions than it offsets, then it should be judged a bad choice. Currently most ethanol produced in the USA is very nearly in this category. In the USA ethanol is primarily made by fermentation of corn starches. While corn yields can be quite high per acre, corn also requires considerable energy inputs in the form of fuel for tractors to till, plant, and harrow the crop, as well as fertilizers, which have the biggest single fossil-fuel-based input, herbicides, and pesticides, all of which are produced using energy from fossil fuels, to grow with maximal yield. In some areas fossil-fuel-driven pumps are used to bring water to the surface to irrigate the corn as well. Finally, land use changes can also affect the carbon balance of corn ethanol. If forests or grasslands are plowed up to plant corn, considerable natural CO_2 storage is lost, lowering the positive carbon value of corn-based ethanol.

There has been considerable debate in the scientific literature over the past fifteen years about how best to account for land use changes in life cycle analysis calculations. These calculations are used to estimate the GHG emissions of various energy sources. Here it is important to point out that CO_2 is not the only GHG and not even the strongest GHG, but it is the most abundantly produced. Scientists often convert emissions figures for other compounds into CO_2 equivalents or CO_2e. This is a good example of an area of study where scientific consensus has not yet been reached, although it has been getting closer in the past few years. A range of studies has estimated that the land use changes for US corn-based ethanol CO_2e increases are around 30g of CO_2e per Megajoule (MJ) of energy released by ethanol as a fuel, although there is still considerable variation (Wang et al. 2011; Hertel et al. 2010; Plevin et al. 2010; EPA 2009; Searchinger et al. 2008). Thus the US EPA's estimate that corn ethanol has 20 percent less CO_2 emissions than gasoline (EPA 2009) does appear to roughly hold up. It should also be noted that some people are regarding the GHG emissions of corn-based ethanol as a 'payback' period, arguing that it could take fifty to 100 years to 'pay back' CO_2 emissions caused by converting land to corn production for ethanol. However, this is a somewhat specious argument, as it compares ethanol only to itself and not to other fuels it is displacing, notably gasoline. Gasoline, as a fossil fuel, introducing carbon formerly stored underground to the atmosphere, has an essentially infinite CO_2 'payback' period and thus does not stand much comparison with ethanol, but this is usually not mentioned (Wang et al. 2011).

It seems that through 2012 land use changes in the USA to increase corn ethanol production have been fairly benign. This does not mean that further increases in corn production will necessarily be benign as more marginal and erodible US cropland is brought into production. Also, there is likely some spillover, or indirect, pressure on developing countries to bring new farmland into production and this new land is much more likely to come from virgin forest and grassland. The EU has tended to put more weight on potential CO_2 emissions increases from land use changes, particularly in developing countries, and is changing its biofuels directives, as discussed in the EU case study at the end of this chapter.

Ethanol from sugarcane is both more efficient and more sustainable than that from corn. Sugarcane stores simple sugars in the stalk rather than complex starches in corn kernels. Starches have to be broken down into simple sugars for fermentation, which is part of the energy cost of corn ethanol. Also, sugarcane is not replanted every year and requires much less in the way of fertilizer, herbicide, pesticide, and irrigation inputs. The stalk residue left over after sugar is removed from sugarcane, bagasse, can be burned as sustainable biomass to generate heat and power to refine the ethanol, further improving its carbon balance. Land use changes are still important, particularly in the tropics, where rainforest may be removed to plant sugarcane. Sugarcane-based ethanol is estimated to be about 50 percent more effective in reducing CO_2 emissions than gasoline (EPA 2009). Unfortunately for the global North, sugarcane grows only in the warm, moist tropics and cannot be grown across most of the USA or Europe.

Another problem with using corn or other crops for biofuels is that they can feed humans and animals. One ends up with a competition between production of crops for biofuels and crops for food, either directly for humans or indirectly through other animals to produce meat for humans. This is the 'food vs. fuel' debate. In the case of corn, world corn prices rose about 30 percent above 2005 levels from 2006 to 2010. This is thought to be largely due to increased use of corn to produce ethanol in the USA (Carter et al. 2012). Similar stories can be told for soybean and palm oil in other parts of the world. The effects on other grain crops are harder to estimate, but it seems likely that at least some of the increase in world food prices does come from the use of crops to produce biofuels, although likely not as much as some opponents of biofuels have claimed. The increase in world food prices has most affected those in the developing world, more of whose income goes to purchase food, often unrefined grains whose prices have risen the most. There is some evidence that increased food prices contributed to the social unrest that led to the Arab Spring (Lagi et al. 2011; Goldstone 2011; Hendrix and Haggard 2007).

There is another problem with ethanol, regardless of how it is made. Unlike gasoline or diesel fuel, ethanol is miscible with water. Ethanol and water combine into a homogeneous solution that can only be separated by vaporizing the ethanol and then recondensing it, which requires considerable energy. Thus ethanol for fuel use must be kept free of water, or it would not combust correctly in an engine. For example, in coastal Maine most boat owners, especially lobstermen, refuse to use ethanol-containing fuels because of the issue of water mixing with the ethanol to create a fuel that will foul engines. Thus at marine fueling stations in Maine you can still get non-ethanol gasoline.

The miscibility issue largely prohibits moving ethanol by pipeline and affects how it can be stored. There is interest in the USA in moving away from ethanol to butanol, a four-carbon alcohol that is less miscible with water and can thus be moved by pipeline. Butanol has a higher energy density than ethanol, 85 percent that of gasoline. There are already strains of yeast that have been engineered to produce butanol instead of ethanol, and a number of companies are considering switching to butanol because of its more favorable chemical properties. The primary holdup is testing all the engine components of a modern car to assure that butanol does not cause more rapid deterioration than ethanol or gasoline.

Non-food-based biofuel: cellulosic ethanol Ultimately it would be better to move away from fermentation of dual-use crops to plants that cannot be used either directly or indirectly for human food. Generally this means turning to cellulose, which is a polymer of sugars that provides support to most plants and is the most abundant bio-molecule on Earth. Most of the mass of wood is cellulose, for instance. Animals cannot directly break down cellulose because of the connections between the sugar molecules, which is why humans cannot eat grass for sustenance. Grazing animals harbor microorganisms that are capable of breaking down cellulose, existing in a symbiosis where the animal provides a home for the microorganisms and they provide food for the animal. There are several technologies on the horizon to convert cellulose into ethanol, cellulosic ethanol, and various other liquid fuels.

Some bacteria and fungi can naturally break down cellulose. One route to utilizing cellulose for biofuel production would be to use cellulose-degrading organisms to break down the cellulose into simple sugars. The sugars would then be purified away to ferment into ethanol or butanol, or else the cellulose degraders would consume them all. Even with the purification, most of the sugar from the cellulose is used for the cellulose degrader's growth and is not available for biofuel conversion, so this is not generally an efficient strategy.

Purification of the cellulose-degrading mechanisms from cellulose-degrading organisms can also be done. The purified cellulose-degrading system can be used to break down cellulose to liberate sugars for fermentation without losing sugars to the cellulose-degrading organism's growth. Many of these cellulose degradation systems, though, are complex and not meant to work on their own; thus they are much less efficient in purified form than they are when working in their host organism. This strategy works a bit better than using the cellulose-degrading organisms themselves, but is still not very effective.

More efficient yet would be to use genetic engineering to transfer the cellulose degrading machinery from a cellulose-eating microorganism to an organism capable of producing a desired biofuel. This would combine both functions in one organism, something that does not exist in nature. Progress has been made on the front of genetically altering several different microorganisms to produce different biofuels more efficiently from various sugars. No real progress has been made on transferring the cellulose-degrading machinery.

Ethanol and other byproducts useful in the plastics and chemical industry can also be made directly from cellulose by chemical catalysis. These methods tend to use fairly high temperatures and often expensive metal catalysts to achieve the conversion. While they can be fairly efficient, most of these systems suffer from a serious problem. Their catalysts are easily fouled by impurities found in most readily available cellulose sources, meaning that the cellulose must be scrupulously cleaned prior to processing, greatly increasing the cost of production. Which system will win out, bioconversion *vs.* chemical conversion, is hard to say at this point. Both systems will require further advances before we can realize the goal of cellulosic biofuels.

Cellulose could come from a mix of sources. Some existing sources are agricultural waste, forest industry byproducts, and even municipal waste. Another source is new cellulose crops such as *Miscanthus x giganteus*, a tall hybrid grass similar to sugarcane without the sugar, that grows rapidly across most temperate regions and produces about three times the biomass of corn with little need for fertilizer or tillage. It is a sterile hybrid that does not produce seeds, but its roots can allow the plant to spread, so it has some invasive potential (Heaton n.d.). In Europe *Miscanthus* is grown as a biomass crop and used in coal-burning power plants to offset some of the coal usage, making existing coal-fired plants more sustainable. Some people argue that this might be a better use for such crops than converting the cellulose into liquid fuels as fuel conversion is an energy transformation and thus must lose some energy to entropy and thus have lower efficiency. Fast-growing trees in plantations, such as pines and willows, can also be used as cellulose feedstocks, particularly in colder climates. There might also be an incentive to return some of the high plains in the USA to more natural grasslands that could provide a low-cost cellulosic crop and would be much better suited to the area than growing the corn, wheat, and soybeans that are planted there now, which require irrigation from groundwater, much of which is unsustainable. There is some concern over using agricultural leftovers such as corn stover, wheat chaff, etc. Removing agricultural waste from fields removes some of the nutrients that future crops need, increasing the use of fertilizers. More importantly it is simply removing the biomass necessary to maintain soil texture and permeability and help absorb those chemical nutrients in the topsoil.

Biodiesel Biodiesel is another biofuel. Most biodiesel is made from vegetable oils such as soybean, corn, canola, rapeseed, and palm seed oils. The bio- in biodiesel refers to the source of hydrocarbon; otherwise it is chemically similar to diesel produced from crude oil by refining. Biodiesel is a hydrocarbon, but it has the advantage of being much cleaner burning than oil-derived diesel. Like its fossil fuel equivalent, biodiesel is made of longer-chain hydrocarbons than those found in gasoline. Biodiesel from crops raises the same range of concerns as ethanol. Most of the crops for biodiesel in Europe are a bit better than corn, but not as favorable as sugarcane. Palm oil plantations in South America and South East Asia are probably no more efficient or even less efficient than corn-based ethanol production and are one of the larger causes of tropical deforestation.

Algae There is one last source of biofuel that may be able to make a difference in the long run. That is biofuel from algae. Algae are single-celled organisms that grow fully in water and are photosynthetic like land plants. Single-celled organisms like algae, bacteria, and related organisms called archaea produce about half of the oxygen on Earth each year by photosynthesis; land plants produce the other half. There is a lot of algal biomass around already and many species to choose from in terms of properties. Many algae can grow in salt water, meaning that they would not compete with humans or crops for fresh water. Some algae can produce long-chain hydrocarbons that can be used to produce biodiesel. Further refining could produce lighter biofuels to replace gasoline for automobiles and jet fuel, essentially kerosene, for airplanes. Genetic engineering can also be used to alter algal metabolism to produce specific hydrocarbon products and increase yield by removing competing metabolic pathways.

A number of companies are working to develop algal biofuel-producing systems. This can be done in desert regions adjacent to oceans or other saltwater sources that again would not compete with cropland. These systems are usually sealed in tall plastic vats or hanging plastic bags to prevent direct evaporation of water and increasing salt concentration, which would eventually prevent algal growth, although some of these organisms naturally tolerate rather high salt concentrations. Air or filtered exhaust from a fossil-fuel-burning power plant is then bubbled through the containers. Solar-driven condensers to further reduce the rate of salt accumulation in the system can recover some of the water vapor leaving the containers with vented air. Crushed limestone can be used to offset acidity produced from sulfur and nitrogen oxides in exhaust and carbonic acid produced by dissolving CO_2 in the water. A problem for the technology at present is rapid removal of oxygen, produced by photosynthesis, as high oxygen concentrations inhibit photosynthesis. This technology is still in its relative infancy and there is considerable room to grow. It appears that fuel from algae would be roughly equivalent to and perhaps slightly better than cellulosic-derived biofuels in terms of CO_2 emission reduction.

Case studies

Brazil Brazil's energy policy centers on self-sufficiency, economic growth, and continued social and industrial development. In terms of electricity generation, Brazil is largely self-sufficient. Hydropower dominates the Brazilian electricity sector, providing about 80 percent of the country's electricity needs. The remaining electricity production comes from natural gas, mostly imported from Bolivia, nuclear power from Brazil's two nuclear power plants, and biomass. Each of those sources provided 3–4 percent of the country's electricity. Below the 3 percent range are oil, coal, and other renewable sources (OECD 2008). Brazil's potential for wind power is very high, but not yet developed. Brazil has long had a biofuels program for its transportation energy needs, as it was recognized early on that sugarcane was an excellent crop for producing ethanol. As early as the 1940s, during World War II, Brazil was producing enough ethanol to supply nearly 50 percent of its transport fuel needs. As in much of the rest of the world, cheap gasoline in the 1950s doomed ethanol. Brazil's military government (1964–85) continued biofuel development programs after the oil crises of the 1970s; it was one of the few countries to do so. Like many developing countries, Brazil was aware of the need to decrease its dependency on foreign companies and countries.

Biofuels are primarily used in the transportation sector. Brazil launched its first biofuel program in 1975 with the National Fuel Alcohol Program (ProÁlcool). ProÁlcool was successful in greatly increasing production of sugarcane-based ethanol and contributing to Brazil's energy independence, and in the economic benefits it brought to the São Paolo region. It has been criticized for its geographic and single crop concentration, the dominance of agribusiness, and exclusion of family farmers (Stattman et al. 2013: 22). Brazil has the most price-competitive biofuel in the world (Sorda et al. 2010: 6981). In 2004 Brazil began a new biofuels program called the National Program of Production and Use of Biodiesel (PNPB is its Portuguese acronym), designed to address the shortcomings of ProÁlcool. It maintained the same goals of energy diversification, energy sovereignty, creating a market for sustainable biodiesel, and focusing on social inclusion and regional development (Stattman et al. 2013: 23). The biodiesel is made mostly from soybeans. Thus far it has been least successful in including small farmers and regional development (ibid.: 23), partly because increased biodiesel use and blending required early on in the program (Sorda et al. 2010: 6982) meant that already-established large farms would be more able to meet demand.

Brazil does not use direct subsidies for ethanol production, but ethanol is taxed at a lower rate than gasoline. Brazil subsidizes biodiesel production in a few ways. The National Petroleum Agency buys set amounts of biodiesel to meet supply targets, which so far have been bought at auction for higher-than-production costs. The government also offers tax incentives to producers if a certain percentage is bought from family farmers (ibid.: 6982).

By 2008 the Brazilian biofuels program had again achieved 50 percent replacement of gasoline in liquid fuels, powering far more cars than in the 1940s, and essentially achieved energy independence for liquid fuels. The energy independence occurs because Brazil's ethanol is produced almost entirely from domestic sugarcane and Brazil has some domestic oil production. Can Brazil continue to produce enough ethanol for a growing number of cars as it continues to develop?

Currently Brazil uses about 7 percent of its arable land for growing sugarcane devoted to ethanol production for fuel, and soybeans for biodiesel. There is considerable room to grow in terms of areas suitable for sugarcane cultivation and there are still more improvements in efficiency that can be squeezed from existing production. The main concern in terms of expanding sugarcane and soybean cropland is the pressure it creates to clear-cut more of the Amazon rainforest.

Brazil's biofuel program has run into problems over the last several years as the global recession and commodities boom of 2008 drove up the price of sugar and ethanol production suffered. Recently there have also been several bad growing years for sugarcane, which have held down production and led to ethanol shortages. In 2011 Brazil even imported ethanol from the USA to make up for shortfalls in domestic production. All of this disruption has raised concerns about how economically sustainable the system will be in the future. Displacement of gasoline peaked in 2008 at 55 percent and bottomed out at 35 percent in 2011. Ethanol production has rebounded by about 10 percent since then, but not quite back to 2009 levels. Part of the problem has to do with the pricing structure for fuel. The Brazilian government sets the prices of gasoline, and in 2012 it sold imported gasoline at a loss (Casey 2013).

The next several years will be critical to the biofuels industry in Brazil. There are increasing numbers of cars as the country experiences economic growth and a remarkable reduction in income inequality. In addition, US tariffs on Brazilian ethanol of 45 cents per gallon in 2010 were allowed to expire in 2011. The possibility of exporting large amounts of ethanol to the USA to help it meet its requirements for sustainable fuels means that a significant market may exist in the future.

The European Union The EU is the world's largest producer of biodiesel. In 2008 the EU produced almost nine billion liters of biodiesel, and almost three billion liters of ethanol. Under the 2003 Common Agricultural Policy reform, there was a direct subsidy on production, with €45 per hectare paid to energy crop growers (Sorda et al. 2010: 6983). In the mid-2000s the European Union was as aggressive in its pursuit of biofuels development as either the USA or Brazil. Recently, however, the EU has shifted its stance on biofuels to a much more 'go slowly' approach. In particular the impacts of land use changes associated with biofuel production appear to have gained more traction in Europe than elsewhere.

A 2009 European Parliament directive reflects both of those factors. It requires a minimum binding 10 percent target for biofuels in transport by 2020, and sets out sustainability criteria for land use (ibid.: 6982). In that same year, the EU Directive on Renewable Energy set a binding target for renewables to satisfy 20 percent of electricity consumption by 2020 (ibid.: 6983). In 2013, the EU Parliament capped biofuels from food-based crops, to favor second-generation biofuels from non-food crops like seaweed and corn stover (European Parliament 2013). This amounts to a reduction in overall biofuel inclusion from earlier mandates.

While these directives, the equivalent of laws, come out of the EU Parliament, it is up to the member countries to decide how to implement the directive domestically to reach the targets. In the 2000s France required blending biofuels into gasoline, and provided tax rebates, which began to be phased out in 2011, and penalties for not meeting biofuel production quotas. French ethanol comes from wheat, corn, and sugar beet (Sorda et al. 2010: 6983). Germany mandates that a certain percentage of transportation fuel be biofuels, and uses quotas and tax rebates to ensure supply. German ethanol comes from sugar beets and grains, and its biodiesel from rapeseed oil. Moving forward, Germany's biofuel quota will be tied to its GHG emissions targets (ibid.: 6984). If a member state does not comply with the directive, the EU can take legal action over the legislative infringement in the European Court of Justice (European Commission 2013).

The United States As mentioned previously, the initial driving factor for bringing ethanol back into the US fuel supply was replacement of MTBE as an antiknock agent in gasoline. The 1978 Energy Tax Act gave tax credits for ethanol blenders, but this tax credit on ethanol was phased out in 2011, along with the tariff on Brazilian ethanol imports, although some other subsidies still exist. Increased ethanol production has been a boon to farmers, rural areas, and the corn lobby, by raising the demand and price for corn.

In 2007 the US Energy Independence and Security Act mandated 15 billion gallons (56.8 billion liters) of biofuels used for transport fuels by 2015 and 36 billion gallons (136.3 billion liters) by 2022. The 2022 total target is to comprise no more than 15 billion gallons of corn ethanol. Cellulosic biofuels are expected to contribute 16 billion gallons by 2022 (Sorda et al. 2010: 6979). The USA produced close to thirteen billion gallons of mostly corn ethanol in 2012 and it is expected that production can be increased. Currently, however, some ethanol plants are idle in the USA because of high corn prices resulting from the drought and concomitant low corn harvest of 2012. Furthermore, the current cap on ethanol in gasoline at 10 percent, the so-called 'blend wall,' means that there is a very real ceiling on demand, which appears to be met, resulting in oversupply and low ethanol prices.

Achieving real growth in biofuel usage to offset gasoline usage in the USA will require either raising the amount of ethanol or butanol blended into gasoline, or convincing car manufacturers to build, and American consumers to buy, more flex-fuel vehicles that can run on higher-percentage biofuels, generally E85, which is an 85 percent ethanol and 15 percent gasoline blend. Both options appear difficult. The current 10 percent cap on ethanol blending is the maximum recommended by engine manufacturers without resorting to the modifications present in flex-fuel vehicles capable of running on E85. Some engineers argue that 15 percent ethanol should not cause problems with current vehicles, but there is little consensus on this issue. Automakers, engine manufacturers, and some environmentalists are against increasing the blend (Peckham 2009). It may be easier to go to higher percentages of biofuel with butanol, which has a lower vapor pressure and avoids some of the mechanical problems associated with higher ethanol percentages, but butanol is not yet approved for use in motor fuels.

Increasing the number of flex-fuel vehicles becomes a chicken-and-egg problem. Consumers are unlikely to buy more flex-fuel vehicles if E85 fuel is hard to get or more expensive than standard 10 percent ethanol (E10) gasoline. If consumers are unwilling to buy flex-fuel vehicles, of course, manufacturers are not interested in making them. The market is unlikely to solve this problem until petroleum-based fuels become much more expensive than they are at present. There is already some evidence that the USA may have reached peak gasoline usage in 2005 and that consumption will continue to slowly decline for the foreseeable future (Pyper 2013), so we are unlikely to see price pressures in the short term. This means that government intervention is the only near-term means of increasing the number of flex-fuel vehicles. There is already some government intervention in the form of incentives for car manufacturers to produce a certain number of flex-fuel vehicles each year. The flex-fuel modifications generally add less than $100 to the cost of vehicle production.

The other problem with widespread adoption of E85 fuel is that there is simply not enough ethanol production capacity in either the USA or Brazil at present to supply the amount of ethanol required to switch a sizable proportion of US gasoline usage to E85 fuel. A more workable solution would be to follow Brazil's example and make lower-percentage biofuel blends available for flex-fuel vehicles and slowly increase the blending percentage as more biofuel becomes available. To reach universal E85 use in the USA will require the full rollout of cellulosic and/or algal biofuels as well as importing sugarcane ethanol from Brazil.

Corn-based ethanol as a biofuel in the USA is marginal in terms of both energy return on energy investment, with an EROeI of 1.3, and CO_2 emission reduction, and was never meant to be the major component of a national, sustainable biofuels program. Rather corn ethanol was accepted as the technology we have ready for deployment while more advanced technologies are developed, with the added benefit of helping to support American agriculture and keep more of the US transportation energy investment at home.

The eventual goal would be to switch much of the corn back to food supply as world agricultural prices rise, as they are likely to as population increases and developing countries consume more calories per capita. The emerging problem is that the deployment of advanced biofuels production has lagged behind what was hoped for.

Conclusion

A fundamental question with biofuels is whether they even make sense to include in an energy portfolio. Is it even possible to supplant all of our current liquid fossil fuels for transportation with biofuels? The simple answer is no; no country, aside from possibly Russia and Canada, which have high land surface to population ratios, has enough arable land, even with some of the more optimistic estimates for cellulosic ethanol production. For example, the 2007 Energy Independence and Security Act in the United States mandates 15 billion gallons of biofuels by 2015. As a point of reference, 15 billion gallons would be about 11 percent of the 2012 total consumption of gasoline, which makes sense if you consider that most gasoline sold in the USA is 10 ethanol, or E10. It appears that the USA actually came close to producing 13 billion gallons of ethanol in 2012.

It is not possible to completely replace fossil fuels with biofuels at the levels of current consumption in the global North. What is possible is to offset some proportion of fossil fuel use and work to reduce future consumption through increased efficiency. This can be particularly effective if combined with greater fuel economy in cars such as hybrids or even switching to more extended-range electric vehicles like the Chevy Volt that can run on electricity for a certain number of miles before turning to burning a liquid fuel. By replacing a proportion of gasoline with biofuels and promoting greater fuel efficiency it should be possible to reduce gasoline consumption by at least 50 percent by 2050 in most of the developed world, and hopefully transfer much of the technology to the developing world as well, where much of the growth in CO_2 emissions from transportation is going to originate.

5 | HYDROPOWER

Energy can be derived from moving water. Water power is hardly a new idea; it has been used for hundreds of years. Water power was the energy source for the beginnings of the Industrial Revolution; later on the switch was made to coal-powered steam engines as they were developed. As we discussed in Chapter 1, water can store potential energy when a dam holds it back. Releasing water from the dam so it flows downhill under the force of gravity makes it possible to extract energy from the moving water. This can be done with a simple water wheel or with a turbine to produce electric current. Power can also be generated from tidal and wave power. The majority of hydropower produced worldwide is from damming rivers. In this chapter we present two cases studies. The first is China's Three Gorges Dam; the other is not a single-case study, but instead focuses on transnational issues stemming from large dam construction. Hydropower carries some extra political issues as rivers do not respect human boundaries and what happens upriver affects people and countries downriver.

We list hydropower with other renewable sources of energy, but with some caveats. Most hydropower reservoirs are refilled by rivers and in that sense are renewable, but dams carry extensive impacts both on natural ecosystems and human populations that are akin to those of fossil fuels or nuclear power. Also, most reservoirs eventually fill up with sediment carried by the dammed-up river over a few decades to about a century. Once filled with sediment the hydropower station can still run using river flow directly, but most of the storage capacity is gone; this removes most of the power output flexibility of hydropower. Hydropower is desirable because it produces almost no emissions or other wastes after construction, it is quite efficient, and hydropower is dispatchable, meaning a dam's power output can often be rapidly increased or decreased to feed electricity to the on-demand electrical grid.

Hydropower around the world

In 2011 hydropower accounted for about 16 percent of global electricity generation (Moller 2012). Like many other energy resources, hydropower potential is not evenly distributed around the globe. Some countries naturally possess abundant, easily tapped hydropower, such as Norway, which has a mountainous spine running the entire length of the country. Norway gets over 95 percent of its electricity from hydropower.

Large developed countries, such as the USA, historically had a high percentage of electricity generated by hydropower, as hydropower was the first large-scale source of electricity. Over the past sixty years, as the US population has grown and per capita electricity use has increased with little increase in hydropower generating capacity, this value has slipped considerably. In 1950 hydropower accounted for about 30 percent of electricity generation in the USA, fell to about 7 percent in 2012, and will continue to fall. Essentially all high-value hydropower dam sites in the USA have been used; there are no current plans to build any new hydropower dams. In fact, a number of smaller, 'low head', hydropower dams are being removed in the USA to reestablish migratory fish habitat, thereby reducing total US hydropower. This pattern repeats for much of the developed world. Dams carry real impacts, and as local political power has grown in most of the developed world it has become more and more difficult to build new, large, hydropower projects.

The top four countries for hydropower, as measured by total installed generating capacity, are China, Brazil, Canada, and the USA (IEA 2010b). According to the Earth Policy Institute, in 2011 China generated 694 billion kWh, which accounted for 15 percent of China's total electricity generation. Brazil generated 430 billion kWh, which accounted for 86 percent of its total generation. Canada generated 377 kWh, which accounted for 62 percent of its total, and the USA generated 328 billion kWh, which accounted for a little more than 7 percent of total generation (Moller 2012). While China and the USA have large inventories of hydropower, they are dwarfed by total Chinese and US electricity consumption and thus represent only a small percentage of the total electricity generated. EROeI for hydropower varies but generally is high, ranging from 60 to about 100.

Many smaller, less developed countries also have high percentages of electricity generated by hydropower. Paraguay, Bhutan, the Democratic Republic of Congo, Lesotho, Mozambique, Nepal, and Zambia generate almost all of their electricity using hydropower; hydropower in Ethiopia accounts for 88 percent of its electricity generation (ibid.). The percentages are so high because of a small total domestic electricity supply generated by just one or two hydropower projects. Paraguay is in the best position in terms of development. The World Bank classifies it as a lower-middle-income country. About 90 percent of its population has access to electricity, and consumes 12 percent of the energy produced; the rest is exported (Factbook 2014). In a more challenging example, less than 10 percent of the population of the Democratic Republic of Congo (DRC) has access to electricity, and 85 percent of the hydroelectricity produced goes to large consumers (Peixe 2013), mainly in the mining industry. As these countries develop further they will need considerable additional generating capacity. How these countries will meet growing demand largely depends on whether they have additional usable hydropower resources and can obtain funding to develop them. Other renewable sources such as geothermal, wind, and solar might be used as well. They will also be tempted to build fossil-fuel-powered plants.

Dams and reservoirs

Not every river is suitable for a hydropower dam. The river must have a reasonable gradient, which is the slope or amount of vertical distance covered per unit of horizontal distance. The river valley should also be relatively narrow. Rivers with steep gradients and narrow valleys are found in hilly or mountainous regions that often have significant natural hazard problems, such as earthquakes and landslides. Flat plains are usually not suitable for hydropower, although dams for flood control or public drinking water may be built in these regions.

Even if the river has a suitable gradient, dam placement is a complicated process. First the local bedrock of the river valley must be assayed for strength and water impermeability. The dam must hold back millions of tons of water and this is accomplished by transferring the weight of the water into the bedrock around the dam, so the bedrock must be strong enough to take the load. Weak rock types such as shale and mudstone or heavily fractured harder rock are unacceptable foundations for dams. The bedrock must also be mostly watertight. This may seem like a given, but it is not. Many rock types allow significant amounts of water to pass through them; they are water permeable. Sandstones, for instance, can be strong enough to support a dam but are often permeable. As water passes through the rock it weakens the rock structure, which can lead to eventual failure of the dam.

Building large dams has become a fairly straightforward engineering task, as long as there is robust oversight of the contracting companies, which may not occur in some countries with serious corruption and/or transparency problems. One key to dam construction is the need to fully understand the seismic hazards of a dam site. Many dams are built in mountainous regions, but the reason those mountains exist is because the Earth's crust has been forced upward, which often involves cracks in the Earth's crust, or faults. Many faults are semi-active and may move only every few hundred to a few thousand years, making them difficult to detect. The entire reservoir must be assessed for seismic hazard, not just the dam site. Filling the reservoir may activate faults. Water weighs about eight pounds per gallon, so weight adds up fast. The potential for large landslides should also be considered, as a landslide into an existing reservoir can create what amounts to a tsunami that can overtop and damage a dam as well as create a lethal flood down the river valley even if the dam is not destroyed.

Hydropower dams have impacts on people living in the area upstream of the proposed dam and the local ecology. A large dam will flood hundreds to a few thousand square miles of land as the reservoir behind the dam fills. This will in many cases lead to the forced relocation of large numbers of people, who may or may not be adequately compensated for their lost land, to say nothing of the potential impacts of relocation on the local culture. An additional impact is that high-quality agricultural land is usually lost when a dam is constructed. This can matter in countries where prime farmland is scarce. Significant local scenic value may be lost as well by the flooding. For instance the filling of the Glen Canyon dam in Utah in the USA buried a beautiful scenic gorge and replaced it with a large reservoir. Archaeological sites are also often victims to dams. Turkey's Birecik Dam flooded the historical city of Zeugma, although a large publicity campaign helped to fund urgent excavations to save many of the artifacts (Brunwasser 2012), but dams in China alone have flooded thousands of archaeological sites.

The filling reservoir will also likely destroy significant local ecological resources. Not only will a large amount of land be lost to flooding, affecting land animals and plants, but the entire river ecosystem is altered by dam construction. Aquatic organisms that once migrated up and down the river in different seasons are blocked by the dam and may not be able to adjust, leading to their diminution or extinction. The Pacific salmon of the northwest United States are a classic example of a species heavily impacted by dam construction. Furthermore, the reservoir itself is a radically different environment from a free-flowing river, and the types of organisms that thrive there will be different from what existed previously.

Ideally both human and ecological impacts should be considered in deciding for or against dam construction in a particular area. Weighing the effects of relocation on human populations and assessing probable ecological impacts is unfortunately not an easy or clear measurement and is thus a contentious issue, as will be discussed in the case studies section of this chapter. In the 1990s the World Bank, whose purpose is to fund large infrastructure projects to bring about development, stopped funding large dams. As the DRC case exemplifies, large dam projects like the Inga 1 and Inga 2 did not benefit the vast majority of the population, but instead supplied most of the power they generated to industry. In 2012, the World Bank agreed to fund a third dam on the Congo river, apparently changing its dam policy (World Bank 2012).

Converting the energy in falling water into electrical current involves running the water through large turbines not unlike those used in harnessing steam power in a fossil fuel or nuclear power plant. At the base of a hydropower dam is a large structure referred to as a turbine house or powerhouse. Water is carried down from the dam, often in tunnels cut in the rock around the dam or through the dam itself, to the powerhouse. Once the water hits the turbine blades and gives up some of its energy to spin the blades it is released back into the riverbed downstream of the dam.

These water releases bring up another environmental impact of dams. Electrical grid operators love hydropower because it is dispatchable; when more power is called for, more water can be released from the dam to generate more electrical current. This is good for electrical grid balancing, but not so good for river ecology. Most animals that have evolved to live in river systems are used to fluctuations in river levels as seasons change, but dams release more water at unpredictable intervals and often not in the same seasons that animals have adapted to, leading to potential life cycle disruptions of aquatic animals. Lastly, the sediment carried by the river is mostly deposited behind the dam; this affects downstream structures such as sandbars that some organisms need to survive. Why do rivers carry sediment? Water is one of the primary erosive features on planet Earth. Slowly wearing down mountains and rivers are the conveyor belts carrying eroded rock to lower-lying regions or the sea. The very gradient that gives the river water the energy that we humans use to generate electrical current also means that more sediment can be carried, as sediment load is a function of the speed at which water is moving. So the higher-gradient rivers more desirable for hydropower are also the rivers that will most rapidly fill their reservoirs with sediment, greatly reducing the usefulness of the dam for hydropower.

Hydropower across much of the developed world is a mature power source, in that little additional growth in generating capacity is expected. This is because of both few remaining suitable sites and an increased awareness of the impacts of hydropower on local human and non-human populations, combined with anti-dam activism in democracies. Instead traditional hydropower will slowly decline as reservoirs fill up or dams are removed because of excessive ecological impacts. The developing world is quite another story; most of the growth in dam building will occur across the developing world where local human representation and valuation of ecological resources are much less assured.

The other hydropower: tidal and wave power

We are used to thinking of hydropower as involving rivers, but any source of moving water carries energy that may be extracted. As the moon orbits Earth its gravity draws up a bulge of ocean water that moves around the Earth, creating the tides. Total tidal range depends on a number of factors, mostly dominated by local geography, but generally ranging from a few inches to several tens of feet. The Bay of Fundy in Nova Scotia, Canada, has some of the largest tidal ranges on Earth at more than thirty feet of difference between high and low tides. There are two types of tidal power: impoundment and free-flowing or hydrokinetic.

Coastal embayments can be found or built that will capture water using movable walls, or sluice gates, to let water in at high tide and prevent it from slowly leaving as low tide approaches. Instead, once a sufficient vertical displacement of water has occurred, generally several hours after high tide, water is released through channels to drive turbines and produce electric current. Some tidal impoundments use reversible turbines so that they can generate some power on the incoming tide and can also pump additional water into the 'basin' as hydrogravitic storage. The downside of tidal impoundment is that its capacity factor, or the amount of time it is capable of generating electric current, is usually quite low for a hydropower project, under 50 percent of the time, which means that it will take longer to recoup the costs of construction.

Tidal impoundment is also not particularly dispatchable, as it can only generate electricity when sufficient vertical displacement of water levels exists, and this is controlled by the timing of the tides, not humans. Human impacts of tidal impoundment are usually quite low, as the area was flooded at high tide anyway. Ecological impacts vary but are generally less than those of traditional hydropower because, again, the area is still flooded twice a day, although this is no longer tied as tightly to the timing of the tides; movement of marine animals is often impaired, however. The La Rance Barrage, built in 1966 in France, was the world's first tidal impoundment power station (Wyre Tidal Energy n.d.). There are several other tidal impoundment power stations in Europe and one in South Korea, built in 2011.

The moving water of tides can also be used directly to turn turbines and produce electric current. This is free-flowing or hydrokinetic tidal power. Water must be moving fairly rapidly for the tide to turn conventional turbines; this occurs only in very limited areas. Traditional turbines can be harmful to marine life, because the turbines act like blenders mounted on the ocean floor. The first grid-connected hydrokinetic tidal energy project in North America was installed in 2012 in Cobscook Bay, Maine (US Department of Energy 2013a). There are a number of hydrokinetic power stations built and planned in the United Kingdom, including 'the largest wave and tidal development zone in the world,' called the Pentland Firth and Orkney Waters Marine Energy Park, in Scotland (Shankleman 2012). Alternatively some groups are looking at unconventional turbines that do not require such rapid water movement, but these systems are still in the early stages of development and it is unknown whether they can be made cost effective or not. Like tidal impoundment, hydrokinetic power has a capacity factor below 50 percent and is not dispatchable.

There is also energy available in waves, but it is much less concentrated than water in a river and focused in an up-and-down displacement rather than in purely forward motion, thus conventional turbines cannot be used. A number of devices have been developed that can harvest energy from wave action, but they all suffer from the basic problem of the low energy density of waves. Thousands of wave generators would be needed to equal one large coal-fired power plant and many hundreds of miles of cables needed to carry the electricity back to shore. Wave power's advantage is that wave action varies less than wind, and changes magnitude more slowly, so wave power would likely have a higher capacity factor than wind or tidal power. However, until wave-powered generators can be made less expensive, but still rugged enough to survive for many years, their cost per kilowatt generated will not be anywhere near as economical as more conventional forms of power.

Case studies

Hydropower in China: the Three Gorges mega-dam China's energy policy was discussed in Chapter 3. The Three Gorges Dam on the Yangtze river in China's central Hubei province is currently the largest hydropower-generating dam in the world; it can produce a maximum output of 22,500 MW of electricity. For comparison, a large coal-fired power plant may produce 500 MW, so the dam is roughly equal to twenty-four or so large coal-fired power plants with essentially no ongoing emissions or wastes. The Three Gorges Dam cannot utilize all its installed capacity constantly, however, because of its other reservoir uses such as irrigation, flood control, and ship navigation. This is quite common for large dams; they serve a number of different purposes, resulting in a capacity factor of 45 percent.

The Three Gorges Dam is 2.3 kilometers (about 1.5 miles) long and 181 meters (about 600 feet) high. The dam was constructed over a seventeen-year period starting in 1994, reaching full power output in 2012. It is one of the largest concrete structures in the world. The reservoir behind the dam flooded about 403 square miles and forced the relocation of 1.2 million people, making it one of the dams with the highest human impact ever constructed. The depth of the Yangtze river gorge means that the reservoir actually has one of the smallest flooded footprints for a large dam worldwide. The dam has affected the ecology of the river, directly leading to the extinction of the Yangtze river dolphin, whose numbers were already very low, and the likely extinction of the Yangtze sturgeon. The reservoir flooded an area rich in biodiversity and human archaeological history. Long-term impacts on the river are likely to be only partially attributable to the Three Gorges Dam. There are several dams downstream of the Three Gorges Dam and several more dams slated for construction upstream of it.

In 2011 China derived about 15 percent of its electricity from hydropower. In terms of total installed generating capacity China is the world's leader in hydropower. Roughly 50 percent of in-construction hydropower projects worldwide are in China. If China stays on its current course, over the next two decades both the Yangtze and Yellow river systems, the third- and seventh-largest river systems in the world by total watershed area, will be converted into a long series of large reservoirs.

The direct human and ecological damage inflicted on the river systems is hard to gauge. The lower parts of both river systems have been heavily populated for thousands of years, with little remaining natural landscape. Over the last twenty years, China's explosive economic growth has come at the price of significant and widespread environmental damage, meaning both rivers were already negatively impacted. Certainly the dam systems will not address the negative effects of pollution, and in some cases will make the problem worse by increasing the amount of time it takes to flush pollution through the river system. The dam systems will help to mitigate large-scale floods, which have plagued both river basins for much of China's history. Equally important to flood mitigation are the massive reforestation projects China is undertaking in both watersheds after decades of deforestation.

Earlier we mentioned that many large-scale dams face protest. In democracies, collective action and protests can influence states' decision-making. This is not to say collective action will always be successful, but it can serve to challenge and influence policies. India's Sardar Sarovar Dam, sometimes called the Narmada dam for the valley where it is located, began construction in 1979. It is a huge structure, whose end height will be 138 meters (about 453 feet). The Save Narmada Movement (NBA in its Hindi acronym) organized in 1985 against the dam project. It was successful in getting the World Bank to withdraw funding from the dam project in 1993. The group has also drawn attention to the lack of compensation for the hundreds of thousands displaced and to questions of the impacts of industrialization on rural societies (Randolph 2010). The first iteration of the Belo Monte Dam in Brazil was stopped in 1989 by a coalition of indigenous groups and environmentalists. Its second iteration, proposed in 2003, faced lawsuits that eventually worked their way to the Supreme Court. Lawsuits were also brought to the Inter-American Commission on Human Rights. Lawsuits have delayed the project, but the dam is under construction (Amazon Watch 2014).

China is not a democracy; the state media rarely cover stories critical of dam projects. Still, we see collective action and protest against dams and relocation policies. The state response to protest tends to be repressive. In Yaowan village, which was to be relocated because of the Three Gorges Dam, 'hundreds of police and paramilitary troops were deployed to stop the protests' (Economist 2002). In 2005 more than 100,000 people protested against the Pubugou Dam project in Sichuan province, which riot police ended (Yardley 2007). However, in 2007 the Chinese government admitted there were environmental problems stemming from the Three Gorges Dam (Yuxia 2007).

Transnational issues The United Nations' International Decade for Action 'Water for Life' 2005–2015 has thirteen focus areas, one of which is transboundary waters. Many rivers are transnational; they often cross several international boundaries and, more critically, often carry water from humid headwater countries downstream to arid countries. Dams are planned domestically to bring benefits to a country, but if put on a river crossing an international boundary or emptying into an international water basin, their effects will be transnational. In this case study, we discuss international dam policy development. We then point to three places around the world that exemplify some of the challenges of large dams on trans-boundary rivers.

Trans-boundary rivers and international institutions There are international institutions, laws, and practices to deal with water-related issues on the 261 trans-boundary river basins in the world (Conca 2008: 218; Biswas 2008). International regimes exist for issues pertaining to the global commons. The oceans, the atmosphere, even Antarctica are global commons. No one state can assert its ownership over a commons. We have global agreements that deal with commons. Some examples are the Montreal Protocol that dealt with CFC-caused ozone depletion, the Kyoto Protocol that dealt with CO_2 emissions, and the International Convention on Whaling. The challenge trans-boundary rivers present for international regimes, though, is that dealing with rivers is not like dealing with other global environmental issues because rivers are not part of the global commons. Rivers are a local resource, and water flow and the needs of local communities have changed over time. International regimes are not normally flexible enough to deal with such variable circumstances (Conca 2006). Even within a country, a river's potential can be harnessed by a state by placement of a dam, and even that often puts the local communities in conflict with the state, to say nothing of the tensions created with those elsewhere along the river.

There are currently 145 agreements dealing with trans-boundary water sources. Thirty-nine percent of those have to do with hydropower, and 37 percent deal with water utilization (United Nations 2014). The 1997 UN Convention on the Law of the Non-Navigable Uses of International Watercourses laid out three obligations – equitable and reasonable utilization, prevention of significant harm, and prior notification of planned measures (McCaffrey n.d.). Thirty-five countries must ratify the Convention for it to become binding. As of 20 December 2013, there are thirty-three countries that are party to the Convention, and four more have signed but not ratified it (Status of the Watercourses Convention 2013).

The World Bank and the World Conservation Union sponsored a conference in 1997 to discuss the growing local and international controversies over large dams (UNEP n.d.). One of the recommendations of that workshop was to establish a World Commission on Dams (WCD), which was created the following year. The Final Report recognizes both the contributions and benefits dams have made to development. Also recognized are that those benefits have often not been distributed equitably and that dams can have unacceptably high social and environmental costs, and lastly that many large dam projects run well over initial budget estimates (WCD 2000: xxviii). To address these issues, the WCD recommended that project planning and implementation should meet five core values: equity, efficiency, participatory decision-making, sustainability, and accountability (ibid.: xxxii). Their specific policy recommendations are:

1 gain public acceptance before initiation of a project;
2 perform a comprehensive options assessment to understand alternatives;
3 address social issues and changing needs for existing dams;

4 work to sustain existing rivers and livelihoods, because 'rivers, watersheds, and aquatic ecosystems are the biological engines of the planet';

5 recognize entitlements and share benefits equitably;

6 ensure compliance;

7 share rivers for peace, development, and security. (Ibid.: xxxiv–xxxvi)

The World Commission on Dams was disbanded after its report came out in 2000, and the United Nations Environment Program's Dams and Development Project has undertaken the task of promoting the values and priorities the report recommended.

Dams on trans-boundary rivers Dams on trans-boundary rivers can be contentious, but the presence of an international or bilateral institution can help to defray some of the tension. Cambodia, Laos, Thailand, and Vietnam have cooperated since 1957 via the Mekong River Commission. That cooperation continued even during periods of unrest in the region among those countries, although it is currently under strain as several member countries now have competing dam proposals for the Mekong. India and Pakistan have cooperated via the Indus River Commission, even through their 1971 and 1999 wars (Conca 2008).

The Danube river passes through eighteen countries. It has been altered for power generation and flood protection since the sixteenth century (International Commission for the Protection of the Danube River n.d.). Hundreds of dams have been built on the Danube and its tributaries, including some that generate power for more than one country. Two of the largest dams on the Danube are the Iron Gate I and Iron Gate II, where it forms the border between Romania and Serbia. As on the Niagara river that marks the border between the USA and Canada, there are power-generating stations in both countries.

In 1993, a dispute over a dam and lock project on the Danube was brought to the International Court of Justice.[1] Based on a 1977 treaty, Hungary and Czechoslovakia agreed to build the Gabcíkovo-Nagymaros Dam, which was really a series of four locks, two built by Hungary and two by Czechoslovakia. Both countries started work on the project, but had agreed to slow down. In 1993, Hungary broke the treaty, arguing it would not build the dam because of environmental and other concerns. Hungary also questioned whether it was obliged to follow a treaty signed with Czechoslovakia when they were both satellites of the USSR, and argued that Slovakia broke the treaty when it diverted waters into a bypass canal in 1992. Slovakia wanted to move forward with the project.

The two countries agreed to bring the case to the International Court of Justice (ICJ). The summary below is drawn from the ICJ's 1997 judgment summary (ICJ 1997). The ICJ recognized that Hungary's concern for its natural environment represented an 'essential interest' of that state, one of the conditions that would allow Hungary to not comply with treaty obligations. However, the ICJ thought Hungary's concern did not reflect 'immediate peril' and was not sufficiently established in 1989, when Hungary broke the treaty. In short, Hungary was not entitled to break the treaty, but it was exonerated for breaking it because of the country's essential interest. The Court also found that Slovakia had not broken the treaty in 1992, so Hungary did not have the right to terminate the treaty. The Court found that Hungary and Slovakia did have to abide by the treaty, and that Hungary had to compensate Slovakia for damage caused by its suspension of the treaty; Slovakia had to compensate Hungary for damage it incurred because of Slovakia's 'provisional solution.'

This case is important because the Court ruled that because of new norms in international environmental law the 1977 treaty is not static, and is open to adaptation to emerging norms of international law. It was a 'groundbreaking case on the application of ecological necessity to treaty obligations' (Deets 2009: 37). Because so many controversial dams are on trans-boundary rivers, they are subject to international law, and, as we see in this case, help to shape international law.

The Nile river basin and Niger river basin in Africa are other sites of contention on trans-boundary rivers. Egypt sees the planned Grand Ethiopian Renaissance Dam on the Blue Nile, a tributary of the Nile, as a threat to its water supply. In 1959 Egypt and Sudan signed an accord allocating water resources on the Nile, but none of the upriver countries was included in that agreement. Egypt insists the 1959 accord still stands. Ethiopia signed a Co-operative Framework agreement with Rwanda, Tanzania, Uganda, Kenya, and Burundi that 'adopts principles of equitable and reasonable use of waters that do not cause significant harm to other states' (Davison and Feteha 2014). The Framework set up a Nile River Basin Commission, which will hopefully enable cooperation in the same way the Mekong and Indus River Commissions do.

Ethiopia's almost-completed GIBE III dam on the Omo river, which empties into Kenya's Lake Turkana, demonstrates the power of two other international forces – activism and critical discourse. Non-governmental organizations (NGOs) like Campagna per la Riforma della Banca Mundiale, Counter Balance, International Rivers, Friends of Lake Turkana, and Survival International have joined together and mounted a global campaign against the dam (Stop Gibe 3 Dam 2014). They have drawn attention to Ethiopia's suppression of dissent, challenges to food security, and ecological concerns they have about the dam.

The groups' actions have helped to shape international discourse taking place at international meetings and on the internet. On the one side are claims of environmental and cultural damage. On the other are those in the developing world who point out the hypocrisy of those from the industrialized world responsible for global warming and all kinds of environmental destruction trying to stop an environmentally and socially responsible project in a poor country (Zenawi 2011: 5). Zenawi (ibid.: 5) repeats the argument that those in the developed world want Africa to remain miserable and poor 'so they can come and visit nature in its pristine state in the winter every so often.' Sentiments from both sides affect lending practices, ideas about development, and reflection on what it means to be an engaged, global citizen.

Conclusion

Regardless of regime type, both democracies and authoritarian systems must face competing needs in their decision-making. Hydropower is a good example of having to balance competing 'goods' like development, modernization, flood control, and low carbon emission power generation with 'bads' like human displacement, damage to ecological systems, and the inequitable distribution of dam benefits.

Wind power is a form of indirect solar power. The sun heats the Earth's surface, warming the air near the ground. This warmer air rises, displacing cooler air and creating wind. There is quite a bit more complexity to the Earth's wind patterns, but the essence is that they are powered by the sun. To capture energy from the wind you need something for the wind to push against. Over five thousand years ago sails to move ships were among the first manmade devices to take advantage of wind power. About fifteen hundred years ago came stationary windmills for grain grinding. More advanced windmills with gearing systems to carry the rotational force of the windmill blades to a rolling grindstone or a saw blade appeared in the 1100s in Europe. Gearing systems or transmissions were important because the windmill blades often turned more slowly than the output device, such as a saw blade needed for cutting timber.

Interest in generating electricity from wind dates to the 1880s, when Scottish academic James Blyth designed and built a homemade wind turbine to power his remote vacation home. By the early 1900s a modest number of wind turbines, generally each uniquely constructed, were generating electricity in Europe and the USA, usually where there was not ready access to hydropower. Hydropower was the first large-scale AC-generating source. The much larger use of wind power in this period was to pump water from underground sources in rural areas, a task still efficiently provided by wind power today.

The first large, grid-scale wind turbines date to the 1930s and 1940s in the USSR and the USA as World War II loomed. The first 1 MW turbine was installed on a hilltop in Vermont in 1941. However, its transmission and generator were not up to the task and failed after only about a thousand hours of operation. They were not replaced owing to wartime material constraints and lack of better available equipment. Wind power then went into hiatus, except for small-scale uses in remote areas, until the 1970s oil shocks revived interest. Many small wind turbines, at capacities of a couple of hundred kW, were installed during the mid-1970s. They had small blades that turned at a high rate of speed and were not particularly efficient. The rapidly turning blades were also essentially invisible to birds, which tried to fly through them and were killed. Environmental advocates derisively referred to some of these early wind turbines in California, an early adopter of wind power in the USA, as 'birdie blenders.' Low oil prices in the 1980s once again helped to kill interest in wind turbines in much of the world.

Not every country gave up on wind power. Denmark, in particular, stuck with wind, one of the few natural resources it possesses in abundance, and became a global center for development of new wind turbine technology. By the late 1980s Danish engineers had come up with larger, more efficient, wind turbines and more reliable transmissions and generators for grid connection. We will return to Denmark in the case studies. This was the start of modern wind power.

Wind power generation has taken off globally this century, going from 17.4 GW in 2000 to 282.4 GW of installed capacity in 2012 (GWEC 2013). This total represented about 5 percent of world electricity generation in 2012.[1] The top wind power generating countries in 2012 were China (75.6 GW), followed by the USA (60 GW), Germany (31.3 GW), Spain (22.7 GW), and India (18.4 GW) (ibid.). The top countries for wind power by percentage of total electricity consumption are all in Europe, which has the longest history with wind energy. In 2012 wind's share of total electricity consumption in Denmark was 27 percent, in Portugal 17 percent, in Spain 16 percent, and in Ireland 13 percent (EWEA 2013). For comparison, in 2012 wind power represented 3.5 percent of total US electricity generation (US Energy Information Administration 2013f).

The case studies presented in this chapter illustrate the importance of policy in meeting energy goals. Denmark and the United States chose differing incentive mechanisms for the development of and investment in wind power generation. The incentives chosen shaped not just the renewable energy sector, but also had local economic, social, and technical implications. As we have seen with many countries' energy policies, they are about more than just where a country will derive its power; they are also tools for economic and social growth. In the case studies presented thus far, the economic and social focus is best exemplified by Brazil's 2004 Biodiesel Program. As we will see for Denmark and the USA, public support for wind power and renewable energy in part reflects the degree to which society is included in renewable energy projects. Energy policy consistency also played a major role in developing a wind industry. Denmark's policy remained consistent for two decades, while US policy has been remarkably inconsistent.

Wind power is forecast to grow rapidly over the coming years, particularly in the USA and China. Wind power in most European countries, except the United Kingdom, is mature, and its growth will be slower. The UK is planning more offshore wind generation. Several European countries are thought to be near the practical current limit of how much electricity can be generated from wind before their electrical grid is destabilized. To understand why there may be limits to how much wind can contribute to a country's electricity generation we need to discuss two problems that both wind and solar power have in common. We will discuss solar power in Chapter 8.

Intermittency and dispatchability

The most important difference between wind or solar energy systems and fossil fuels, hydropower, geothermal power, or nuclear power is that wind and solar power are intermittent power sources. The sun does not always shine and the wind does not always blow. Intermittency is a real problem for our electricity grid, as it is currently configured. Remember that the grid is an on-demand system. Electricity is not stored in the grid; it is only transmitted, almost instantaneously, from generator to user. When more electricity is needed, it must be generated to balance the grid. Wind and solar have the dual problem of not always being available (intermittency) and of not being dispatchable. That is, power output cannot necessarily be increased as needed. For instance, the amount of electricity generated by a wind turbine is a function of how hard the wind is blowing, not of how much electricity is needed by the grid at a given instant.

There are solutions to both the intermittency and the dispatchability issues, but they come with costs. One solution to both problems is to build more wind and solar generating capacity than is strictly needed. If one needs 150 MW, and on average your renewable source is producing electricity only 50 percent of the time, then you build 300 MW of capacity. Scalability, the ability to easily make a project larger or smaller, is an additional benefit of both wind and solar power. However, as you might surmise, building twice as much capacity as you need is going to be about twice as expensive, meaning your power is twice as expensive as the cheapest fossil fuel, usually coal or natural gas, with which you can build much closer to just what you need in terms of generating capacity.

Another solution is to distribute generation over a wide geographic area. This strategy takes advantage of the law of averages – that if the wind is not blowing or the sun is not shining in one area, then it is likely to be blowing or sunny somewhere else. Wide geographic distribution can help reduce the amount of redundant generating power needed, but cannot fully offset intermittency, particularly for solar at night. Dispatchability is likewise improved by spreading wind or solar generating capacity over a wide area, but it is not completely ameliorated either. This is one reason the EU has pushed for the largest electricity market possible, to take advantage of renewable power spread out across an entire continent. This will likely also be a driving factor in unifying the three-headed US grid system discussed in Chapter 1.

Energy storage likewise strengthens the grid against both intermittency and dispatchability problems. However, as discussed in Chapter 1, it is very difficult to store electric current, which means converting electricity into another form of energy and then back again when electricity is needed. Cost and reliability of storage systems are also issues. Well-proven technologies such as hydrogravitic and compressed air energy storage are fairly expensive. Some types of chemical batteries, such as liquid metal batteries, may be able to help if they can be made economically, which remains to be seen.

Yet another option is to back up intermittent systems with other generating capacity that is more dispatchable. As mentioned in the last chapter, hydro-power is an ideal option but not one that will be expanded in most of the developed world. The generation III+ and generation IV nuclear power plants, some of which are under construction, are more capable of rapidly raising or lowering their electrical output than today's nuclear plants are, a design referred to as 'load following,' and could help. Lastly, from a CO_2 generating perspective at least, there is the option of fossil-fueled backup generation. For fossil fuels, actually only modern combined-cycle turbine-driven natural gas plants are truly dispatchable. Most coal-fired plants require considerable lead time to feed more coal into their boilers to increase electrical output. Ironically, coal gasification, part of Carbon Capture and Sequestration (CCS) technology, would make CCS coal plants more dispatchable.

Most current electric grids will have at least some problems with grid stability as intermittent sources approach about 20 percent of total daily electricity generation, and some grids will have problems at even lower percentages. Currently some European countries are above this rather mushy 20 percent threshold and are able to stabilize their grids by exporting extra power to surrounding countries. Germany, for instance, has had grid reliability problems as it tries to integrate large amounts of wind and solar power into its existing grid (Schröder 2012). However, it should be noted that there is no fundamental constraint to adding more transmission capacity and energy storage to the grid to accommodate higher percentages of intermittent power sources (Mai et al. 2012). The primary hurdle is financial, not technological. Who pays for the grid upgrades? This is particularly problematic in balkanized or highly divided grid systems where there are incentives to protect local ratepayers even if they could benefit in the future from the grid improvements.

Modern wind turbines

Like their predecessors, modern wind turbines have gearing systems to step up the rotation captured by the turning blades to produce 60 Hz electricity, or whatever frequency is in use locally, while the blades turn more slowly. The blades on a large 1.5 MW wind turbine may appear to be turning slowly. However, the blade is often about forty meters or 120 feet long, and the speed at the blade tip may be in excess of eighty kilometers per hour (about fifty miles per hour). The amount of energy captured by a wind turbine increases at the square of the diameter of the blade sweep. This is one reason why large wind turbines are more cost effective. Another is that it is cheaper to build one large transmission and generator than several smaller ones.

A typical 1.5 MW wind turbine is 60–80 meters (about 200 feet) tall, with blades about forty meters (110 feet) long, and has an installation cost of \$4–5 million. The wind does not blow all the time so a wind turbine will not generate electricity 100 percent of the time. A typical yearly average would be about 25 percent of theoretical capacity or capacity factor. At a capacity factor of 25 percent, and assuming 15 cents per kilowatt hour,[2] the turbine would produce about \$500,000 worth of electricity per year. Its payback time would be about ten years, and probably a bit longer owing to ongoing maintenance costs. EROeI for onshore wind is generally about 20.

Wind turbines are getting progressively bigger. The 1.5 MW turbine mentioned above was a standard size installed from 2005 to 2010. Larger turbines came on the market in the late 2000s and are now starting to achieve market penetration. The average turbine installed in 2014 will probably be 2.5 MW. Very large turbines capable of producing 10 MW or more have been designed, and a few have been built, but are very tall at 91–122 meters (300–400 feet), and it is unclear whether they will be commonly used.

Placement of wind farms Large groupings of wind turbines are called wind farms. Deciding where to put a wind farm is critical to its success. Most developed countries have wind speed data going back thirty to fifty years, which allows pretty good predictions of average daily wind speeds. Generally wind turbines produce maximum output at wind speeds of 32–48 kilometers per hour (20–30 miles per hour). At very high wind speeds, usually above 80 kph (50 mph), the turbines will actually turn themselves off to prevent damage to the turbine's transmission and generator. So wind farms are best placed in areas with frequent wind speeds in the 32–48 kilometers per hour range.

Wind speed is not the only consideration for wind farm placement. Modern wind turbines are less dangerous to birds than earlier wind turbines, but still should not be placed in proximity to large numbers of birds. For instance, migratory pathways of geese and ducks are best avoided, even though this may mean avoiding a favorable placement on high ground above a lake or river. Wind turbines have also been shown to have detrimental effects on bat populations, particularly those situated on high ridgelines on the eastern coast of North America (Curry 2009). Bats are important predators of numerous insect species and significant reduction in their numbers would mean more agricultural loss and increased pesticide usage.

Many people also object to wind farms for aesthetic or financial reasons. Certainly wind farms alter the appearance of the landscape around them. At 61 or more meters (200 feet or more) tall they can be seen for several miles. In close proximity they produce a noticeable whine that can be aggravating. Lastly, those that see the turbines are often not the ones directly profiting from them. Leasing fees for the land a turbine sits on go only to the owner of that land. Wind farms also usually contribute to the local tax base, which may reduce property taxes or other fees paid by local residents that do not get direct leasing payments.

Offshore wind farms Most wind power capacity installed to date has been on land. As the technology has developed, however, a number of countries have begun building offshore wind farms in the ocean or on large lakes. There are several advantages to offshore wind farms. The wind is steadier along coastlines, with capacity factors approaching 40 percent. Also, if they are located far enough offshore, there are no permanent human residents around to complain about the landscape effects. Offshore wind areas are also often proximal to power-hungry areas of high population density in Europe and along the East Coast of the USA and China, meaning that losses from power transmission can be minimized.

The disadvantages of offshore wind power are also sizable. The support towers for the turbines must be built to withstand wave action, which tends to be aggressive in areas of high wind, where most offshore wind farms would be situated. The corrosive action of salt water is also a problem for metal components. Construction and maintenance costs are considerably higher for offshore wind. Lastly the electricity must be brought back to land, which requires the construction of submerged high-voltage power lines, an expensive proposition. Although close proximity to populated areas likely offsets this cost, compared to more remote onshore wind power.

To date most offshore wind projects have been in Europe. As of the end of 2013 three large offshore wind projects came online in the UK alone, totaling some 962 MW of generating capacity. These include the London Array, the world's largest offshore wind farm, with 175 turbines generating 630 MW at maximum output. However, development of several offshore wind farms in Germany is currently on hold owing to higher than expected costs (Fröhlings-dorf 2013). Estimates for the cost of offshore wind-generating capacity have gone up considerably from earlier projections. In 2011 a UK study estimated levelized cost for offshore wind electricity at 16.9 pence/kWh ($0.27/kWh) based on actually built projects. For reference, the same report's levelized cost estimate for new-built nuclear power in the UK was 9.6 pence/kWh (Mott MacDonald Inc. 2010). Currently offshore wind power is viable only with considerable government subsidy. It is not clear whether improvements in technology can bring down prices in the future, as turbine-based wind power is a fairly mature technology; there is not a lot of improvement left to make.

Small-scale wind power

In some areas wind can also be used to power individual homes, although it is not usually the least expensive option. Simple wind turbines generate DC current, which must be converted to AC to run most household appliances. More of a problem, though, are the rapid fluctuations in power output that a wind turbine can produce as wind speed can vary rapidly. Usually this requires some sort of buffering system, capacitors, or batteries to store energy and feed it into a typical household at a steady rate. Unlike solar panels, even small-scale wind turbines cannot usually be attached directly to a house, requiring a separate supporting structure. All of these factors make small-scale wind power a fairly expensive option for residential power. An interesting use for small-scale wind power is building heating, which can be powered directly with the DC current and which usually does not require current buffering, helping to keep costs down. However, a backup heating system would be required for most locations for when the wind is not blowing.

Lastly, some municipalities have taken steps to tightly regulate or even outright ban residential wind turbines. This is due to complaints similar to those against large turbines, namely that they are obtrusive in terms of both sight and sound. Some newer small wind turbine designs use vertical blades, or impellors, that produce much less noise than traditional horizontal blades, but it remains to be seen whether these newer designs will help alleviate local concerns about small-scale wind power.

The real future for small- to medium-scale wind power lies in the developing world, where isolated wind power farms could produce electricity for local residents without requiring expensive long-distance transmission lines to be built. In other words, it may be possible for some developing nations to avoid the large investments in traditional electrical grids if decentralized local power generation is used. This would be similar to the way many developing nations have abandoned installing a traditional landline phone system infrastructure, and gone straight to cellular. See the Kenya case study in Chapter 8 on solar power for more discussion of this possibility. Without energy storage or backup generating systems wind power would be intermittent, but this would not be outside the norm for many countries. Backup power could be solar or some mix of fossil-fueled generating capacity and/or energy storage, although the price of redundant systems will be hard to justify for cash-strapped countries.

Case studies

Denmark Denmark began producing oil from its own offshore reserves in 1972. As in most of the cases we have discussed so far, the 1973 oil crisis shaped Denmark's energy policy to focus on moving toward renewable sources of energy, even though the country had some domestic crude oil supply in the North Sea. At the time of the crisis, Denmark was highly oil dependent, importing 90 percent of energy supply. In Denmark, the way the shift toward renewables happened was strongly influenced by grassroots movements. There was a good deal of organization against the use of nuclear power, as well as movements organized to promote green energy sources like wind. These grassroots energy movements collaborated with energy companies, private firms, and some politicians to promote energy policy, in what Hvelplund calls 'innovative democracy.' Government policy responded to citizens' actions and set policies that would enable the development of wind power generation (Mendonça et al. 2009: 385). The policies included 'mandatory grid connection for decentralized generation,' which, as described above, helps to address the intermittency and dispatchability issues, implementation targets, and a kWh subsidy (Saidur et al. 2010: 1749). Denmark's energy policy specifies a target reduction in carbon emissions, which are also influenced by its EU and Kyoto commitments.

Since the 1980s, even though Denmark's economy has grown, its energy consumption has remained relatively constant, and its CO_2 emissions have been reduced (Danish Energy Agency 2012: 2). It has been successful for three reasons. First, while the wind industry was maturing, the energy policy consistently focused on reducing consumption, increasing efficiency, and supporting renewable power. Wind turbines became a major export for Denmark in the early 1980s. It was strongly influenced by US federal and state energy policies, discussed below, that supported renewable energy. By 1986, when oil prices were continuing to decline, a change in US incentives caused demand for wind turbines to drop. Denmark maintained its energy policy goals. The wind industry survived the lean years when turbine exports fell off because of state support and subsidies. During that time engineers in Denmark developed a new 0.6 MW turbine, which lowered costs by 20 percent and became the first commercially successful large wind turbine (Mendonça et al. 2009: 385). Denmark became the world's leader in turbine technology. This is not to say everyone was on board with wind power. 'The large power companies, the Association of Danish Industries, and certain sectors within trade unions did not support government policy regarding the wind industry' (ibid.: 385).

Secondly, Denmark chose policy tools with effective disincentives. In 1977 the government imposed taxes that increased over time on electricity, oil and natural gas. In 1982, coal was taxed, and later a carbon tax was introduced (OECD n.d.). In 2010 Danish households paid a 56 percent tax on electricity, though industry and district-heating schemes paid a reduced fee for electricity from combined heat and power plants.

Thirdly, Denmark chose policy tools that both reflected public sentiment and allowed for public support of wind projects. In the late 1970s, the Danish parliament passed legislation to enable local wind cooperatives within municipalities to invest in wind power. Cooperatives, for centuries common in agriculture, are part of Denmark's political culture. Setting up that system for wind power was not seen as outside the norm (Mendonça et al. 2009: 384). The first wind power cooperative was established in 1980. Cooperatives were very local. One of the requirements was that cooperative members live within 3 kilometers of the turbine (ibid.: 385). Cooperatives and the opportunity for investment provided the local buy-in, constituting support that is largely absent in the New York case, discussed next.

In the early 1990s Denmark borrowed the feed-in tariff (FIT) idea, which was initially created in the USA in the 1970s. Utilities had to buy renewable power from generators in their area at a price set by the government, which compensated the renewable energy developers for the environmental benefits of the power they generated (Lipp 2007: 5482, quoted in Mendonça et al. 2009: 386). The investment credits and cooperatives resulted in 120,000 Danes owning shares of wind farms by the early 1990s. In 1996 Denmark started an offshore wind policy to help meet a CO_2 emissions target of 50 percent below the 1990 level. By 2001, 80 percent of wind turbines were owned either individually or as part of a cooperative by 175,000 households (Mendonça et al. 2009: 385–6).

The 1999 Electricity Reform Agreement abolished the FIT in favor of a Renewable Portfolio Standard (RPS) and tradable green certificates (ibid.: 387). The reform introduced competition, but also included renewable quotas for consumers, and a target reduction of CO_2 emissions (Saidur et al. 2010: 1749). However, the reform has been difficult to implement, leading to postponed implementation of the RPS. Switching to the RPS mid-stream, after years on the FIT, proved difficult. Effectively the RPS was never implemented. Instead transitional rules centered on a premium tariff for new projects and a FIT for grandfathered projects were used. A premium tariff means that the electricity produced by wind is sold at market rates, but that the producer gets a defined premium payment for producing renewable electricity.

As the government changed policy tools, public support for wind power generation declined. The distance rule for cooperative membership expanded several times, to 10 kilometers, to neighboring boroughs, to those who work in an area, to all of Denmark, and in 2000 any European Union citizen could join the cooperative (Mendonça et al. 2009: 388). As membership rules have changed, public support for onshore wind has declined.

Denmark has mandated that 50 percent of electricity consumption must come from renewable sources by 2020. The country also wants to be independent of fossil fuels by 2050 (Danish Government 2011). The government sees onshore and offshore wind projects as a large part of gaining that independence. Wind's share of electricity production grew from 2 percent in 1990 to 18 percent in 2001 (Saidur et al. 2010: 1749), and met 30 percent of electricity consumption needs in 2012 (Danish Wind Industry Association 2013).[3]

As discussed in Chapter 2, an electric grid cannot store excess electricity without building in energy storage. Denmark at times produces so much power from wind that it pays neighboring Norway and Sweden to import the extra electricity. These countries, which both have extensive hydropower resources, are then able to decrease their hydropower output and save water in their hydropower reservoirs to be converted to electricity later when needed (Kanter 2012). Denmark has also introduced policy measures to increase the number of electric cars, which could potentially be used as a giant distributed battery. Lastly Denmark has a number of CHP electricity plants that can decrease their electrical output. Energy is still needed for the hot water to heat homes and businesses in the heat part of CHP, so extra electricity can be used to heat water, which can then be stored in insulated tanks (Kelly-Detwiler 2013). When the wind dies down the CHP plants fire back up again. Denmark can also export electricity to Germany, and with grid interconnect upgrades could export electricity to the UK.

The United States The USA was also hit hard by the 1973 oil crisis, in particular because it was one of the targets of the oil embargo. This case study highlights the interplay between federal and state policies, inconsistencies in US energy policy, and the disregard for building public support that have held back the installation of renewable energy such as wind power.

In the mid-1970s, the State of California offered a 55 percent tax credit on renewable energy development, which was followed by the federal-level 1978 Public Utility Regulatory Policies Act that allowed non-utilities to produce power. California also passed the first energy efficiency standards for appliances, set energy efficiency building codes, and created the California Energy Commission (Galbraith 2010), which crafts the state's energy policy (California Energy Commission 2013). The federal-level Energy Tax of 1978 used Investment Tax Credits, residential and business tax credits, on renewable energies, which previously had been available only to the oil and gas industries (Mendonça et al. 2009: 380). California imported thousands of turbines from Denmark for the Altamont Pass wind farm,[4] the first of its large wind farms and other wind projects. The residential wind and solar tax credits were allowed to expire in 1985, when oil decreased greatly in price, effectively ending the installation of large wind farms in the USA.

In 1992 Congress created a Production Tax Credit (PTC) of 1.5¢/kWh for large-scale wind projects. The PTC was allowed to expire in 1999, which led to a 93 percent decline in wind development the following year. It expired again in 2001, and then a third time in 2003, followed by 70 percent drops in development (ibid.: 380). Congress let it expire again at the start of 2014. When the PTC was in place for several years wind power generation grew, specifically in large-scale wind projects that had little economic impact on local communities. As you can see in Table 6.1, wind power installation is correlated with the presence of the Production Tax Credit. As discussed in Chapter 1, uncertainty makes long-term planning difficult. As of 2011, other US states, including Iowa, Michigan, North Dakota, and South Dakota, have crafted state-level tax incentives to encourage community-owned wind projects.

The US Department of Energy called for 20 percent of electricity consumption to come from renewable sources by 2030 (US Department of Energy 2008). Many US states have their own Renewable Portfolio Standards (RPS), sometimes called Renewable Energy Standards (RES). California's RPS requires a third of electricity to come from renewable sources by 2020 (California Public Utilities Commission 2013). New York's RPS requires 30 percent of electricity consumption to be from renewable sources by 2015 (DSIRE 2013).

TABLE 6.1 US installed wind capacity, by year

Year	Installed capacity	Federal Production Tax Credit (PTC)
1999	2,472 MW	Expired 7/99
2000	2,539 MW	Enacted 12/99 Ticket to Work and Work Incentives Improvement Act of 1999
2001	4,232 MW	Expired 12/01
2002	4,687 MW	Enacted 3/02 Job Creation and Worker Assistance Act of 2002
2003	6,350 MW	Expired 12/03
2004	6,723 MW	Enacted 10/04 Working Families Tax Relief Act of 2004
2005	9,147 MW	Continues via Energy Policy Act of 2005
2006	11,575 MW	Energy Policy Act of 2005 in effect
2007	16,907 MW	Energy Policy Act of 2005 in effect
2008	25,410 MW	Tax Relief and Health Care Act of 2006 in effect
2009	34,863 MW	American Recovery and Reinvestment Act of 2009
2010	40,267 MW	American Recovery and Reinvestment Act of 2009 in effect
2011	46,916 MW	American Recovery and Reinvestment Act of 2009 expired 12/11
2012	60,005 MW	No PTC
2013 (as of 30 Sept.)	60,078 MW	American Taxpayer Relief Act of 2012, expired 1/14 $.023/kWh

Source: US Department of Energy (2013a)

The way states structure incentives makes a big difference in terms of who can afford to install renewable energy, as exemplified by a comparison of New York and New Jersey. New York provides a grant through the New York State Energy Research and Development Authority (NYSERDA), and tax credit for residents who install a renewable energy source such as wind or solar on their properties. New Jersey established a renewable energy certificate trading platform. New Jersey residents must pay the full cost of installing a wind or solar system up front, and then earn renewable energy certificates for the power they generate. The certificates are then auctioned to public utilities, which can generate income for the owner, but that income is variable.

Opposition to wind farms and wind turbines in the USA centers on concerns over placement, heath, and existing zoning rules. Mendonça et al. (2009) argue that if wind projects could be community owned it would cut down on local opposition to wind farms. Community owned is different than individual homeowners in the community getting lease fees, as is currently common in the USA. Community ownership keeps economic benefits such as profits from wind power generation in the local economy. Community involvement and outreach are important to gain public support for wind turbine installation before seeking approval from local regulating bodies, regardless of whether it is community-owned or not. A comparison between Delaware's Bluewater offshore wind project and a proposed offshore wind farm in Lake Ontario, New York State, demonstrates this point well.

Delaware's proposed Bluewater wind park Delaware is a small state on the East Coast of the USA, centered among highly populated mid-Atlantic states. In 2005, Delaware restructured its electricity market and removed price caps (Svenvold 2008: 78). The result was a large increase in residents' utility bills. In response, the state's legislature passed a law allowing Delaware's electric distribution companies to own and operate electricity-generating plants (General Assembly of the State of Delaware 2006). Bids to build a new power plant included plans for a coal-burning plant operated by NRG, a natural gas plant operated by Conectiv, and a 200-turbine offshore wind park operated by Bluewater Wind (Svenvold 2008: 79).

From the beginning, Bluewater focused on public relations. They had computerized models of what the wind farm would look like from the shore for Delaware's citizens. They hired consultants to understand the effects on migrating birds. The company's communications director organized town hall meetings and visited local talk shows (ibid.: 79). Delaware's governor endorsed the natural gas plant, but public opinion was firmly behind the wind project, with 78 percent approving the hypothetical wind farm located 6 miles offshore, and 90 percent approving power from offshore wind, even if it meant higher electricity prices (Firestone et al. 2008: 2). See Svenvold (2008) for a summary of the political fight in Delaware's legislature.

Eventually the state public utility, Delmarva, and Bluewater Wind signed an agreement to build the wind park. In late 2009 NRG acquired Bluewater Wind, and moved ahead with the wind park project. However, as of January 2012, the offshore wind park is on hold. According to NRG, the US Congress's elimination of the Department of Energy's loan guarantee for offshore wind and the failure to extend the PTC made the program unfinanceable (NRG 2011).

New York Power Authority's proposed Great Lakes offshore wind farm Oswego, New York, is located on the southeastern shore of Lake Ontario. The county draws tourists for sport fishing and visiting historical sites. The county is no stranger to electricity generation. There are small-scale hydropower plants on the Oswego and Salmon rivers, three nuclear reactors in the county, and an oil- and natural-gas-powered station in the city of Oswego. In December 2009, the New York Power Authority (NYPA), the state-owned electric utility, put out a request for proposals for its Great Lakes Offshore Wind (GLOW) project. It then went to the county legislatures bordering Lake Ontario to seek site approvals.

On 12 March 2010 the authors attended an Oswego County Legislature meeting because we had heard the day before that the legislature was voting on a proposed offshore wind farm in Lake Ontario. During the public comment period of the meeting it became clear that very few people in the room, including the elected legislators, understood how wind power works, what its environmental effects are, what the wind farm would look like from land, and what its effect on tourism might be, other than the assumed negative impact. There was a great deal of misinformation and suspicion that information was being withheld by NYPA on the details of the project.

In fact, the request for proposals was still open at that point, so even NYPA did not have full information on the project. However, even if they had received the proposals by then, their policy is to not release the information until a developer is chosen (Oleck 2010). The legislature that day had basically three options – approve the wind farm, oppose the wind farm, or table the decision so that the legislators would have the time to get more information. They voted to oppose the wind farm.

Juxtaposing the Delaware and Oswego cases illustrates that getting public support is crucial. In the Oswego case, several participants at the meeting mentioned that the turbines would mar the view of the lake at sunset. Aesthetic criticisms of wind turbines are common. NYPA should have anticipated public concerns, and could have brought with them conceptualized images of the wind farm. The current panoramic view from downtown Oswego starts to the west with two tall and four short smokestacks from an oil and natural gas electric plant, a beautiful lighthouse, a working harbor protected by concrete break walls, and a cooling tower from a nuclear power plant a few miles to the east. This is not a public that is used to a pristine lake view. Yet there was no effort on NYPA's part to mount a public relations campaign, despite the fact that the public relations campaign by Bluewater Wind had clearly been so influential in Delaware just a few years before.

In 2011, NYPA ended the GLOW project, citing economic concerns (NYPA 2011). According to the US Department of Energy, 25 percent of wind projects are delayed or withdrawn because of site approval concerns (cited in Mendonça et al. 2009: 383). Most local governments do not have zoning ordinances for wind turbines, which is another challenge to installing wind power.

Conclusion

Wind power is the first intermittent renewable energy source to gain a significant foothold in electricity generation at the entire country level. This is largely because the technical hurdles to developing cost-effective large wind turbines were not too great – although it should be pointed out that advances in material science in the period between 1940 and about 1985 helped considerably by making new metal alloys and plastic components available. Additional advances in wind turbine cost can really only be achieved by increasing the size of the turbine and we may be near the practical limit for onshore systems at around 2.5 MW per turbine. Offshore wind would benefit from fewer large turbines, and indeed some recently installed offshore turbines are now 3.5 MW each, possibly with room to grow.

A number of countries are now approaching a point where further inclusion of intermittent energy sources, such as wind and solar, risk destabilizing their electrical grids. Improving the grid to handle more intermittent sources will require more interconnection, meaning construction of transmission lines, and energy storage, both of which are expensive and sometimes contentious. Managing future global growth of wind power will require effective policy tools.

Denmark and the USA exemplify the increase in usage of wind power worldwide, and they achieved the increase by using different policy mechanisms. Denmark chose an FIT, while the USA chose a Renewable Portfolio Standard. Both policy tools were successful in bringing about an increase in wind power generation. Inconsistencies in US energy policy and on again/off again short-term tax incentives make for an uncertain investment environment. These factors have reduced how much wind power generation could have been built in the USA over the past fifteen years.

7 | GEOTHERMAL ENERGY

Geothermal refers to extracting heat from the Earth. The earliest examples of geothermal energy were various types of in-ground houses that helped keep their residents warm in the winter. The ground holds heat and stays much warmer than the air in winter. In a few areas hot water from the ground has also historically been used to heat homes, in what is called 'passive' geothermal. We begin this chapter with a discussion of passive geothermal. We then move to the more active uses of geothermal such as electricity production. There are three case studies included in this chapter – Iceland, Turkey, and Australia. Iceland is rich in high-temperature resources, and is the top country in terms of the percentage of electricity consumption met by geothermal. Turkey is rich in low-temperature resources, primarily used for district heating. Australia is rich in unconventional geothermal resources.

About twelve gigawatts (GW) of geothermal electricity production was installed worldwide as of 2012. This is about 0.2 percent of global electricity production, but is a significant proportion of total electricity production for some countries, such as Iceland (30 percent), the Philippines (27 percent), and El Salvador (25 percent). The USA has the most installed geothermal generating capacity at about 3,100 MW, but this is a very minor proportion, 0.3 percent of total US generating capacity. Passive geothermal heating with hot groundwater can make a substantial impact on a country's total energy usage, as evidenced by Iceland, which heats most buildings and provides indoor hot water with geothermal hot water. Combined with geothermal electricity production, this means that Iceland gets a large share, 60 percent in 2011, of its total energy requirements from geothermal sources, which is the highest in the world (Orkustofnun 2012). Most countries do not have as much readily accessible geothermal energy, but there are other geothermal technologies that do not require hot rock near the Earth's surface.

Passive geothermal

Passive geothermal uses the ground essentially as a heat 'battery' – that is, the thermal mass of the ground, or water in lakes and ponds, is used as a heat sink in summer to absorb extra heat and as a heat source in winter. This technology is called a geothermal heat pump. Air-based heat pumps have been around for several decades and are simpler in that they use fans to pull air through the heat pump to remove heat in summer or extract heat from the air in winter. The problem with air-based heat pumps is that the air

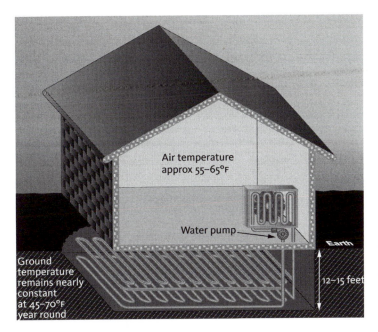

Air temperature approx 55–65°F

Water pump

Earth

Ground temperature remains nearly constant at 45–70°F year round

12–15 feet

7.1 Geothermal heat pump schematic (*source*: Courtesy Shutterfly)

temperature changes a lot more than the ground temperature does because of the mass differences involved. Air does not weigh much, cannot store much heat, and thus its temperature changes more rapidly. The ground stores far more heat and its temperature thus changes slowly. Air-source heat pumps work fine in the summer for cooling, but they don't work well in the winter for heating in locations where it gets below 4°C (about 40°F) for long periods. Geothermal heat pumps are only modestly more efficient than air systems in the summer but much more efficient in the winter. In the tropics, where little or no heating is required, air-based heat pumps are sufficient.

Geothermal heat pumps are most efficient in locations where the mean annual ground temperature is between 7 and 13° Celsius (45–55° Fahrenheit). This would encompass much of the continental USA, parts of Argentina and Chile, Europe, China, Japan, Australia and New Zealand. Mean annual ground temperature is the temperature of the ground below the frost line about 0.7 meters (1–2 feet) below ground, and is effectively the average of summer and winter temperatures over many years. The mean annual ground temperature is not affected much by a few hot summers or abnormally cold winters. During the warm summer months energy can be pulled out of indoor air by a refrigeration unit, cooling the indoor air, and then sent into the nearby ground using a network of pipes carrying a fluid. Over the summer the ground will warm slightly as energy is dumped into it from the warm circulating fluid. In winter the same circulating fluid can be used to extract heat from the warm ground to raise the temperature of indoor air, slowly cooling the ground. A schematic is shown in Figure 7.1.

A geothermal heat pump does not extract energy from the ground to power its own operation. Rather it uses electrical energy to transfer heat from the building to the ground in summer or heat from the ground to the building in winter. The advantage is that for many mid-latitude regions it can entirely replace a fossil-fuel-burning furnace (using coal, oil, or natural gas) and an air conditioner, resulting in substantial savings on heating and cooling costs. However, it may increase a building's total electricity usage.

The downside of geothermal heat pumps is that they are fairly expensive to install. An average system in the USA will run to about $40,000. The main reason for the expense is that geothermal heat pumps require about a half-mile of tubing be installed in the ground to give the system a sufficient thermal reservoir, or heat storage, for heating and cooling applications. In more rural areas the tubing can be laid in trenches 4–6 feet deep, 3–5 feet wide and about fifty feet long; in urban areas with less surface space vertical pipes going down 200–300 feet can be used. Lakes and ponds can also be used as thermal storage for geothermal heat pumps. These systems can be somewhat cheaper to install than underground ones as there is no digging involved; the piping is just sunk into the pond or lake. However, shallow lakes and ponds will have more seasonal temperature variation than the ground and thus will be less efficient as heat sinks or sources.

The payback time for a residential geothermal heating system in the USA will be about ten years, somewhat longer if you finance the system rather than paying for it up front. This payback time assumes state and/or federal tax credits of about 30 percent of the system cost, which have been available, but are dependent on renewal and vary from country to country if they exist at all. The heat pump should last longer than a furnace; most geothermal systems are rated for twenty-five to thirty years, as opposed to about fifteen to twenty years for a furnace or boiler. Lifetime savings over thirty years can total $30,000 or more over the original cost of the geothermal system, depending on the cost of fuel for the furnace it replaces. If you plan to be in a house for twenty years or more, a geothermal heating system is a good investment.

Residential and commercial geothermal heat pumps could offset significant oil and natural gas use for building heating. In the USA, for instance, more than a million households, particularly in the northeast, still heat with oil furnaces, which are getting progressively more expensive to run and produce significant pollution. Switching these residences to geothermal heat pumps would reduce oil consumption and pollution. A significant proportion of the residents, however, are not likely to be able to afford a $40,000 up-front cost without some form of financing assistance.

In Chapter 1 we discussed sub-national drivers of energy policy. One of the new buildings on our college's campus illustrates two examples of sub-national action in the absence of a national climate policy. The Richard S. Shineman Center for Science, Engineering and Innovation was designed to meet the requirements for LEED (Leadership in Energy and Environmental Design) Gold certification. The US Green Buildings Council, a non-profit non-governmental organization, developed the ratings system for green buildings, and its certification is now sought after. In 2007 SUNY Oswego's president joined with several other college and university presidents to sign the President's Climate Commitment, and set a goal of reducing the college's carbon footprint by 40 percent by 2050. The Shineman Center is one of the first structural steps toward reaching that goal. The building's heating and cooling come from 240 geothermal wells dug 152 meters (500 feet) into the earth, which keep the building at a steady 21°C (70°F). Geothermal heating and cooling are estimated to reduce the building's energy cost by 12 percent annually, and reduce emissions by 33 percent (SUNY Oswego 2013).

A more intensive use of geothermal heat is to bring naturally occurring geothermal hot water to the surface for use in residential and commercial heating. This concept is usually referred to as district geothermal heating, taking a cue from the co-gen concept of using hot water produced by electric generating power plants to heat local residences. Wells are bored to bring the water to the surface and insulated pipes distribute it to individual houses. As the water cools, it is often discharged into local surface water sources, rivers, streams, and lakes. District geothermal heating is only appropriate in relatively limited geographic regions where sufficient hot water is near enough to the surface to be economically accessible, and where the replacement rate of the water is high enough. Such regions include parts of Iceland, Turkey, Japan, and the western USA, among others.

Geothermal electricity production

A more active use of geothermal energy is to produce electricity. To be able to produce electricity there must generally be a source of about 200+°C groundwater available. Only a few regions on Earth have ready access to such sources near the Earth's surface, so this power source is regionally restricted. These regions are volcanically active, as liquid rock (magma) near the Earth's surface is a heat source for very hot groundwater.

To produce electricity the hot water is brought to the surface and run through a heat exchanger to heat surface water, or other fluids in newer 'binary' systems, into steam used to turn turbines. Using the hot groundwater directly is generally a bad idea. Hot water underground has a nasty tendency to dissolve salts and minerals out of the rock through which it travels. When the temperature and pressure of the water drop, some of the dissolved material comes out of solution and can be deposited on surfaces. This is particularly destructive to equipment such as turbines. The groundwater also tends to be acidic, which can further damage equipment.

Naturally hot groundwater is not a truly renewable resource. The rate at which heat is drawn out of the ground in the form of hot water is almost always higher than the rate of replacement from deeper in the Earth. The exception may be extraordinary places such as Iceland, where new magma – high-temperature, liquefied rock – is continuously rising to the Earth's surface. The amount of energy stored in areas with naturally hot groundwater can be vast, but the temperature will generally slowly decline until it is too low to allow electricity production. For example, Larderello, Italy, is the oldest geothermal plant in the world. Meaningful power production started in the early 1920s and continues to this day. However, the amount of steam produced has fallen by 30 percent since peak production in the 1950s (REUK 2007) and will continue to slowly fall. Larderello is approaching 100 years of power production, more than recouping the cost of building turbine plants and transmission lines. Length of time until temperature falloff will be highly variable with location and depend on local geologic conditions, and can be hard to predict. Thus geothermal hot water for electricity production and district heating is a sound investment, but one must realize for long-term planning that these resources will not last forever.

Enhanced Geothermal Systems (EGS or hot dry rock geothermal) While the areas with naturally occurring groundwater hot enough to use directly for electricity production are quite limited, there are larger regions with what is referred to as 'hot dry rock' geothermal potential. In these cases the rock, usually at a significant depth of 2–10 kilometers (6,500–32,800 feet), does not have much volume of water associated with it. Water can be brought down from the surface, heated by interaction with the hot rock and then brought back to the surface for use in electricity generation. There is increasing interest in using some of these areas to produce steam for electricity production. In some of these configurations horizontal drilling is used to avoid the problem of the hot water picking up material from the surrounding rock by simply encasing the entire below-ground loop in piping. In other scenarios water is pumped down one borehole and retrieved through another a short distance away. Hydraulic fracturing must be used to increase the ability of water to travel through the rock.

Few EGS plants have been built to date. A number of shallower systems, less than two kilometers deep, have been operating worldwide for several decades. The deepest currently producing system is in Europe at Soultz-sous-Forêts, on the border of Germany and France. The plant was built as a scientific pilot project in the late 1980s, and was connected to the grid after the introduction of FIT in 2010 (French Geological Survey 2012). The wells at Soultz are 4.5–5 kilometers deep and have been producing steam since 2008. Soultz is a prototype system delivering only 1.5 MW, but is serving as a test bed for technologies to expand EGS. One important piece of data that researchers working on EGS hope to glean from the work at Soultz is how long a well will produce water hot enough to drive a turbine.

One of the current unknowns making financing for EGS projects difficult is how long wells will last before the heat stored in the rock is expended. To understand this limitation, one needs to envision what the power plant would look like. At the surface, an EGS power plant has a turbine house and cooling system like any other steam-driven electric plant, and is connected to the grid by power lines. Adjacent to the power plant would be a number of deep wells, probably about eight to twelve wells in total spread over 1–2 square miles. Several wells would be injection wells, sending water from the steam house down into the ground to be heated; the rest of the deep wells would be return wells, bringing high-temperature water back up to be sent to the turbine house. This set of injection and return wells would constitute one well field. The area around the electric plant would be divided into sectors, each of which would be the eventual site of one well field. Probably only one to two well fields would be in use at a time. As the temperature of the return water decreased in the initial field, a second well field would be drilled. As the temperature in the second well field slowly decreased over time a third well field would be drilled, and so on. This means that each set of deep wells will only be usable for a certain, currently unknown, length of time. Eventually, all of the hot deep rock within a reasonable distance of the plant, probably a 2–3-mile radius, would be exhausted, and the power plant would close.

A steam-based electric plant usually has a service lifetime of about thirty years and costs about one third of an EGS plant, so it would be ideal if the area around the plant could provide hot water for about thirty years. The heat at Soultz is holding up after five years of production, but the volume of water being brought back to the surface is less than what was planned.

The potential for EGS is enormous, but it is unknown whether EGS will be economically viable in the foreseeable future. There are vast amounts of heat stored in the Earth's crust. For a color-coded map of deep heat resources across the USA at various depths ranging down to 10 kilometers, see MIT (2006); similar maps exist for Europe and Australia. The estimated energy available to EGS from rock under the USA, at a rather conservative assumed 2 percent of total heat extraction, is approximately enough energy to power the USA for about 2,800 years at current consumption rates (ibid.).[1] It is important to realize that once this heat is removed it will not be replenished for several thousand years or more.

The main problem in extracting this energy is getting to it in the first place. As you may have noted earlier, EGS wells will be at a significant depth. For reference, the deepest oil well to date was drilled in 2009, ironically by the Deepwater Horizon that would be destroyed a year later in the Gulf oil disaster of 2010. The well in the Tiber oil field in the Gulf of Mexico was drilled to 10.6 kilometers in 1.2 kilometers of water, for a total bore depth in rock of about 9.4 kilometers. So wells down to about 10 kilometers are technically feasible. A key difference between deep wells for oil as opposed to EGS is rock temperature. Most commercially available drilling technology, particularly steered drills for directional drilling, are limited to about 65°C (150°F). Rock temperatures in excess of 200°C at the bottom of bores for EGS will require development of more thermally robust equipment. Such development seems to be attainable with existing materials.

Three main physical factors are barriers to EGS use: induced seismicity, water availability, and fracturing technology. Owing to the likely amount of water to be injected with EGS, there is a real possibility of activating long-dormant cracks or faults in the Earth's crust. Preliminary work on one EGS project in Switzerland was terminated after water injection triggered a 3.4 magnitude earthquake (Deichmann and Giardini 2006). Such a low-magnitude earthquake would be felt only locally and do little damage, but the concern was that continued water injection could trigger a larger earthquake. Small earthquakes would be common with EGS development, and are common today with deep coal mining, for instance. The key would be risk assessment. How likely would EGS be to initiate a significantly damaging earthquake? The results would likely depend on the seismic history, bedrock geology, and surficial geology (some materials near the surface are very susceptible to, and can magnify, ground movement) of an area. Some areas would have to be off limits to EGS development owing to the risk of inducing earthquakes.

Water consumption by EGS is also a problem in areas with limited water resources. Not all of the water injected underground comes back to the surface and considerable water is used for cooling at the surface in the electricity generating plant. The last barrier is technical and theoretically could be overcome. Hydraulic fracturing works well in relatively weak rock such as shale. EGS, on the other hand, will often be deployed in hard, crystalline rocks such as granite, which are very challenging to fracture effectively with existing technology. Between induced seismicity and water availability, large sections of the western USA that are favorable for EGS may not be feasible to develop. Significant portions of the humid eastern USA may be off limits owing to concerns about induced seismicity as well. This may seem odd, as much of the East Coast is relatively quiet, seismically. However, areas that are not currently seismically active may have stress stored up and awaiting a trigger to be released. Unfortunately detecting such stored stress is very difficult at present.

There are a number of unknowns with EGS that make estimating the economics difficult. EGS is nascent technology. The estimate in the 2006 MIT-led report on EGS for the US Department of Energy (MIT 2006) was that EGS would not be economically viable without a carbon tax or other method of making fossil-fuel-powered electricity generation significantly more expensive than it currently is. What may happen in the USA is that shallower EGS sites in the western USA will be developed first, followed later by utilization of deeper heat resources in the eastern USA as the technology improves and costs come down. Currently the USA, the EU, Iceland, and Australia are pursuing EGS in a limited way. Australia's recent experiences are discussed below.

Case studies

Iceland Iceland is an example of a renewable-energy-rich nation. Iceland has tremendous geothermal potential, largely because the island is actively growing. Iceland is situated directly atop the mid-Atlantic ridge, a point where the Atlantic seafloor is tearing apart and forming new oceanic crust as magma rises up from below the seafloor and hardens. There are several active volcanoes in Iceland. Consequently, Iceland has quite a range of thermal features, including hot springs and geysers. Geothermal hot water has long been used in Iceland to heat buildings.

Iceland produces about 30 percent of its electricity from geothermal energy. Almost all the rest comes from hydropower, making Iceland the global leader for renewable electricity generation. Geothermal hot water is used to heat most buildings. Consequently, only 23 percent of Iceland's total energy budget is devoted to fossil fuels. This is the lowest percentage among developed countries. Almost all fossil fuel use is in the transportation sector, which is responsible for 80 percent of the country's GHG emissions. Iceland is pursuing electric vehicles as well as hydrogen for hydrogen-fuel-cell-powered vehicles, and synthetic hydrocarbon fuels produced from geothermal energy or hydropower.

Iceland is a constitutional republic with a parliament and a separately elected president. Iceland's parliament, the Althingi, established in 930 CE, is one of the oldest parliamentary systems of government in the world. Its central and municipal governments legislate energy policies. Iceland is a party to the European Economic Area of the European Union and is a signatory to the Kyoto Protocol, so it has commitments to those institutions. It is a candidate for EU membership. For Kyoto's first commitment period from 2008 to 2012, Iceland's target was to limit its GHG emissions to no more than 10 percent above 1990 levels. Iceland did not meet its first commitment,[2] owing primarily to the expansion of heavy industry, especially aluminum production (Ministry for the Environment 2010). It introduced a carbon tax in 2009, and it takes part in the EU's GHG emissions trading scheme (ibid.).

In 1998 Iceland committed to being 100 percent fossil fuel free by 2038 (Sverrisson 2006). However, relatively little progress has been made on hydrogen development as a transportation fuel. Admittedly hydrogen fuel cells are only now becoming efficient and reliable enough to power personal vehicles. What should matter is that Iceland has set a long time horizon and clearly signals its commitment to its energy policy, which should allow for research and development and innovation in technology. However, Iceland currently seems more interested in attracting to the island energy-intensive industries, such as aluminum smelting, that use cheap electricity and/or geothermal heat directly in industrial processes. In fact just one industry, aluminum smelting, used 71 percent of Iceland's electricity production in 2011 (Orkustofnun 2012).

Iceland was strongly affected by the 2008 recession. Its banks were badly overleveraged with debt and failed completely. Iceland's people decided not to bail out the banks and consequently Iceland has been rebuilding its economy for the past five years. The government fell, and the country rewrote its constitution. It has not had much extra revenue to spend on non-essential projects, which may also explain some of the lack of progress on following through on the 1998 pledge.

There is considerable additional geothermal power potential in Iceland. One interesting proposal, currently being tried at pilot plant scale, is to use geothermal energy to convert CO_2 into methanol, a one-carbon alcohol (Bullis 2013). The methanol could be used as a transportation fuel, although methanol makes a poor fuel. Initially most of the methanol will go into the chemicals industry. The CO_2 is extracted from geothermal water and not the atmosphere, but the process is intriguing. A similar technology using concentrated sunlight may someday become important and is covered in Chapter 8 on solar power.

Turkey Turkey is a rapidly developing nation of about eighty million people on the southeast edge of Europe. Most of the country technically lies in Asia, and the country is a bridge physically, economically, and culturally between Europe and the Middle East. Several pipelines cross Turkey, bringing oil and natural gas from Central Asia and the Middle East to Europe. Turkey is a republican parliamentary democracy. It is a candidate for EU membership, and liberalized its electricity market to bring it in line with EU policies. Differences on some issues have halted the accession process for now. Turkey joined the UNFCCC in 2004 and signed the Kyoto Protocol in 2009. Turkey is an Annex I country, putting it in the category of industrialized countries which must lower emissions, but at several of the annual Conference of Parties to the UNFCCC Turkey was recognized as being in a different situation than other Annex I countries (UNFCCC 2013b).

Turkey's energy policy goal is energy security. Turkey has a rapidly growing economy that is particularly vulnerable to imported energy sources. It is second to China in terms of the increase in demand for natural gas and electricity (Ministry of Foreign Affairs 2011). In 2005 Turkey imported 79.3 percent of its total energy requirement (Erdogdu 2009: 2537), and only slight progress has been made since. Thus Turkey has considerable incentive to expand renewable power. Its strategy to achieve energy security includes diversifying where it gets its energy, increasing renewables, and nuclear energy, increasing energy efficiency, and contributing to Europe's energy security (Ministry of Foreign Affairs 2011).

Turkey's renewable sources include hydropower and geothermal power.

Turkey has a few wind farms, and continues to build large dams in the eastern part of country. There it faces the same challenges discussed in Chapter 5 on hydropower, namely conflicts with downstream countries Syria and Iraq, insufficient environmental impact assessment and resettlement programs, and the submersion of historical sites. We discuss Turkey in this chapter, because of its geothermal potential.

Geologically, Turkey lies in the Alpine-Himalayan tectonic zone, which runs from the Swiss Alps across southern Europe through Turkey, Iran, southern Russia, and Afghanistan, to the Himalayan mountains of India. All along this region tectonic forces are deforming the Earth's crust as continental plates grind against each other. Consequently there is considerable seismic activity across the entire region. Along with the seismic activity comes the potential for considerable geothermal energy.

Turkey began to tap its geothermal resources in the 1980s and has seen considerable development since the late 1990s. Currently Turkey has about 200 MW of geothermal electricity production, just 0.4 percent of its total electricity generation. This is largely because the existing geothermal sources in Turkey are mostly low-temperature, less than the 150°C which is usually considered to be the minimum for electricity production. However, Turkey is still estimated to have about 3,000 MW of untapped geothermal electric potential (Erdogdu 2009). The problem of induced seismicity in a region prone to powerful earthquakes will likely severely limit if not curtail the possibility of using EGS in Turkey.

Many geothermal resources in Turkey may be low-temperature in relation to what is needed for electricity production, but they are still hot enough to be useful for building heating and residential hot water. Much of western Turkey's Aegean coast, as well as select other regions of the country, have good potential for low-temperature geothermal. From 2002 to 2012 use of geothermal hot water in district heating increased from 30,000 to 90,000 homes, representing about 162 MW of thermal energy (TurkishPress.com 2013). From this beginning, there is considerable room to grow. Turkey is the seventh-richest country in the world in terms of geothermal potential, with an estimated 31,500 MW of untapped geothermal heat potential, which could represent up to 15 percent of its total energy budget and heat half of the homes in Turkey (Erdogdu 2009). The question is how to take advantage of the potential.

Turkey's renewable electricity standard (RES) is to have 25 percent of its electricity generation come from renewable sources by 2020. The government has used policy to encourage private investment in energy sectors to meet rising demand. Turkey's policy tools include European-style feed-in tariffs, the RES, clean energy tax incentives, and government procurement policies (Pew Charitable Trusts 2012: 49). In 2012 the Turkish government also provided value-added tax exemptions on purchases or imports, custom duty exemptions for imports, exemptions from other fees and charges, and waived license fees for smaller producers (KPMG 2013). The 2013 Electricity Market Law gives a discount on the transmission system utilization fee and stamp tax exemptions for investment-related documents, and an 85 percent discount on leases and rights to transmission lines for ten years (ibid.). Interestingly, Turkey offers a high FIT for wind electricity that is generated with turbines manufactured in Turkey, in order to encourage domestic wind power manufacturing (Şimşek and Şimşek 2013).

Prior to the 2013 Electricity Market Reform the FITs were low, which may explain why renewable electricity had not seen as rapid a deployment in Turkey as it has in places with higher FIT rates, such as Germany. Higher FITs should spur investment. Turkey seems to have learned from other countries' policy missteps. Germany has had to revise its high FIT, because it led to an over-installation of solar PV and higher fees passed on to consumers. Turkey's FITs are locked in for only ten years. At the time of writing, it is too soon to tell whether the 2013 policies will result in more renewable power generation coming online in Turkey.

Australia Australia is a country of 23 million people, the world's twelfth-largest economy by GDP, and has the fifth-highest per capita wealth in the world. Historically, Australia's major exports were agriculture-related; however, over the last fifty years Australia's rich natural resources have taken over exports. In 2011, for instance, 102.1 billion Australian dollars' worth of coal and iron ore were exported, mainly to China, representing 58 percent of all resource exports (IEA 2012).

Australia is a federal state with a bicameral parliamentary legislative branch and a prime minister appointed by the ruling party or coalition. Much as in the United States, Australia's states have their own legislatures and considerable legislative power to push back against federal initiatives, and/or lead the way on their own.

Coal and natural gas accounted for 89 percent of Australia's electricity generation in 2012. Renewable sources, primarily hydropower with 6 percent of total generation, made up the rest (Energy Explorer 2013). Geothermal energy did not contribute significantly in 2012, but interest has been high over the last ten years. One would not typically think of Australia as rich in geothermal energy. Australia has no volcanoes and has not been volcanically active for many millions of years. Nevertheless, Australia has significant deep geothermal potential, largely due to heat from the radioactive decay of naturally occurring radioisotopes, rather than magmatic activity. Most of Australia's geothermal energy is from a deep dry-rock resource, so EGS is the only practical way to tap into the energy.

About a dozen companies have been developing EGS resources in Australia over the past ten years. Two pilot-scale plants, 1–2 MW each, are currently operational in the Cooper and Paralana basins. The cost of EGS-produced electricity was 26.9 AUS cents/kWh in 2011 (Gurgenci 2011: 83). This is two to three times more expensive than onshore wind power or natural-gas-fired power, putting it just a bit higher than the cost of offshore wind power. Clearly, further reductions in the cost of electricity produced by EGS will be necessary to make it cost competitive. Interestingly, the 2006 MIT-led study of the USA came to about the same estimate for EGS power costs and concluded that some sort of carbon pricing mechanism would be required to make EGS power cost effective (MIT 2006).

Australia signed the Kyoto Protocol in 2007 and since then has taken a number of steps to encourage renewable energy and reduce CO_2 emissions. A carbon tax was enacted in 2011 and feed-in tariffs provide support for renewable power (Department of Infrastructure, Energy, and Resources 2013). However, the election of Tony Abbott and the Liberal/National coalition in September 2013 may reverse some of the initiatives of the past few years. In particular, Abbott supports repealing the carbon tax.

The interest in EGS in Australia was likely driven by two factors. First, the goal to produce more power from renewable energy, with its concomitant policy supports such as the FIT and carbon tax, provided enough incentives to encourage investors to move into the sector. The second was that Australia has a robust oil and natural gas industry and there is considerable drilling expertise in the country. However, by late 2013 Geodynamics, the company behind the Cooper basin pilot EGS plant, had written off the cost of the entire plant (Parkison 2013). It was unable to find anyone to buy its power, and the outlook for renewables looked less viable. However, the Cooper basin is also the site of a new potential tight oil and gas reservoir that may be developed with hydraulic fracturing technology. If HF takes off in the Cooper basin, then there may be more need for already-developed power as people move into the area to support HF development.

In a larger sense the current cooling of interest in EGS in Australia can be tied to two trends. One is the recent policy shift away from favoring renewable energy at the federal level, which creates uncertainty for companies wanting to invest in EGS in Australia. The other is that electricity demand in Australia is actually falling, making profit margins for all electricity generators in Australia thinner.

The reasons for falling electricity demand in Australia are also twofold. Strong exports of mostly base commodities like coal and iron ore are driving up the value of the Australian dollar, which is making it harder to manufacture products profitably in Australia.[3] The manufacturing sector in Australia has been in decline for more than ten years (Mitchel 2013). Of course, this trend is seen in much of the developed world as manufacturing shifts to lower-cost countries; however, it has been particularly pronounced in Australia and is exacerbated by the high value of the Australian dollar. Contraction in the manufacturing sector has lowered industry's electricity demand. The second factor bringing down electricity demand in Australia is solar photovoltaics (PV). Australia is well positioned for solar energy, and while grid-level solar systems have not been deployed on a large scale by utilities, small roof solar for residential use has become very popular with 1.1 million rooftop PV systems now installed (Milman 2014).

In a sense this is two renewable sources squaring off against each other. Currently solar has the upper hand as it is relatively inexpensive, much of Australia is very favorable for solar power, and individuals can choose to install systems. However, as intermittent sources such as solar PV and wind begin to contribute more to the grid, the point of instability could be reached unless there is improvement in the existing grid system, which is expensive. So solar will have its day – pun intended – but there will be a need for base load and nighttime power generation that solar PV cannot supply. In Australia either that capacity will be met with coal and natural gas or with solar thermal, energy storage, and, potentially, EGS, depending on policy directions.

Energy from the sun is in many ways the quintessential form of energy on Earth. Fossil fuels represent concentrated solar energy captured long ago by living organisms, wind is generated by the uneven heating of the Earth's surface, and even hydropower would not exist if not for the sun's energy striking the oceans and causing water to evaporate to eventually create rain over land. Living systems, such as the Amazon rainforest we discussed briefly in Chapter 1, are almost entirely fueled by the sun's energy. Agriculture is in essence the use of self-replicating solar energy collectors (plants) to produce food for humans. Humanity is just now on the cusp of being able to use solar energy directly, on a large scale, to power our society.

Solar energy is ubiquitous, at least while the sun shines. Solar, like wind, is an intermittent energy source but with relatively predictable daily, seasonal, and weather-related interruptions. The amount of energy in the sunlight that strikes the Earth's surface is more than enough to power all of human civilization many times over. That energy, however, is very diffuse, containing only about one kilowatt per square meter of energy at noon, at the Earth's equator, on a sunny day. Moving farther north or south reduces the amount of energy available, owing to the tilt of the Earth's axis of rotation and the rounding of the globe. Clouds also reduce the available energy, so cloudy regions are less suitable for solar energy utilization. One can calculate how much energy strikes the Earth's surface at a particular location, called insolation.[1] For instance, in London (UK) on a sunny day in June you would collect at best 4.2 kW/m² per day, whereas in Cairo, Egypt, in June on that same sunny day you could collect 6.7 kW/m² per day. Sunny days in Cairo, I suspect, are a bit more common than sunny days in London. Of course, this is the maximal energy available at a particular location; the efficiency of the solar energy collector is another limiting factor in how much usable energy can be obtained. Solar energy collection systems can be broken down into two main categories: passive and active.

Passive solar

The simplest use of passive solar is heating buildings. We humans utilize tremendous amounts of energy heating buildings and using heat for industrial purposes. Passive systems utilize energy from sunlight as low-grade heat energy. Using sunlight to generate heat does not involve additional energy transformations, as electricity generation would, and so it can be quite efficient. As you may surmise, this is also one of the more ancient uses of solar power. Mud brick houses have been used for millennia in hot, arid regions where day and nighttime temperatures may differ by 25°C (about 50°F) or more. Thick walls of dense material provide insulation from the day's heat, but slowly warm up during the day. At night they release their stored heat, warming the building. The walls' heat loss at night leaves them ready to provide cooling for the next day. There are some modern takes on the humble mud brick, the most obvious being fired clay bricks of various types. Concrete and rammed earth, which is loose soil put between solid supports and then compacted into a solid material, can also be used. Even used tires filled with earth and straw bales covered with concrete stucco have been used.

Other architectural points that influence solar heating are recessed windows, which allow low-angle light into the house in the morning and evening but prevent near-vertical light around midday from entering and heating the building during the warmest part of the day. Putting more windows on building faces that receive the most sun to increase light and heat the building can also help. Letting light in without letting heat out has been helped greatly by the development of high-efficiency windows.

These simple concepts can reduce the need for building heating and cooling from 20 to 90 percent, depending on how aggressive one wants to be with their implementation. The passive house (*Passivehaus*) initiative, for instance, first begun in Germany, requires lowering energy input to the house for heating and cooling to no more than 15 kWh/m² (or 1 Btu/ft²). This is about a 75 percent energy reduction over what is currently required in US buildings that qualify as energy efficient at 15 Btu/ft² (NREL 2013). Passive houses are sufficiently energy efficient that they do not need a regular heating system and instead rely on passive solar heating, waste heat from appliances, and even the body heat of the residents to heat the building. The passive house technology is currently about 10 percent more expensive than standard construction, a cost that will be more than made up for over the life of the building.

Passive solar construction techniques also can be readily applied in large-scale commercial settings. An interesting example of this is the Minneapolis Mall of America in the famously cold state of Minnesota. The mall is the largest or one of the largest in the world, with an area of about four-tenths of a square kilometer (4.2 million square feet). Part of its rooftop, 32,376 square meters (8 acres), is covered in glass to permit sunlight to penetrate into building spaces that are designed to maximize the gain and storage of the solar energy. During the fall, winter, and spring seasons an inside temperature of 21° Celsius (70° Fahrenheit) is maintained from the solar energy, heat from electrical equipment, and body heat of all the humans (40 million per year) who visit or work there. Energy is needed only in the warmer months to cool the building (Mall of America 2014).

Another passive solar technology is water heating. It is fairly simple to capture the sun's energy in water, largely because water has a high specific heat. It takes a lot of energy to change the temperature of water, making it a good energy storage material. Loops of flexible piping can be laid on a rooftop or in raised beds and water pumped through them to an insulated storage tank for later use. This may seem like a boring way to reduce your fossil fuel use, but consider this – in 2010 about 18 percent of total home energy use in the USA was for water heating, and most of that energy came from natural-gas-, electric-, or oil-burning hot water heaters (US Energy Information Administration 2013g). Some countries with sunny climates, including Israel since 1980 and Spain since 2011, require new homes to include solar hot water heaters to reduce energy usage.

China has also gotten into the solar hot water game, and as is usual for China, they have done so in a big way. In 2011 roughly 68 percent of installed solar hot water heating worldwide was in China, representing 151.6 GW of thermal power (REN21 2013: 46). Solar hot water makes the most sense in areas that have plenty of sunshine and at least moderate temperatures. In China and most of southern and central Europe solar hot water heaters are equivalent to or cheaper than electric or natural gas hot water heaters, owing largely to the price of electricity and natural gas in those areas. In most of the USA cheap natural gas, low electricity rates, and relatively high labor costs for installation make solar hot water uneconomical. Only in the southwest and south central USA, and Hawaii, are solar hot water heaters currently economical. The State of Hawaii requires them on all new single-family residences.

Active solar

Active solar means the conversion of solar energy into electrical power or some form of stored energy, such as using sunlight to make hydrogen gas from water. Electricity can be generated directly with photovoltaics, materials that can absorb the energy in sunlight and convert some of that energy into electrical current. Electrical current can also be produced by concentrating solar energy into a small area that heats water or other compounds to temperatures high enough to use steam turbines to generate electricity, called concentrated solar or solar thermal.

Photovoltaics The term photovoltaic (PV) refers to a material that when struck by photons of sunlight produces an electric current. The PV material absorbs some of the energy from photons of sunlight and converts it into a voltage potential that can be transferred out of the absorbing material. Only certain materials have this property; one of them is the element silicon. The first PVs used crystalline silicon. The problem with crystalline silicon is cost. The first PV systems of the 1960s were so expensive they were used only on satellites that cost hundreds of millions of dollars apiece. At that total price you are not likely to notice a few million dollars in solar panels, but you are

8.1 Concentrating solar, with Stirling engine (*source*: US-NREL image #19881)

not going to put them on your house. The price of crystalline silicon panels has come down over the past several decades, with a dramatic decrease since 2006. This is due to both improved fabrication technology and growth of the solar panel manufacturing sector, with concomitant economies of scale. A typical crystalline solar panel in 2012 ran to about four dollars per watt for installed residential systems, a bit less for larger commercial and grid-scale systems. By the end of 2013, the price of installed PV systems had fallen to $2.59/watt in the USA (Solar Energy Industries Associates 2014).

You will sometimes encounter the term 'junction' used in reference to solar panels. This term refers to the number of photon-absorbing layers in the solar panel. A single-layer solar panel can usually absorb only over a narrow range of light's wavelengths; the rest of the light striking the panel is wasted, or worse leads to heating of the panel, thereby reducing efficiency. By adding additional layers that contain mixtures of other materials to modify their absorption properties you can broaden the range of wavelengths that are absorbed and converted to electrical current. However, each layer you add also reduces the overall efficiency and increases the cost of the panel. For instance, a single-junction solar panel might convert 20 percent of the light that strikes it into electricity. Adding a second layer that absorbs over a different wavelength range might add 6 percent conversion, but also causes a 2 percent reduction in overall efficiency, for a total efficiency of about 24 percent. Diminishing returns with additional layers mean it is usually not worth going beyond two or three layers, or double- and triple-junction solar panels. How efficient can a solar panel get? This depends on the configuration of the solar panel. For a single-junction solar panel under normal sunlight the thermodynamic limit is 33.7 percent. For double- and triple-junction PV

8.2 Concentrating solar, with PV field (*source*: US-NREL image #13740)

panels the limit is higher, approaching 60 percent for triple-junction PV (Vos 1980). Concentrating sunlight on the PV material with lenses raises the limit, called concentrating solar PV. These systems use lenses or parabolic mirrors to concentrate sunlight onto small areas of high-efficiency PV material or micro-heat engines to generate electricity. Such systems decrease the amount of PV material needed and increase the efficiency of energy conversion.

The image in Figure 8.1 is a concentrating solar system in which the parabolic mirrors focus heat to drive a heat engine, called a Stirling engine, which generates electricity. This technology is available now, has low maintenance requirements, and is good for remote areas with modest power needs. The image in Figure 8.2 is an array of smaller parabolic mirrors focusing concentrated sunlight onto small patches of high-efficiency PV material.

Regardless of the theoretical limit, most commercial solar panels are not limited by thermodynamics but rather by price of fabrication. Typical installed residential solar systems use crystalline single-junction panels with around 20 percent efficiency. Efficiency for single-junction crystalline silicon panels will probably not increase much more. The best chances for future efficiency increase probably lie with concentrating PV and materials other than silicon.

There is also non-crystalline silicon PV technology, called thin film or amorphous silicon PV. We have to be careful with the thin film term because it is also used to refer to a range of other materials that are produced as thin films. Not all of these technologies use silicon. What unites them is the thin film production technology and the fact that they are usually somewhat flexible, although this varies between different types of thin film PV.

Thin film silicon panels are cheaper to produce than crystalline silicon PV, but they have a lower efficiency of around 14 percent, meaning you have to buy more panels to produce the same amount of electricity. Thin film silicon also suffers from a more rapid falloff in its efficiency over time. Crystalline solar panels can last thirty years or more, whereas thin film silicon loses significant efficiency after six to eight years. The thin film silicon panels can be made somewhat flexible, however, and thus are more suited for some applications. A reasonable EROeI for crystalline silicon PV as of 2012 was about 6–8 and may have the potential to rise further, but varies by manufacturing process and installation location (Lundin 2013). The reason for the low EROeI is the large amount of energy and material that go into producing crystalline silicon PV. That is one of the points some environmentalists make against solar PV, that its manufacture uses considerable energy and that much of that energy currently comes from fossil fuels. EROeI for thin film silicon is about 8–10 owing to its less energy-intensive manufacturing process, but this value too varies considerably depending on material and manufacturing process.

There are a host of up-and-coming solar PV technologies (for a recent review, see Tyagi et al. 2013). Which technology will win out in the long run is hard to say at this point. Currently crystalline panels have the edge on thin film silicon, owing largely to economies of scale, higher efficiency, and longer lifespan. However, future development of various thin film PV technologies may be able to catch up sufficiently on a cost basis with crystalline silicon PV, as there seems to be more room for improvement of thin films. Some PV technologies also use relatively rare elements in their construction. If we begin deploying solar PV at large scales this could result in material shortages and increasing prices for certain PV technologies.

Currently single-junction crystalline PV panels can produce electricity at prices comparable to those of electricity purchased through the grid in a number of localities – much of western Europe, for instance, and some US states. This is a much-hoped-for development and is referred to as grid parity. Achieving grid parity with other electricity generating sources means that solar PV should be able to more effectively compete with those other sources, many of which are fossil fueled. Grid parity is also a sign of a more mature technology needing less subsidy support.

Both residential and grid-scale deployment of solar PV will require changes to the existing electrical distribution grid. As described in Chapter 6 on wind, solar is an intermittent energy source, whereas the grid is an on-demand system. Thus extensive overcapacity, wide geographical distribution of generation with concomitant grid expansion, backup generation, or energy storage will be required to meet twenty-four-hour-a-day energy needs. Nighttime will require much more energy storage than seems currently feasible, even with the promising development of liquid metal batteries, as discussed in Chapter 1. Solar PV can be an important contributor to our energy mix, but because of intermittency and lack of nighttime generating power it is not going to be feasible to run a society solely on solar PV. Luckily there are some other solar energy technologies that can help with both daytime intermittency and nighttime energy needs.

Concentrated solar with thermal storage PV converts sunlight directly into electrical current. However, you can also capture the heat energy in sunlight and use that energy to boil water to make steam and generate electricity through conventional steam turbines. This technology is referred to as concentrated solar or solar thermal. The authors prefer the term solar thermal, as it is directly explanatory and avoids confusion with concentrating solar PV technology.

Solar thermal electric plants can be built to store some of the heat they capture from sunlight, called solar thermal with thermal storage (STTS). These STTS plants come in two configurations, trough and power tower. In the trough arrangement, long U-shaped troughs lie along the ground or on racks a little above the ground. The inside of the trough is coated with reflective material and the trough's shape reflects sunlight onto a pipe going through the middle of the trough, as depicted in Figures 8.3 and 8.4.

8.3 Parabolic solar trough field (*source*: US-NREL image #11070)

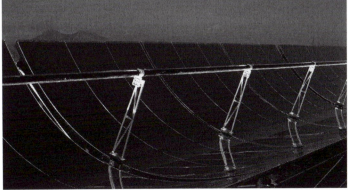

8.4 Parabolic solar trough (*source*: US-NREL image #16604)

The trough's central pipe carries water or inorganic oil. Inorganic oils have a higher energy density than water and can be heated to several hundred degrees Celsius, making them potentially more efficient. The hot oil is then used to boil water to either immediately produce steam to spin turbines or to store in an insulated tank for later use. STTS plants use water directly as the thermal fluid heats the water to high-pressure steam in the trough and then it is either used to spin turbines or is sent to an insulated building, where it gives up its heat to a solid or liquid heat sink for thermal storage. The water or oil is then sent back out into the trough field to be heated again. The stored heat can be used later to heat water into steam to generate electricity when clouds obscure the sun or after the sun has set.

The choice of water or inorganic oil for circulating thermal fluid is partly based on experience. Trough systems were the first large-scale solar thermal plants to be built back in the late 1970s and 1980s. Generally they were built as straight solar thermal, without heat storage. Some of the older oil-based systems have had high maintenance costs, which have tended to drive newer systems back toward simpler water designs. There were about 2,600 MW of trough plants in service at the end of 2013, primarily in Spain (about 1,500 MW) and the USA (about 800 MW), and Abu Dhabi, United Arab Emirates (100MW), although many other countries, including Morocco and South Africa, have plants in the planning stages. Most of these existing plants run as straight solar thermal with no thermal storage; thermal storage raises the cost of the plant considerably. The Andasol plant in Spain is a modern trough STTS complex consisting of three separate 50 MW plants with 7.5 hours of molten nitrate salt-based thermal storage and a capacity factor of 41 percent. All three phases of the plant, totaling 150 MW, cost just over $1.2 billion to build; it was completed in 2012.

The power tower arrangement uses a field of mirrors to reflect sunlight onto a central pillar, or power tower. At the top of the pillar is a holding tank for water or various inorganic salts that are solids at room temperature but liquids at several hundred degrees Celsius. The turbines, heat exchangers, cooling system, and thermal storage units are situated in or near the base of the tower. The mirrors are motorized to follow the sun as it moves across the sky, keeping reflected sunlight focused on the top of the power tower.

The advantage of STTS plants is that they can save energy for later use. This helps to solve the intermittency and nighttime problems of solar power. Most STTS plants cannot actually store enough energy to get through an entire night at full electric output; rather they manage some fraction of full output for about sixteen hours a day. Current thermal storage is too expensive to build enough extra capacity to get through the night; that may change. However, late night demands for power on the grid tend to be quite low so the base-load capacity of other generating sources would be more able to get the grid through the rest of the night.

8.5 Power tower solar thermal plant (*sources*: Schlaich Bergermann und Partner, SBP Sonne GMBH; US-NREL image #19807)

There are only a few power tower STTS plants now in operation, again mostly in Spain and the USA. The first modern power tower STTS, PS10, an 11 MW demonstration plant in Seville, Spain, was brought online in 2006. A full-scale power tower plant will come online in the USA in early 2014. Solar-Reserve's 110 MW Crescent Dunes plant is in Tonopah, Nevada. The plant will cost about $900 million, which is more costly than a conventional coal or natural gas plant of the same capacity at around $180 million. However, the STTS plant will not require any fuel for its entire lifespan and will generate little CO_2 after its construction. Nevada Power, which has an RPS, has signed a twenty-five-year power purchase agreement with the plant for $0.135/kWh (Wesoff 2011). At that rate the plant should generate around $65 million per year in revenue (at about the planned 500 GWh of electricity production), less operating costs (only labor, no fuel!), maintenance, and financing costs – it should still pay for itself in about twenty years.

Trough systems are generally cheaper to build than power towers. Power towers, however, can operate at higher temperatures as much more reflected sunlight is concentrated at the top of the tower. Higher temperature means higher thermodynamic efficiency. Levelized costs for modern plants of either type of STTS are hard to gauge at this point as most plants have not been in operation for long. There is a suspiciously large range of values, particularly between government agencies and the renewable energy websites. Some of this discrepancy may represent time lag, as government agencies use data from older solar thermal systems. A reasonable value is around $0.24/kWh, and it is believed that the learning curve will be steep for the next few years, meaning levelized costs may come down rapidly (Hernández-Moro and Martínez-Duart 2013). EROeI for STTS plants of either type is around 10. There should be considerable room for cost reductions for thermal storage as the technology improves (for a technology review, see Cartlidge 2011).

The future of solar power

There is only modest room for further improvements in single-junction crystalline PV in terms of efficiency; costs will continue to come down a bit more, but there are not likely to be large further reductions. Some thin film technologies could show more dramatic improvements in efficiency and may eventually replace crystalline PV. Concentrating solar PV may be a real game changer in the future, particularly for commercial and grid-scale systems.

Another recent development that is likely to expand in the coming decades is hybrid solar–natural gas electric plants. As their name implies, these plants are solar thermal plants while sunlight is available and run off natural gas in cloudy conditions or at night. The plants use a shared set of turbines to generate electricity, and steam is produced either by solar heating or by fuel combustion as needed. These plants are particularly suited for areas where twenty-four-hour electricity production is vitally needed for grid support, as they essentially have built-in backup power capability. These types of plants are a reasonable bridge technology between fully renewable and fossil-fueled electricity generation. Once they are built, though, the companies that own them will expect to be able to run them for twenty to thirty years, so there is the danger of creating a new entrenched industry that would resist attempts to fully de-carbonize electricity generation.

Further into the future we should have solar PV materials that can be sprayed onto surfaces or incorporated into a flexible thin film that can be molded to surfaces, taking the place of paint. The efficiency of such a material would not have to be particularly high, probably around 6 percent would be sufficient, but its cost would have to be low. As the Amazon rainforest shows us, the way to deal with powering a complex system with sunlight using low-efficiency conversion is to use a huge surface area. Spray-on or wrap PV, coupled with more efficient PV deployed on rooftops of most buildings, could make urban areas electricity-sufficient during the day and produce enough extra electricity to make a dent in the amount of energy used in transportation, either with plug-in hybrid vehicles or converted to hydrogen gas for hydrogen fuel cell vehicles. The hydrogen or other chemical potential energy storage could also be used to help get the grid through the night by conversion back into electricity, although this would be a lower-efficiency use of the hydrogen.

An intriguing use of solar energy is to store it the way plants do, as chemical energy. Artificial photosynthesis of sugars from atmospheric CO_2 is a long way off, but solar water-splitting systems to produce hydrogen from water using solar energy are being developed in solar-panel-like form (Service 2011). Eventually these systems might compete for roof space with conventional solar panels to produce hydrogen for your hydrogen-fuel-cell-powered car. This assumes hydrogen fuel cell costs come down. Arrays of such solar-powered water-splitting systems, if they can be made cheaply enough, could produce hydrogen for shipment via pipeline. The hydrogen could be used in cities for fuel-cell-powered cars or to produce electricity for grid support. Economical deployment of hydrogen-producing solar cells is probably still ten to twenty years away.

Power-tower-type arrangements can also be used to convert water to hydrogen and/or make simple hydrocarbons such as methanol from CO_2 (Roeb and Sattler 2013). In this case the chemistry operates at tremendously high temperatures, in the range of 1,000°C or more, and with substantial pressure. Like the solar water-splitting panels, these systems would store solar power in chemical bonds until it was needed at night or for transportation fuels. As with the hydrogen-producing panels, there is still substantial work to be done with these systems, but they exist at research-lab scale and there is room for substantial improvement.

Eventually we will need to tap into the ultimate solar power location, space. Solar PV in space at the Lagrange point between the Earth and the Sun, the point where the gravity of the Earth and Sun balance each other and little to no fuel is needed to hold position, would be the most efficient possible. In space there are no clouds and the sun never sets, meaning that power can be collected continuously. Energy could be beamed back to Earth using microwave radiation that can easily penetrate the Earth's atmosphere with minimal energy loss, and the beam could be made diffuse enough to carry energy without any real worry that it could be used as a weapon.

To achieve space-based solar, though, we will need a much more cost-effective system for getting into space and likely need to do most of our solar panel manufacturing on the Moon. The Moon makes a nice way station as it has much less gravity than Earth, meaning that objects to be sent to other locations in the Solar System require far less energy to escape the Moon's gravity than they do Earth's. Also, the Moon has accessible construction materials on the surface, meteorites that have accumulated over the Moon's four-billion-year history. Solar PV on the Moon is a possibility too, a certainty, I would say, for Moon-based manufacturing. However, to send reliable energy back to Earth from the Moon would mean having to ring the entire Moon in solar panels, as only half the Moon is illuminated at any one time, and you would still have to deal with power loss about twice a year during lunar eclipses. Space-based solar is not here yet, and will not be for a while, but the US military is looking at the possibility of satellite-based solar power for remote military bases where it is expensive and dangerous to bring in other energy sources. First we need to get solar power working better here on Earth.

Case studies

Germany Germany was a founding member of the European Union. It is a federal republic, where the chancellor is the head of government and the president is the head of state. The legislature has two houses, a council, to which states send representatives, and an elected parliament with proportional representation. Germany is a party to the UNFCCC, and signed and ratified the Kyoto Protocol. German energy policy is firmly committed to sustainability, GHG reductions, and environmental protection. The country has committed to decrease overall energy-sector GHG emissions to 40 percent below 1990 levels by 2030.

No other country has installed more solar PV-generating capacity than Germany over the past twelve years. As of the end of 2013, Germany had 35.3 GW of installed solar PV, roughly equivalent in peak electrical output to seventy large coal-burning power plants. This meets a little over 5 percent of total electricity consumption on a twenty-four-hour average, but can spike to about 50 percent of immediate total electricity consumption during daylight hours on a sunny day. Germany also boasts a robust solar PV manufacturing sector, and has created many jobs in the country for manufacturing and installation of solar PV systems. This is a tremendous success for renewable energy, but Germany is still working out some of the related challenges, such as proper levels for renewable subsidies, grid stability, utility company financial health, and the proposed phasing out of nuclear power.

The primary driver behind the rapid growth of solar PV in Germany has been a feed-in tariff implemented by the *Energiewende*, Germany's energy plan. This plan calls for 50 percent renewable electricity generation by 2030, 65 percent by 2040 and 80 percent by 2050 (Federal Ministry for the Environment, Nature Conservation, and Nuclear Safety 2010). The plan also stresses decentralized power generation and co-gen over large-base-load electric generating plants, which sounds eerily similar to Thomas Edison's vision for the US grid from Chapter 1. A FIT sets guaranteed prices for electricity produced from various renewable sources for a set number of years – twenty for solar, fewer than ten for wind. The tariff is paid by a surcharge added to electric bills in Germany. Residential users pay the full rate; large industrial users pay a percentage of the full rate.

Germany has faced a few challenges in terms of getting the subsidy for solar PV right. The FIT, when it was first crafted, led to a sharp rise in installations in 2010 and 2011, which exceeded the government's target for PV installed capacity by 100 percent (Leepa and Unfried 2013: 536). In response German legislators built a tripwire into the energy plan, which decreased the FIT on a quarterly, and then monthly, basis as the subsidy rapidly increased. The FIT reduction was meant to slow down solar PV installation. The effect of the planned decrease, however, incentivized people to install solar PV systems before the tariff got even lower, resulting in even more generating capacity, the cost of which was passed on to consumers (ibid.: 537). In 2012 the total tariff cost to consumers in Germany was €20.4 billion, which added about €0.05/kWh to residential electricity rates (Economist 2013). Germany already has some of the highest residential electricity rates in the developed world at around $0.35/kWh, compared to the US average of about $0.12/kWh, although one recent analysis found that the amount of solar-power-generated electricity feeding onto the grid during peak usage hours has decreased the cost of electricity by 7 percent (Tveten et al. 2013: 761).

Because solar receives the credit for twenty years, albeit at a slowly declining rate, much of the cost rebate for already-installed solar PV will continue for years to come. However, government officials are floating the idea of lowering the FIT for new installations. Some German solar producers have also declared bankruptcy because of decreased demand for PV in Germany and increased competition from Chinese-produced PV. Whether this contraction in the German solar industry continues or the industry stabilizes remains to be seen.

Germany will also likely be the first country to face the hurdle of dealing with large-scale grid integration of intermittent solar and wind power. Currently, when solar power output spikes on a sunny day, much of the resulting electricity is exported to surrounding countries, often at steep price discounts, as German utilities are required by the feed-in tariff to buy all electricity produced from solar. This practice is essentially dumping electricity into surrounding countries' electric markets and is creating political blowback against Germany. Ultimately Germany will need to find a way to stabilize its grid without such 'dumping' events.

One way to do that would be to increase interconnections and spread the electricity around the country and to other countries more efficiently, but this will entail building more transmission lines. Normally this would be done by power utilities. However, the power utilities in Germany, and across Europe in general, are in poor financial shape. Initially this was due to over-building power plants in the late 1990s for an anticipated spike in electricity demand that never materialized. Even worse, the financial crash of 2008 further eroded demand for electricity. All of this happened before the rise of renewables. Where wind and solar have exacerbated the problem is that these power sources have reduced the value of electricity at peak demand, where utilities used to make most of their money (Economist 2013). This is a classic case of corporate inertia – the established utilities were not interested in getting into solar panel leasing or other means of riding the renewable wave, and now they are suffering for their lack of vision. It is very difficult for base-load electric plants in Germany to make a profit these days. It seems Germany will have to evolve a new system of paying for grid construction and maintenance if it wishes to continue increasing renewable's share of total power generation, as the established utility companies are in no shape to do so.

Another way to use 'excess' electricity in Germany would be to convert the excess electrical current into a storable fuel such as hydrogen, which could be used for transportation or converted back into electricity at night. Currently conversion of the energy in electricity to hydrogen is not particularly cost effective, but hydrogen could help Germany to reduce reliance on gasoline and diesel in its transportation sector, often the sector most intractable to de-carbonization.

Germany has also committed to ending nuclear power by 2022. Nuclear currently produces about 16 percent of Germany's electricity. Without nuclear power to back up intermittent solar and wind there will likely have to be more reliance on fossil fuels to produce electricity. Additional solar PV or wind power is unlikely to bridge the gap, owing to both the intermittency issues and reduced future growth rates to keep the FIT from driving electricity rates through the roof. Coal will likely be the fossil fuel of choice as natural gas is expensive in Europe, but this will drive up CO_2 emissions. Essentially Germany must choose between keeping CO_2 emissions low or getting rid of nuclear power.

Kenya Kenya is a parliamentary republic where the president is head of both state and government. Its parliament is elected by proportional representation. The World Bank classifies Kenya as a low-income country. In 2005 about 46 percent of its population lived below the poverty line, down from 50 percent in 2000. The World Bank (2013a) thinks the poverty rate has declined to somewhere between 36 and 42 percent, but no official household survey has been conducted since 2005. In 2010 only about 18 percent of Kenya's population had access to electricity (World Bank 2013b). Access to electricity is positively correlated to improving health and education, overall living standards and quality of life, as well as economic growth (Niu et al. 2013; Kanagawa and Nakata 2008). Kenya's electric grid is currently confined mostly to urban areas and would have to grow dramatically, at considerable expense, to reach more Kenyans.

It may be possible for Kenya to avoid building an integrated electrical grid. Consider the evolution of its phone system. According to the International Telecommunications Union, Kenyan landline phone subscriptions peaked in 2009 at 664,100. In 2010, they dropped substantially to 381,750. By 2012 there were only 251,500 subscribers. Most Kenyans now use cell phones instead of land-based phone lines. In 2012 almost thirty million Kenyans, about 70 percent of the population, were cell phone subscribers (ITU 2014). Technological advances enabled high phone connectivity in Kenya, at a far lower cost than having to build a land-based phone system. Phone systems are easier to run as distributed networks than electricity distribution systems, however, so bypassing the need for a traditional electricity grid will be harder.

Kenya's energy policy mission is to 'facilitate provision of clean, sustainable, affordable, reliable, and secure energy services at least cost while protecting the environment' (MEP 2013) and is designed to achieve the goals of the 2008 *Vision 2030*, meet development needs, and protect the environment. Overall, Kenya wants to make the country attractive to investors, so it will move ahead on transparency initiatives, develop mechanisms to share benefits between the national and county governments, and streamline licensing.

As a low-income country, Kenya will likely have to rely on foreign investment and technologies to implement its energy policy. The cap-and-trade mechanism of the Kyoto Protocol was meant to address the need for capital and technology. For example, Kenya, which exports mainly agricultural products like black tea, would likely have carbon credits available for sale on international carbon markets. The sale of those credits would provide a revenue stream. The Clean Development Mechanism (CDM), related to the cap-and-trade system, would allow companies in the Annex I countries to earn credits by investing in new projects in non-Annex I countries that would result in additional CO_2 reductions. The CDM was meant to address the need for technology transfer. Many post-colonial countries have faced considerable challenges in developing infrastructure or shifting economic patterns from what they were under colonialism. Foreign investment does not necessarily mean the creation of high-wage jobs for locals, or that the company's profits will be invested in the local economy. In order to ensure that energy development also profits the domestic economy, Kenya set a minimum 30 percent local equity participation for foreign investment in the energy sector (ibid.: 11).

Kenya plans to exploit fossil fuels to expand electricity production in the short term. It discovered petroleum reserves in 2012, and will facilitate building the infrastructure to extract, refine, store, and dispense petroleum. It is continuing to explore for on- and offshore reserves (ibid.: 18). The government wants to decrease the country's overreliance on biomass for heating. In 2013, 69 percent of the country's energy requirements came from firewood and charcoal (ibid.: 52). The Ministry of Energy and Petroleum correctly is not counting biomass as a renewable fuel in the energy mix, because the rate of current consumption is unsustainable. Kenya expects the oil reserves will expedite the move from biomass. Kenya taxes fossil fuels to encourage conservation and efficiency. It is also pursuing bio-methane as an energy source, with a goal of building 5,000 small-scale biodigesters by 2017 (ibid.: 58).

Solar cook stoves can replace some of the need for wood and charcoal fuel. In 2009 Jon Bøhmer, a Norwegian based in Kenya, won an environmental prize for creating a very inexpensive cardboard solar cooker that costs about six dollars (Forum for the Future 2009). Solar cook stoves have been popular in Kenya, though their popularity reflects a learning curve on the part of locals and the development community. Daniel Kamman, a physicist who has been conducting workshops in East Africa since the 1980s, carries out week-long workshops with women in local communities, who learn to build and use the solar oven technology. He found that the technology is successful only when the community is receptive to getting it, and knows how it works so that they can maintain it. Secondly, the international development community based their actions on Western norms, and would often only interact with men, assuming they were the agriculturalists and heads of household. The development community's approach to gender and development has gone through several iterations, and today an empowerment or capacity-building policy uses an approach similar to Kamman's.

Kenya wants 70 percent of its electricity generation to come from renewable sources. Kenya has considerable conventional geothermal potential and intends to generate 5,500 MW of geothermal electricity by 2030. In 2012 50 percent of Kenya's electricity generation came from newly developed hydropower. Large and small hydropower will continue to be developed. Kenya also plans to use considerable solar power.

Kenya is well positioned for solar power. It sits astride the equator in East Africa and has many sunny days. Kenya's energy policy uses short- and medium-term strategies to implement its solar policies. They include education, setting standards, and providing incentives. In 2012 Kenya passed Energy (Solar Water Heating) Regulations requiring the installation of solar hot water at premises with hot water requirements of more than one hundred liters (26 gallons) per day. Existing homes have five years to comply. Local authorities and all new construction have an immediate requirement (Energy Regulatory Commission 2012).

By 2012, the country had installed PV systems on 945 public buildings such as schools and health centers that were far from the existing grid (MEP 2013: 59). Their target is to install solar PV on half of the remaining off-grid public buildings by 2017. The government will also distribute solar-PV-powered lanterns to its population to replace kerosene (ibid.: 60). Kenya is building or converting power stations into hybrid – solar/wind, solar/diesel – stations, a compromise to cut CO_2 emissions while providing backup power (ibid.: 59). Kenya's policy incentives for renewable electricity include its renewable energy standard from 2008, a FIT, and net metering. The FIT for small-scale (up to ten MW) is $0.12/kWh for on-grid, and $0.20/kWh for off-grid. Large-scale solar has a $0.12/kWh FIT for on-grid (Oimeke 2013).

For years Kenya has had among the highest per capita usage rates of solar power in the world, in the form of very small-scale solar power systems. The systems are largely for cell phone and battery-powered light charging; some of the solar systems are domestically produced (Hicks 2004). Another strength of solar power in Kenya lies in home-based systems that are not connected to the national grid. As of 2010 about 300,000 such systems had been installed, representing approximately 10 MW of generating capacity (Ondraczek 2013). Kenya has had some success in rural development with the establishment of electric micro-grids built from these small solar PV systems and other types of generation such as small-scale wind (Kirubi et al. 2009). The higher off-grid FIT should incentivize the installation of residential solar PV for these micro-grids. However, as stand-alone systems they are vulnerable to local daytime cloudiness and loss of power at night.

The issue is whether reliable local grids can be forged from such micro-grids without the expense of significant energy storage or backup generation.

Forging these distributed sub-grids into a national grid would mean some level of interconnection with associated transmission-line construction. The ideal would be a compromise – a distributed national electric grid with modest interconnectivity and enough energy storage to avoid the need for, and massive expense of, a fully integrated national electric grid. This type of partially distributed electrical grid could serve as a model for other developing countries.

9 | CONCLUSION: WHERE DO WE GO FROM HERE?

As we have seen in the scope of cases presented in this book, different countries have different energy policies, and the goals that an energy policy encompasses also vary. Energy policies reflect the country's national interest, and national interest is in turn constituted by many different factors. Some countries have committed to addressing their GHG emissions, and see addressing climate change as part of their national interest. Others want to pursue development in a way that benefits society and does not degrade the environment. We often hear that there is a North/South divide when it comes to international agreements on climate change, and while it is true that there are some divisions, countries of the South, which will be more deeply impacted by climate change than wealthier countries, also conceive of their energy policies as bringing about economic and social growth, but doing so in a sustainable way. At the same time we see countries in the North, for example the United States, which have so far spent a lot of time talking about addressing GHG emissions and climate change, without following it up with actions designed to address those goals. Many other countries face similar problems with difficulty changing course or charting a new course.

Business as usual

It would be quite easy to continue as we have been, using the same old fossil-fuel-based energy. This is the business-as-usual approach. It is easy because it requires no new approaches or actions. Things done a certain way are understood to be normal, so it takes some doing to move us off that inertial path. The way that we understand the world shapes how we act. We often will not question an institution, practice, or behavior that has existed for a long time, but we are very critical of and reticent about change. As we noted in the chapter on nuclear power, many people are afraid of the radiation from nuclear waste and nuclear power plants, because the idea of nuclear radiation is very scary. But we are exposed to radiation on a daily basis without thinking about it (see PBS 2014). For example, when we fly, racking up the frequent-flyer miles comes to mind, not racking up millirems of radiation exposure by flying at over 30,000 feet. Fossil fuels also present their own dangers, which do not prompt calls for a paradigm shift. Since 2010 North America alone has experienced oil spills, natural gas pipeline explosions, coal mine explosions, and explosive train wrecks, and 300,000 West Virginians could not drink, bathe in, or cook with their water because of chemicals used in the coal-cleaning process leaking into the river that supplies their drinking water.[1]

Those who benefit from business as usual are not likely to embrace change, which is why we will often point to entrenched interests as a problem. Beyond that, once institutions, practices, and beliefs become entrenched, they are the norm – they are what we consider to be normal. Challenging what is normal is an uphill battle. First, it requires thinking outside the box and imagining another way of doing things. Secondly, our institutions, practices, and beliefs support the status quo. For example, today when we talk about cost–benefit analysis, most people would assume we are talking about economic costs and economic benefits. 'The bottom line' means profit or loss.

Economic rationality shapes not only economics, it also shapes politics and society. When politicians sought to address CO_2 emissions, their solution was to create a market of the atmosphere. That is not surprising, given that the current paradigm for both politics and economics is dominated by neoliberalism. In economics, neoliberalism means a focus on economic openness, where goods and capital (but generally not labor) can cross borders as easily as possible. In politics, neoliberalism means a focus on privatization, low taxes, small government, and a belief in the efficiency of markets. As we discussed in Chapter 1, there are some situations where markets fail. A market cannot deal with a free good, for example. There are other conceptualizations of 'the bottom line.' A focus on what is commonly called the triple bottom line reflects a different conceptualization of what we should be measuring in decision-making. The triple bottom line looks at the economic, ecological, and social and political equality of the variety of choices before us. It does not privilege the economic concerns over environmental or social ones. The cost of upgrading the inefficient grid system provides a good example.

The electrical distribution grid in most developed countries is one of the things that will have to change. In the chapter on wind power we discussed the problems of intermittency and dispatchability common to wind and solar, the two most abundant and easily accessed renewables. There are four main ways of dealing with these problems: overcapacity (building more than you need), geographic distribution, energy storage, and backup generation capacity. Of the four solutions, geographic distribution is the lowest-cost option. To achieve greater geographic distribution, however, will require building more transmission lines, which has faced opposition in many developed countries.

The electrical grids in many developed nations, particularly the USA, are old and in need of investment to modernize infrastructure. The additional expense of designing grid improvements to enable a greater percentage of renewables would likely not be much higher than the base improvement investment; this opportunity should not be missed. In the USA, further steps will have to be taken to unite the three regional interconnects, a process that has already begun (Siluk 2011).

There was a time when utility insiders spoke of 'fundamental limits' to wind and solar power's contribution to the grid, as if there were unbreakable barriers to going above say 20 percent of total generation capacity from wind. One does not hear that so much anymore, with several European countries now above that threshold range. It is true that the grid must be improved to accommodate higher percentages of renewables and that some of the countries that have gone to higher percentages of renewables have fallen behind in doing so and thus are experiencing grid destabilization and financially stressed utilities. These are solvable problems and investment in the grid infrastructure is needed anyway.

The take-home message for the grid is that with sufficient geographic distribution of generation and sufficient interconnection the grid should be able to accommodate significant percentages of renewables, perhaps upwards of 50 percent. Higher percentages are possible but will require some mix of more energy storage, overcapacity, and backup generation capacity. For example, one grid improvement that would help with renewable integration is a smart grid. The cost estimate for installing a smart grid in the USA is $150–170 billion over the next twenty years (Amin 2011). According to Amin, the benefits outweigh the cost by a large margin. Budgeting the costs requires being proactive; policymakers have the political will, and view the smart grid and building microgrids as one goal in a long-term energy program. Not budgeting it means the business-as-usual reactiveness; the costs will be borne annually by lost electricity on a less efficient grid, and the economic losses that come with power outages.

Note that this is one area where countries like Kenya, as discussed in the solar chapter, are in a somewhat better position, because they are closer to starting from scratch.

Climate change in the driver's seat

In 2006 the UK-commissioned *Stern Review on the Economics of Climate Change* argued that climate change represented a threat to economic growth and that strong, early action on climate change outweighed the economic costs (Stern 2007: ii). Small island nations, such as the Maldives, are already spending hundreds of thousands of dollars on mitigation efforts to prevent the rising seas from swamping their countries (Island President 2011). While it is impossible to declare that any one weather event is the result of climate change, the IPCC's (2007b) Working Group on Impacts, Adaptation and Vulnerability report warned of an intensification of tropical storms in the North Atlantic and stronger storm surges exacerbated by rising ocean levels. The cost associated with Superstorm Sandy, which hit the US East Coast in October 2012, was $65 billion (National Climatic Data Center 2013).

For most of human history, economic growth has been positively cor-related with greenhouse gas emissions. As we saw in the case of Denmark, however, that does not mean that reducing GHGs necessarily means no or slow growth. Denmark's economy grew enormously after 1980 without the accompanying rise of GHG emissions. In 2014, the 'Global Commission on the Economy and Climate set up by the UK, Norway, Sweden, Indonesia, South Korea, Colombia and Ethiopia will release an updated assessment of the economic costs and benefits of addressing climate change' (Clark 2013). Note that economics is still the motivating factor of decision-making. Dealing with the constraints that climate change places on us requires us to use our imaginations and creativity to address development challenges regardless of whether we are in a developed or developing country.

The take-home message on climate change is that we should set policies while we still have an array of policy choices before us that will keep us from passing the 2°C (3.6°F) temperature rise the international community agreed to in 2010 at the Cancún Conference of Parties to the UNFCCC. The longer we wait to deal effectively with GHGs, the fewer the policy options we will have and the more expensive they will become.

Energy policies that sufficiently address climate change will be based on alternative conceptualizations of development, the public good, rights and responsibilities, citizenship, and energy security.[2] Sustainable development for all countries will mean using the triple bottom line of people, planet, profit, or equity, ecology, economy, or whatever other alliterative mechanism you like that recognizes that the economy, society, and the environment are inherently intertwined, in our analyses of risk and costs and benefits.

Pros and cons of various electricity generation methods

We have talked about a wide range of energy sources for generating electricity. Now it is time to try to draw together some of that information. First, we have a few general observations. The upfront costs of many renewables are high, particularly for hydropower and large-scale solar power. This tends to discourage adoption because investors are leery of being able to recoup their investment. However, once they are built the operation and maintenance costs of most renewable power plants are quite low and they emit little CO_2. The opposite is true of fossil fuels. Upfront costs are relatively low, and consist mostly of construction costs. Fuel is paid for on an ongoing basis and is often seen as less of a concern because we are used to the concept of paying for fuel. The back-end costs, which mostly are externalities and not calculated as costs, are, however high. They range from acid rain and smog, to global warming and climate change. In essence, as mitigation and adaptation costs for dealing with climate change go up, we will be paying the back-end costs of two centuries' worth of fossil fuel burning. Until we can link the back-end costs of fossil fuels to their actual price in the marketplace, it will be hard to move away from them.

The second observation is that choosing between two types of electricity generation can often be summarized as: how do you want your pollution? Burning fossil fuels sends the combustion products up the smokestack to join the global commons of the atmosphere, for everyone to 'enjoy.' With nuclear power emissions are not an ongoing concern, but you are left with spent fuel that will be dangerous for at least ten thousand years to come. Essentially the pollution is highly concentrated in the spent fuel that theoretically can be handled with proper regulation and oversight. Hydropower displaces people and destroys local ecologies; its 'pollution' is literally built in. The three core renewables – wind, solar, and geothermal – produce less pollution overall (with the possible exception of solar PV, whose energy, water, and mineral resource consumption during manufacturing are quite high) but still have their issues. Solar and wind take up space, can be aesthetically displeasing, and are intermittent sources of power. Geothermal, barring the advent of widespread EGS deployment, is confined to localized regions with hot groundwater and still emits more CO_2 than most people realize. Many hot groundwater resources have appreciable dissolved CO_2 that is released when the water is brought to the surface.

There is no perfect energy source – all come with tradeoffs, and we must understand what those tradeoffs are. Table 9.1 summarizes the pros and cons of various electricity sources discussed in this book.

As mentioned in Chapter 1, EROeI and LCOE values can be useful for comparing different energy sources but do not take into account a range of externalities such as pollution, environmental degradation, and military spending to ensure access to an energy resource. Also keep in mind that comparison of EROeI values requires some thought – see the longer discussion of EROeI in the terms section of Chapter 1. An EROeI below 3 does not yield enough net energy to allow for maintenance of a society, as little to no energy is left for the end user (the net energy cliff concept). Care must also be taken for very high EROeI values as they carry little percentage increase in net energy; for instance, the difference between an EROeI of 25 and an EROeI of 50 is only a 4 percent increase in net energy.

An extension of LCOE would be to include an estimate of the cost of some externalities with fossil fuels. A study from Europe (ExternE 2006) came to the conclusion that a variety of externalities (not including military spending) would roughly increase the cost of coal by about 75 percent (to about $0.17/kWh) and add about 30 percent to natural gas (to about $0.10/kWh). The costs of other generating sources (biomass, nuclear, hydropower, wind, and solar PV) were not appreciably affected.

Lest champions of renewables get too excited, there are also modifications to renewables' LCOE that are not usually worked in. As we said earlier in this chapter there will have to be improvements to the electrical grid to support larger proportions of intermittent power sources. There will also have to be backup power generation for some fraction of the capacity of the intermittent

TABLE 9.1 Comparison of different energy sources for electricity generation

Energy source	Pro	Con	Levelized[1] cost US cents/kWh	EROeI[2]
Fossil fuels	High energy density Portability Ease of use (combustion)	High CO_2 emissions May have other emissions Not evenly distributed worldwide	Coal: 10.0 Coal w/CCS: 13.5 NG: 6.6 NG w/CCS: 9.3	80 10
Biomass	Easily obtainable Can be sustainable	Food vs. fuel Limited by land area	12.0	40–70
New nuclear	Low CO_2 emission Load-following designs	Expensive to build Potential for accidents Spent fuel is a long-term problem	11.3	≥4
Hydropower	Low-cost electricity with low CO_2 emission Often dispatchable	Limited sites Human and ecologic impacts	8.9	60–100
Onshore wind	Low-cost electricity with low CO_2 emission Widespread availability	Intermittent source Aesthetic and some ecologic damage	8.7	18
Offshore wind	Low CO_2 emissions Can be proximal to population centers	Intermittent Expensive	22.1	n.d.[3]
Geothermal (non-EGS)	Low CO_2 emissions	Limited sites	8.9	n.d.
Solar PV	Low CO_2 emissions Widespread availability	Intermittent Expensive	14.4	6–8
Solar thermal with thermal storage	Low CO_2 emissions Widespread availability	Partial intermittency Currently expensive	26.0	n.d.

Notes: 1. Levelized Cost of Electricity (LCOE) values from US Energy Information Administration, 'Levelized cost of new generation resources in the annual energy outlook 2013; www.eia.gov/forecasts/aeo/er/electricity_generation.cfm; 2. EROI values largely from Murphy and Hall (2010: 102–18); 3. No data – EROeI values for these sources are not well discussed in the literature power source. Both of those costs can be added to the installation costs of intermittent power sources, driving up their overall cost. Costs go up rapidly, however, as you increase the percentage of total generating power you are getting from that source. At 10 percent of total generating capacity from solar the cost of solar might not be driven up too much, but by the time you get to 30 percent from solar you will see significant price increases. The US National Renewable Energy Laboratory (NREL) has done a modeling study on the effects of going to various levels of renewable energy ranging from 20 to 80 percent by 2050 for the USA that is worth a look (Mai et al. 2012).

Hopefully it is evident by now that having a mix of electricity generating capacity is usually a good idea, although some countries have managed fine without much diversification where they can rely on a non-intermittent and not directly polluting source. Some prominent examples include Iceland with hydropower and geothermal, Brazil with hydropower, and France with nuclear power. However, both Brazil and France face significant barriers to their reliance on hydropower and nuclear power. In Brazil, new hydropower will be expensive to build and increasingly involves either displacement of large numbers of people or destruction of Amazon rainforest habitat. France has lost some of its will to rely on nuclear power and seems unwilling to shoulder the price of new nuclear plant construction, which will soon be needed to replace aging nuclear stations. So what would be a good mix? There is no perfect answer and to a large extent it will depend on the particular circumstances within a country.

To answer that question for ourselves, we divided the energy sources up into three tiers, but we differ on what should be included in each tier. For one of the authors, the divisions assume an absolute premium on low CO_2 emissions that has not been instituted in a number of countries, such as the USA. He also weights current cost quite heavily. His top tier includes hydropower, geothermal, and onshore wind. Next are natural gas, biomass, coal with CCS, and nuclear. On the third level are traditional coal, offshore wind, solar PV, and STTS. As we stated in Chapter 8, STTS has a lot of room to improve and will likely move up to the second tier. Solar PV is teetering on the edge of the second tier and should move up with some further modest improvements.

The other author also assumes a premium on low CO_2 emissions, but does not weight current cost as heavily. In her opinion, the cost of mitigation and adaptation due to climatic change will be high anyway and money spent now should be viewed as an investment in avoiding future climate-change-related expenses. Additionally, the perception of cost as high or low reflects a country's priorities. New cost estimates for the US wars in Afghanistan and Iraq top $4 trillion. In that light, a solar thermal power tower is a bargain. For that price we could have had roughly four thousand STTS plants built in the USA (probably more factoring in economies of scale, although new transmission line construction would also be a considerable expense) with a capacity of around 450 GW, offsetting roughly 60 percent of the 2012 total of about 780 GW of fossil-fuel-powered electricity generation (US Energy Information Administration 2013h). For her, Tier 1 includes STTS, geothermal, and onshore wind. Tier 2 includes solar PV, hydropower, offshore wind, nuclear, sustainable biomass, and natural gas. Tier 3 includes coal with CCS.

Thinking beyond electricity

In the introduction to this book we noted that electricity generation constitutes usually only about one third of a developed country's total energy expenditure. We have mostly focused on electricity generation because electricity is the same output no matter what the energy input is, so it is possible to mix and match different types of generation and easier to compare them. It is also where renewables have really started to get an appreciable percentage penetration of total capacity and so it makes a good case study for decarbonizing our energy infrastructure. However, it is only about 33 percent of the problem and is one of the easiest sectors to address. The other energy use sectors – transportation, industry, and commercial/residential – are to varying degrees less amenable to replacement of energy inputs from renewable sources. We will review some of the major hurdles and possible solutions for each sector, although it will not be an all-inclusive review as each sector could easily be a separate book unto itself.

Transportation It is the transportation sector which is most keenly addicted to fossil fuels, and with good reason – the energy density and portability of gasoline and diesel are unmatched. Thus it will be the transportation sector which lags on switching to renewable energy. Beyond the simple-to-conceive but hard-to-solve problems of energy density and portability is the existing infrastructure problem. If we were to switch to all-electric vehicles, when that becomes possible, we would have to build tens of thousands of new charging centers to replace today's gas stations. We would also have to either phase out or switch all our vehicles over to electric power.

What technologies are likely to help get the transportation sector off fossil fuels? Electricity is often cited, and it would be a good choice, if it were possible with existing technology. We already have a distribution system for electricity, the grid. All that would be needed are the aforementioned charging stations. Unfortunately we simply do not have the battery technology for all-electric vehicles yet. The best current batteries, lithium ion, are good enough for hybrid vehicles that do not draw down the batteries too aggressively and thus are less likely to run into battery degradation issues. There is also the problem of low energy density; with lithium ion batteries having about one eighth the energy density of gasoline, cars are going to have to get much lighter and more efficient to help make electric cars a reality. There are some all-electric cars on the road today, most notably the Tesla S sedan and the Nissan Leaf. It will be interesting to see how the batteries for these vehicles hold up over the coming years. Nissan guarantees its batteries for eight years/100,000 miles, and in 2013 started an extended-warranty battery replacement program (Nissan 2013). If new battery technology, such as the lithium–air battery currently under development, can be coupled with lighter and more efficient vehicle designs, then electric cars will be more of a possibility.

In the early 2000s, hydrogen was all over the news and the 'hydrogen economy' was soon going to magically transform our world. That has not happened. The reality is that hydrogen-powered fuel cells, the most efficient way to extract energy from combining hydrogen and oxygen to produce water, are just now becoming cost effective and reliable enough to power personal vehicles and a few are starting to appear (Lindberg 2013). Storage of hydrogen in vehicles remains a problem; even at very high pressures it is difficult to store enough hydrogen in a car to get what we gasoline-addicted drivers would consider a reasonable driving range. The third issue is generating the hydrogen. Currently the cheapest means of generating hydrogen is from natural gas. Considerable technological improvement of solar-based or chemical catalysis-based systems, likely combined with a carbon pricing mechanism, will be required to make hydrogen production from non-fossil fuels economically attractive. Breaking down water with electricity, electrolysis, to produce hydrogen also works, but is not efficient and is more costly than producing hydrogen with natural gas. Converting extra electricity produced by intermittent renewables such as wind and solar to hydrogen via electrolysis would be preferable to dumping the electricity into the ground to keep the grid balanced and could represent a source of some hydrogen, although it would not be very cost effective.

We have mentioned that biofuels alone are not a tenable solution to the transportation de-carbonization issue (see the conclusion to the biofuels chapter). There simply is not enough arable land, even with algal and cellulosic biofuels fuels thrown in. What may be possible is an all-of-the-above approach combined with increasing vehicle efficiency. Biofuels can be used to offset some gasoline. Hydrogen may play a role in some areas. Plug-in hybrids, hybrid electric vehicles whose batteries can be recharged but which can also run on liquid fuel, can also contribute. We are right on the threshold of having good enough batteries for truly reliable plug-in hybrids. There is not going to be a silver bullet for de-carbonizing the transportation sector and it is likely to be the last to be fully de-carbonized.

We also want to clarify that the above discussion about meeting transportation needs is based on the assumption that we want to continue our current transportation patterns in a way that emits less CO_2. It is also true that a cultural shift toward pedestrian-friendly cities with bike lanes and efficient public transportation can also help to meet decreased emissions goals. Group-owned, robotically driven vehicles, for instance, could also dramatically reduce the number of vehicles in most developed countries.

Industry The primary use of energy in industry beyond electricity is process heat – heat used to make material pliable, change its chemical structure, or for use in drying. Most process heat currently comes from combustion of fossil fuels, usually coal or natural gas, although some comes from converting electricity to heat, which is not an efficient process and is usually only done with electricity from hydropower or nuclear. More emphasis should be placed on using the 'waste' heat from current electricity generation for process heat, although waste heat from electricity generation will not be hot enough for some industrial processes. It should be possible to get process heat from the sun via solar thermal as well, either through power-tower-type arrangements, where high temperatures are needed, or through parabolic troughs for lower-temperature processes. Solar thermal will be more expensive upfront than current fossil fuel heat, and companies will likely need some sort of incentive to consider the longer payback horizons with solar thermal.

The most intractable issue with de-carbonizing industry may be finding alternatives to the actual carbon content of fossil fuels. Currently most plastics and asphalt for roads, along with waxes and lubricants, come from fossil fuels. These uses combined constitute about 8 percent of worldwide fossil fuel use; replacing that volume of material will not be easy. Some can come from carbon crops, as with production of biofuels, but will compete with biofuels and food production for land. It may eventually be possible to obtain some carbon inputs using the high temperatures of solar thermal power towers to convert CO_2 into simple hydrocarbons, but this is not anywhere near economical yet. For the foreseeable future most of the carbon for plastics and other manufactured goods from carbon are likely to continue to come from fossil fuels. There is actually a school of thought that a hundred years or so from now, as fossil fuels become tremendously expensive to obtain, the last remaining economically extractable reserves should be put aside for just such purposes.

Commercial/residential Besides electricity, building heating/cooling and hot water are the main energy inputs to maintaining commercial and residential spaces. Most of these needs could be addressed by the types of passive energy strategies outlined in the solar energy chapter under passive solar combined with solar hot water collectors, making this sector perhaps even more amenable to conversion to renewable energy sources than the electric generation sector. Adding in solar PV paint or moldable PV in the future, and roof-mounted panel PV now, most buildings could be made largely electrically self-sufficient for daylight hours, with a grid connection or backup power required for heavily overcast days. What is lacking in most developed countries is effective policy to make it happen, although that is slowly changing. Also, retrofitting existing buildings is always going to be more expensive than building passive features into new buildings, so exporting this technology and knowhow to the developing world is vital to help those countries avoid constructing millions of energy-intensive buildings. Sustainability of construction materials is another issue, but that is beginning to be addressed as well.

The Rosenfeld Curve, Jevons paradox, and the energy efficiency trap We have mentioned several times that increases in efficiency will be important if we are to wean ourselves off fossil fuels. The Rosenfeld Curve refers to a graph of California's electricity usage over time showing that from 1973 to 2009 usage increased by only about 10 percent whereas electricity usage in the rest of the country more than doubled. This trend is usually attributed to California setting many energy efficiency standards in the wake of the first oil crisis in 1973. Arthur Rosenfeld, a former physics professor and former head of the California Energy Commission, pioneered the call for efficiency standards, thus the name of the curve. The causal link between the graph and energy efficiency standards has been called into question recently (Levinson 2013), and certainly using aggregate data to prove something like the effect of energy efficiency policies is not very, well, efficient. It is likely that not all of the difference between California's minimal electricity usage growth rate and the much higher national rate is due to efficiency standards. However, the reverse is also true – that a significant portion of the effect is likely attributable to efficiency standards, so they are worth pursuing if they are well designed and implemented.

For the broader USA the trend toward a less energy-intensive economy has accelerated since the 1960s. From 1973 to 2011 the energy intensity (the amount of energy required to generate one dollar of GDP) has fallen by an average of 2 percent per year (US Energy Information Administration 2011), and there was an average 1 percent per year decrease going back to around 1900. Energy intensity is not energy efficiency. For instance, a major contributor to the energy intensity decline in the USA has been the flight of heavy industry such as steel smelting to other countries, but it does give us an idea of the trend. The hope is that more national energy efficiency policies could push that yearly percentage decline higher. As we try to move away from fossil fuels we will need more efficient energy systems for the simple reason that alternatives to fossil fuels simply do not have as high an energy density, and thus to move away from fossil fuels we will need to learn to do what we do today with less energy input.

There is a darker side to energy efficiency that is also worth mentioning. This is in the form of two counterintuitive traps related to energy efficiency gains. One is an economic theory called Jevons paradox and the second is complacency that gains in energy efficiency will be sufficient to reduce CO_2 emissions without having to move away from fossil fuel use. Jevons paradox refers to the observation that increasing the efficiency of a fuel will tend to drive demand for more of that fuel. It was conceived in the 1860s, looking back at the great expansion of coal use in the Industrial Revolution. Jevons paradox refers to fuel efficiency, not total energy efficiency, and it is thought that carefully crafted policy that does not decrease the actual end cost of a commodity much can avoid most of the effects. It does serve to inform policymaking, though, as poorly crafted energy efficiency policy could well hurt overall gains in reduction of fossil fuels through the economic effects of the paradox.

The second point is fairly straightforward and really refers back to the business-as-usual concept. This is the false impression that as long as we can increase efficiency enough to cut carbon emissions we do not have to do the hard work of dramatically reducing fossil fuel consumption. Easy to understand, unfortunately, does not make it easy to avoid.

Getting the policy right

The fundamental lesson that comes across in all of the case studies is that to have a shot at being effective, energy policy must be goal-, not crisis-, driven. Countries that articulate clear goals will end up with energy policy that is consistent. Across the various case studies presented in this book, we see that countries go about crafting and implementing their energy policy using different tools and to different ends. See the Appendix for a listing of countries and the policy mechanisms they use to encourage the adoption of renewable energy sources. We have not undertaken a deep enough analysis here to state that one policy tool is better than another. What we have seen is that policies need to be crafted based on an understanding of the local context, and should be subject to revision when needed. For example, Brazil's first comprehensive energy policy, ProÁlcool's, goal was to bring about energy independence. As discussed in Chapter 4, one of the shortcomings was that sugarcane development was concentrated in large agribusinesses near São Paolo. The 2004 revision of energy policy introduced rules, mechanisms, and incentives to ensure that other areas of the country as well as small farmers would also benefit from biofuel production. Another good example is Germany's revision of the FIT for solar power generation, as discussed in Chapter 8.

We can draw three broad conclusions from the case studies presented in support of this argument. First, consistency matters for success. Most oil-importing countries were greatly affected by the oil crises of the 1970s, which in some cases instituted and in all cases shaped energy policy. Many countries reacted to the 1973 oil crisis with ad hoc policies that were short lived. Countries that had consistent energy policies became industry leaders, as we saw with Brazil with biofuels, and Denmark with wind. Policies are consistent when the policy's goal is considered part of the national interest. Political realists argue that it does not matter who a country's leader is – the leader will act in the country's national interest. If the goals of the energy policy are articulated and accepted as legitimate, the fundamental policy will withstand political power shifts. For the oil-exporting countries, the crisis came in the 1980s when oil prices crashed. Although most oil-producing countries realized the dangers of relying so heavily on a globally traded commodity, they have also had a very difficult time shifting away from business as usual, subject to the same reasoning and explanations as the oil importers.

A second conclusion, related to the first, is that successful policies are those that decrease uncertainty. Consistency is important not just for purposes of research and development and technological innovation. Consistent policies to achieve clearly articulated goals decrease uncertainty. Uncertainty inhibits research, investment, and policy implementation. A consistent energy policy guides the bureaucracy that works toward achieving its goals. Heads of state change every few years, but the bureaucracies they preside over that implement and carry out the policies do not.

The third conclusion is that subsidies are required to level the playing field for new technologies. Direct and indirect subsidies exist for older, fossil-fuel-based technologies, but they are not often recognized as subsidies. We have talked a lot about the negative externalities of fossil fuels, some of which should be understood as forms of indirect subsidies. There are also direct subsidies and historical subsidies for fossil fuel sources that are not part of the discourse on complaints about subsidies.[3] We would argue the subsidies should also be transparent, as a check against corruption and cronyism benefiting a few individuals instead of meeting the energy policy's goals. Subsidies will create political entrenched interests if they benefit the few rather than the many, which can inhibit needed policy revisions.

Policy recommendations We do not want to recommend specific policies here. Instead, we will borrow some of the criteria Mendonça et al. (2009: 395) suggest for policy analysis. They are reminiscent of the recommendations put together by the World Commission on Dams regarding dam policies. Policymakers should consider the following:

1. Local acceptance – how does the proposal account for and influence local acceptance? As we saw in the cases of local wind cooperatives in Denmark and the comparison of two offshore wind farm case studies in the USA, local acceptance is key.

→ knowledge of the local context

2. Benefits – whose interests are furthered or protected? This is an issue that comes up often with large hydropower projects, where dams displace and dispossess often poor and marginalized communities to benefit urban communities. But we see it elsewhere as well. In the last decade the history of oil extraction in both Nigeria and Ecuador has been one of conflict and power struggles. For example, oil extraction in Nigeria takes place in the Niger Delta, but communities in the delta live in poverty and do not see much of the oil wealth. The same could be said for indigenous communities living in Ecuador's Amazon region. While indigenous communities in Ecuador have filed lawsuits against foreign-owned oil companies, Nigeria has seen attacks on the oil pipelines and kidnapping of foreign workers (BBC News 2006). In 2011, the country of Sudan split in two when South Sudan voted to secede. The two regions had fought a civil war years before that ended only when Khartoum, Sudan's capital city located in the northern part of the country, agreed to a revenue- and power-sharing scheme with rebel leaders from the south, where the oil is extracted.

→ need for transparency

3. Transition – how does the policy link to previous and supporting policies? This is relatively straightforward, but it speaks to two important aspects of policy-making. The first is to understand where and how this decision fits into the country's overarching policy goals. The second has to do with identifying potential shortfalls and structural or ideational challenges to implementing the new policy, and also where the new policy dovetails with already existing ones.

Conclusion

What factors would you privilege when making an energy policy? You should now have a better understanding of the science behind how various energy sources work, as well as some of the limitations of those sources. You also can draw on some examples of how different energy sources have been promoted in different national contexts. We conclude this book with a homework assignment.[4] How would you design your country's energy policy? Be specific. What sources would you privilege? What challenges will those sources bring? How would you address those challenges? Does your town or city have an energy policy? What is your state or province's energy policy? What is your country's energy policy? How closely does that policy match the ideal policy you designed? A published example of such an analysis exists for the United Kingdom in the book by David McKay, *Sustainable Energy – without the Hot Air* (McKay 2013).

We leave you with these questions to make our final point. You should have a voice in the energy policy debate. Do not leave it to government or politicians to tell you what sources will be privileged, and do not assume that those making the policy understand how energy works or know what policies have or have not worked elsewhere. Given the challenges of energy security and climate change, we all have a stake in energy policy. Your informed voice should be in the debate, analyzing claims about energy sources and policy proposals. You now have the necessary tools.

APPENDIX: RENEWABLE ENERGY SUPPORT POLICIES

Legend:
- ● national level policy
- ○ state/provincial level policy

HIGH INCOME COUNTRIES

Category	Policy	Australia	Austria	Barbados	Belgium	Canada	Croatia	Cyprus	Czech Republic	Denmark	Estonia	Finland	France	Germany	Greece	Hungary	Ireland	Israel	Italy
PUBLIC FINANCING	Public competitive bidding/tendering				●	●				●			●				●	●	●
	Public investment, loans, or grants	●	●	●	●	●	●		●	●	●		●	●	●	●		●	●
FISCAL INCENTIVES	Energy production payment										●	●		●					
	Reductions in sales, energy, CO$_2$, VAT, or other taxes						●			●	●			●	●	●		●	●
	Investment or production tax credits			●	●	●			●				●	●					●
	Capital subsidy, grant, or rebate	●		●	●	●	●	●	●	●	●	●	●	●	●	●			●
REGULATORY POLICIES AND TARGETS	Tradable REC	●	●		●				●	●			●	●				●	●
	Heat obligation/mandate													●			○	●	●
	Biofuels obligation/mandate	○	●		●	●		●	●	●	●	●	●	●	●	●	●		●
	Net metering			●	○	○				●									●
	Electric utility quota obligation/RPS				○	○												●	●
	Feed-in tariff/premium payment	○	●			○	●	●	●	●	●	●	●	●	●	●		●	●
	Renewable energy targets	●	●	●	●	○	●	●	●	●	●	●	●	●	●	●	●	●	●

Japan

Luxembourg

Malta

Netherlands

New Zealand

Norway

Oman

Poland

Portugal

Singapore

Slovakia

Slovenia

South Korea

Spain[1]

Sweden

Switzerland

Trinidad and Tobago

United Arab Emirates

United Kingdom

United States

Notes: 1. In Spain, the feed-in tariff (FIT) and net metering programs have been temporarily suspended by Royal Decree for new renewable energy projects; this does not affect projects that have already secured FIT funding. The value added tax (VAT) reduction is for the period 2010–12 as part of the stimulus package.

Countries are organized according to GNI per capita levels as follows: 'high' is US$ 12,476 or more, 'upper-middle' is US$ 4,036 to US$ 12,475, 'lower-middle' is US$ 1,026 to US$ 4,035, and 'low' is US$ 1,025 or less. Per capita income levels and group classifications from World Bank (2012). Only enacted policies are included in the table; however, for some policies shown, implementing regulations may not yet be developed or effective, leading to lack of implementation or impacts. Policies known to be discontinued have been omitted. Many feed-in policies are limited in scope of technology.

Source: See note 1 for this section.

Global overview of renewable energy support policies — Upper-middle income countries

		Algeria	Argentina	Belarus	Bosnia and Herzegovina	Botswana	Brazil	Bulgaria	Chile	China	Colombia	Costa Rica	Dominican Republic	Ecuador	Grenada	Iran	Jamaica	Jordan	Kazakhstan
PUBLIC FINANCING	Public competitive bidding/tendering	●	●		●	●			●				●			●	●	●	
	Public investment, loans, or grants		●				●	●	●		●			●					●
FISCAL INCENTIVES	Energy production payment		●						●						●				
	Reductions in sales, energy, CO$_2$, VAT, or other taxes		●	●		●	●	●	●	●	●	●		●	●	●		●	●
	Investment or production tax credits		●				●		●				●				●	●	
	Capital subsidy, grant, or rebate		●		●	●		●	●	●			●						
REGULATORY POLICIES AND TARGETS	Tradable REC																		●
	Heat obligation/mandate						○		●	●			●						
	Biofuels obligation/mandate		●				●	●	●	●							●	●	
	Net metering						●		●			○	●		●		●	●	
	Electric utility quota obligation/RPS									●	●								
	Feed-in tariff/premium payment	●	●		●		●		●				●	●		●		●	●
	Renewable energy targets	●	●		●	●	●	●	●	●	●	●	●			●	●	●	

● national level policy

○ state/provincial level policy

UPPER-MIDDLE INCOME COUNTRIES

Latvia

Lebanon

Libya

Lithuania

Macedonia

Malaysia

Mauritius

Mexico

Montenegro

Palau

Panama

Peru

Romania

Russia

Serbia

South Africa

St Lucia

Thailand

Tunisia

Turkey

Uruguay

LOWER-MIDDLE INCOME COUNTRIES

Armenia

Cameroon

Cape Verde

Côte d'Ivoire

Egypt

El Salvador

Renewable energy support policies (● national level policy; ○ state/provincial level policy)

Category	Policy	Fiji	Ghana	Guatemala	Guyana	Honduras	India	Indonesia	Lesotho	Marshall Islands	Micronesia	Moldova	Mongolia	Morocco	Nicaragua	Nigeria	Pakistan	Palestinian Territories[2]	Paraguay	Philippines	Senegal
PUBLIC FINANCING	Public competitive bidding/tendering		●			●	●	●	●				●	●			●			●	
	Public investment, loans, or grants		●			●	●	●					●	●		●	●			●	●
FISCAL INCENTIVES	Energy production payment						●		●											●	
	Reductions in sales, energy, CO_2, VAT, or other taxes	●		●	●	●	●	●	●	●		●		●				●	●	●	●
	Investment or production tax credits	●	●			●	●	●	●											●	
	Capital subsidy, grant, or rebate		●				●	●	●							●	○			●	
REGULATORY POLICIES AND TARGETS	Tradable REC						●														
	Heat obligation/mandate						○														
	Biofuels obligation/mandate		●	●			●	●										●	●	●	
	Net metering		●				●		●		○				●					●	
	Electric utility quota obligation/RPS						●	●												●	
	Feed-in tariff/premium payment		●			●	●	●	●				●	●	●	●	●	●		●	●
	Renewable energy targets	●	●	●	●	●	●	●	●	●	●	●	●	●	●	●	●			●	●

● national level policy
○ state/provincial level policy

Sri Lanka

Sudan

Syria

Ukraine

Vietnam

LOW INCOME COUNTRIES

Bangladesh

Burkina Faso

Ethiopia

Gambia

Guinea

Haiti

Kenya

Kyrgyzstan

Madagascar

Malawi

Mali

Mozambique

Nepal

Rwanda

Tajikistan

Tanzania

Togo

Uganda

Zambia

Note: 2. The area of the Palestinian Territories is included in the World Bank country classification as 'West Bank and Gaza.' They have been placed in the table using the 2009 'Occupied Palestinian Territory' GNI per capita provided by the United Nations (US$ 1,483).

Source: REN21 (2013) *Renewables 2013 Global Status Report,* Table 3, pp. 76–8. Available at: http://ren21.net/Resources/Publications/REN21Publications.aspx

NOTES

Introduction

1 The Anthropocene is a proposed new epoch, or division, in geological history, reflecting the dramatic impacts humans are having on the Earth, not just in climate change but also in biodiversity and other areas. The current geological epoch, or previous if the new epoch is accepted, is the Holocene, which goes back to the end of the last ice age approximately twelve thousand years ago. There is also debate on when the new era should be considered to have started, with arguments for both the years 2000 and 1800, among others.

2 We use the terms 'global North' and 'global South' throughout this book, since they are currently the terms used most frequently in the discourse on development. Global North refers to developed, industrialized, countries. Global South refers to countries that are 'developing' (a term which has its own genealogy and connotations and has fallen out of favor), which were formerly part of the 'third world.' We note, however, as have many before us, that the terms are not geographically accurate, as there are 'developing' countries north of the equator and industrialized countries south of the equator.

3 This is vividly demonstrated by NASA images showing what the Earth looked like at night at the beginning of the twenty-first century (see www.nasa.gov/mission_pages/NPP/news/earth-at-night.html). As one can clearly see, the global North, as well as some cities in the global South, consume a huge amount of energy.

4 For a color-coded map of Annex I and non-Annex I countries that are sized relative to the GHG emissions, see www.grida.no/graphicslib/detail/total-co2-emissions-from-fossil-fuel-burning-cement-production-and-gas-flaring_af46.

5 In the USA since about 2009 some politicians have referred to cap-and-trade systems as a carbon tax. This is incorrect. In cap-and-trade systems companies that overuse allowed emissions have to buy additional pollution credits, a cost that can be passed on to customers. A carbon tax is a tax levied on goods because those goods at one or more points in their production or consumption are connected to CO_2 emissions. A carbon tax would likely be levied on gasoline, for example. That additional cost is directly borne by the consumer.

6 Throughout this book the term 'dollar' or symbol '$' refers to the US dollar, unless otherwise specified.

1 Basic energy and policy concepts

1 Recently it has come to light that there was a society based on more sustainable agricultural practices in the Amazon basin. See Charles C. Mann's *1491: New Revelations of the Americas before Columbus*, Vintage Books, New York, 2006.

2 See Stephanie Sammartino McPherson, *War of the Currents: Thomas Edison vs Nikola Tesla*, 21st Century Press, Missouri, 2012.

3 There is a growing literature questioning the notion of 'the good life' and what considerations should go into defining standard of living. Those debates are beyond the scope of this book, but we do recognize that standard of living and quality of life are different measures, are open to debate, and that the teleology of 'development' to being a 'top consumer' is not necessarily a laudable goal. See Princen (2014) and Martínez-Alier et al. (2010).

2 Fossil fuels

1 Note that fossil fuel consumption data used for this statistic includes fossil fuels consumed for non-energy uses such as asphalt and plastics. In a review of the literature, calculating all fossil fuels seems to be the standard. The REN21 *Renewables 2013 Global Status Report*, p. 19, Figure 1, shows fossil fuels at 78.2 percent of global energy consumption in 2011, but they exclude non-energy use of fossil fuels.

We calculate 91 percent in 1997 based on 1997 data on consumption by fuel type in the *BP Amoco Statistical Review of World Energy 1999*, p. 38, www.bp.com/assets/bp_Internet/globalbp/STAGING/global_assets/downloads/S/Statistical_review_of_world_energy_1999.pdf, accessed 17 January 2014.

2 See Shaffer (2009: 3–6) for a broader discussion on the many connections between oil and politics.

3 When comparing oil prices across years, one has to make sure that the cost is in constant dollars. The value of a dollar in one year is not the value of a dollar the next year because of inflation. Here we use 2007 constant dollars, because that is what our source data used. The nominal (not adjusted for inflation) value of oil was $3.14 per barrel in 1973, and $12.44 in 1974. There are several websites that will calculate the value of a dollar for different years, if you want to plug in those numbers and see what the value is in the year you are reading this.

4 Large amounts of water are used in all fossil fuels extraction. One can find several comparisons in the literature that make fracking natural gas look like the better choice. For example, fracking natural gas uses 50 percent less water than coal mining (Laurenzi and Jersey 2013: 4896). On the other hand, fracking uses much more than renewable energy sources. Many publications dismiss the concern about the amount of freshwater used by comparing it to how much water is used to water lawns and golf courses in arid areas (Blackmon 2013; Nicot and Scanlon 2012). While valid, this also masks the unsustainability of keeping up lawns and building golf courses when it does not make ecological sense. Those are contested practices, addressed by programs such as the California American Water District rebates for replacing lawns, Sacramento County's Storm Drain Project rebate for installing a rain garden (see Ellis 2012 for an example), and the City of Santa Monica's Landscape Rebates and the sustainable garden program (City of Santa Monica 2013). The comparisons we choose to make shape how and what we think about our energy options. Seen in one light, the business-as-usual view, HF of natural gas is a rational option to decrease our GHG emissions. If we look toward a paradigm shift toward a sustainable future, HF of natural gas and tight oil

becomes a siren's call, keeping us on the same, unsustainable path, and distracting us from shaping a new reality.

5 For a humorous and informative historical account, see the *Daily Show with John Stewart* segment 'An energy independent future' from 16 June 2010, www.thedailyshow.com/watch/wed-june-16-2010/an-energy-independent-future.

6 More information on the Sustainable City is available at www.kacare.gov.sa/en/.

3 Nuclear power

1 The natural abundance of U238 – 993 out of every 1,000 uranium atoms on Earth is the U238 isotope (the rest is mostly U235 with a tiny bit of some of the rarer isotopes as well).

2 For a good and approachable review of radioactivity, nuclear weapons design, and nuclear history, look at Richard Muller's *Physics for Future Presidents*, W. W. Norton & Co., Inc. New York, 2008.

3 The calculator is available at www.nrc.gov/about-nrc/radiation/around-us/calculator.html.

4 The World Nuclear Association website has side-by-side heat maps showing the evacuation areas and the radioactive contamination plume in mSv/year over Fukushima seven months and eighteen months after the accident. Available at www.world-nuclear.org/info/Safety-and-Security/Safety-of-Plants/Fukushima-Accident/. If the link does not work, the website's page tree is: World Nuclear Association website>information library>safety and security>safety of plants>Fukushima accident.

5 Wikipedia has a nice summary page under 'nuclear reprocessing.'

6 Overview of in-progress reactor designs can be found at www.world-nuclear.org/info/Nuclear-Fuel-Cycle/Power-Reactors/Advanced-Nuclear-Power-Reactors/.

5 Hydropower

1 The International Court of Justice was established in 1945 as part of the United Nations. The Court uses international law to settle disputes brought to it by countries, and to give advisory opinions to UN agencies.

6 Wind power

1 Based on data provided by REN21 (2013).

2 US average residential electricity was

about $0.13/kWh in 2013 (US Energy Information Administration 2013f).

3 For a live breakdown of Denmark's power generation, see energinet.dk/Flash/Forside/UK/index.htm.

4 The Altamont wind farm should never have been sited where it is, because of its impact on bird populations, and California now has much stricter siting regulations.

7 Geothermal energy

1 The calculation is 100,000 ExaJoules (EJ) – an EJ is 10^{18} Joules. One EJ is about 278 billion kWh. So the potential is 278,000,000,000 times 100,000 (MIT 2006). At that point, geothermal would not be available for heating purposes.

2 Based on a calculation performed by the author at the UNFCCC GHG data site. Iceland's base year of 1990 total GHG emissions excluding LULUCF/LUCF (land use changes) was 3,508 Gigagrams (Gg). Ten percent of that is 351 Gg, so the 2012 target should be no more than 3,859 Gg. In 2011, the last inventory year available on the UNFCCC website at the time of writing, Iceland's total was 4,413 Gg. Iceland's peak year was 2008 with 4,994 Gg. See the UNFCCC's flexible GHG data queries page at unfccc.int/di/FlexibleQueries/Event.do?event=go for more information.

3 This is a common phenomenon called Dutch Disease, after the experience the Netherlands when it started exporting oil, but the 'disease' can occur with any valuable export commodity. The Netherlands' domestic textile manufacturing declined greatly, because imports effectively became cheaper and could not compete with domestically produced goods once the value of the currency rose. The phenomenon also affects the domestic

labor market. See Michael L. Ross, 'Oil, Islam, and women,' *American Political Science Review*, 102(1): 107–23 (February 2008).

8 Solar energy

1 There are a number of calculators on the web to determine insolation. For an example, see solarelectricityhandbook.com/solar-irradiance.html.

9 Conclusion

1 We refer here to: the Deepwater Horizon (BP) oil spill in the Gulf of Mexico in 2010; multiple pipeline explosions, the most recent (2014) in New York City and Adair, Kentucky; the Upper Big Branch coal mine explosion in 2010; the derailment and explosion of a train carrying crude oil in Lac-Mégantic, Quebec, in 2013; and the 2014 Freedom Industries chemical spill into the Elk river in Charleston, West Virginia.

2 These ideas come out of the sustainability literature. It is beyond the scope of this conclusion to go into great detail here. See Thiele (2013); Simon Drezner, *The Principles of Sustainability*, Earthscan Publications, London, 2002; Brian Doherty and Marius de Geus (eds), *Democracy and Green Political Thought: Sustainability, Rights, and Citizenship*, Routledge/ECPR Studies in European Political Science Series, 1996; Princen et al. (2002).

3 For a breakdown of subsidies by fuel source type, see US Energy Information Agency, *Direct Federal Financial Interventions and Subsidies in Energy in Fiscal Year 2010*, 2011, www.eia.gov/analysis/requests/subsidy/.

4 We give this assignment in the class we co-teach on which this book is based. It usually goes down quite well.

BIBLIOGRAPHY

ADEME (n.d.) *Energy Policies*, French Environment and Energy Management Agency, www2.ademe.fr/servlet/KBaseShow?sort=-1&cid=96&m=3&catid=17575, accessed 31 December 2013.

Akhonbay, H. (2012) *Saudi Arabia's Energy Policy: A Disciplined Approach to Forward-looking Policymaking*, Center for Strategic and International Studies, August, csis.org/files/publication/120831_Akhonbay_Saudi ArabiaEnergy_Web.pdf, accessed 22 December 2013.

Al Jazeera (2013) *The Secret of the Seven Sisters*, 26 April, www.aljazeera.com/programmes/specialseries/2013/04/20134410523148 7582.html, accessed 1 January 2014.

Amazon Watch (2014) *Brazil's Belo Monte Dam*, amazonwatch.org/work/belo-monte-dam, accessed 9 January 2014.

Amin, M. (2011) 'Toward a more secure, strong and smart electric power grid,' *IEEE Smart Grid*, January, smartgrid.ieee.org/january-2011/67-toward-a-more-secure-strong-and-smart-electric-power-grid, accessed 18 January 2014.

Aucott, M. L. and J. Melillo (2013) 'A preliminary energy return on investment analysis of natural gas from the Marcellus Shale', *Journal of Industrial Ecology*, 15(5): 668–79.

Axelrod, R. S., S. D. Vandeveer and D. L. Downie (eds) (2010) *The Global Environment: Institutions, Law, and Policy*, 3rd edn, Washington, DC: CQ Press.

Axelrod, R. S., S. Mirand, A. Schreurs and N. J. Vig (2011) 'Environmental policy making in the European Union,' in R. S. Axelrod, S. D. Vandeveer and D. L. Downie (eds), *The Global Environment: Institutions, Law, and Policy*, 3rd edn, Washington, DC: CQ Press, pp. 213–38.

Barradale, M. (2008) *Impact of Policy Uncertainty on Renewable Energy Investment: Wind Power and PTC*, US Association for Energy Economics Working Paper no. 08-003, January, www.iaee.org/en/students/best_papers/Merrill_Barradale.pdf, accessed 22 December 2013.

Baxter, C. (2012) 'Big Coal: decades of deception', *Polluter Watch*, 10 September, www.polluterwatch.com/blog/big-coal-decades-deception, accessed 16 December 2013.

BBC News (2006) 'Nigerian oil fuels Delta conflict,' *BBC News*, news.bbc.co.uk/2/hi/africa/4617658.stm, accessed 26 January 2014.

— (2013) 'Russia deal saved Ukraine from bankruptcy – PM Azarov,' *BBC News*, 18 December, www.bbc.co.uk/news/world-europe-25427706, accessed 6 December 2014.

Biello, D. (2010) 'Are new types of reactors needed for the US nuclear renaissance?', *Scientific American*, 19 February, www.scientificamerican.com/article.cfm?id=are-new-types-of-reactors-needed-for-nuclear-renaissance, accessed 28 December 2013.

Biswas, A. (2008) 'Management of transboundary waters: an overview,' in O. Varis, C. Tortajada and A. K. Biswas (eds), *Management of Transboundary Rivers and Lakes*, Berlin: Springer-Herlag Publishers.

Blackmon, D. (2013) 'Water for fracking, in context,' *Forbes*, www.forbes.com/sites/davidblackmon/2013/07/01/water-for-fracking-in-context/, accessed 17 December 2013.

Bipartisan Policy Center (2012) *The Executive Branch and National Energy Policy: Time for Renewal*, PDF, November, bipartisanpolicy.org/sites/default/files/BPC_Governance_Report_0.pdf, accessed 3 January 2014.

Brasier, K. J., M. R. Filteau, D. K. McLaughlin, J. Jacquet, R. C. Stedman, T. W. Kelsey and S. Goetz (2011) 'Resident's perceptions of community and environmental impacts of natural gas in the Marcellus Shale: a comparison of Pennsylvania and New York cases,' *Journal of Rural Social Sciences*, 26(1): 32–61.

Brooks, S. (2012) 'High-stakes gas prices,' *Know*, 10 April 2012, www.utexas.edu/know/2012/04/10/energy_poll_gas/, accessed 30 December 2013.

Brunwasser, M. (2012) 'Zeugma after the flood', *Archaeology*, www.archaeology.org/issues/44-1211/features/252-features-zeugma-after-the-flood, accessed 8 December 2013.

Bullis, K. (2013) 'Company makes CO_2 into liquid fuel, with help from a volcano,' *MIT Technology Review*, 28 November, www.technologyreview.com/news/521031/company-makes-co2-into-liquid-fuel-with-help-from-a-volcano/, accessed 10 January 2014.

Burmistrova, S. and N. Zinets (2014) 'Russia raises gas prices for Ukraine by 80%,' *Reuters*, 4 April, uk.reuters.com/article/2014/04/04/uk-ukraine-crisis-gas-idUKBREA330C520140404, accessed 4 April 2014.

California Energy Commission (2013) *California's Energy Policy*, www.energy.ca.gov/energypolicy/, accessed 13 January 2014.

California Public Utilities Commission (2013) *California Renewables Portfolio Standard (RPS)*, www.cpuc.ca.gov/PUC/energy/Renewables/, accessed 13 January 2014.

Cardis, E., L. R. Anspaugh, V. K. Ivanov, I. A. Likhtarev, K. Mabuchi, A. E. Okeanov and A. E. Prisyazhniuk (1996) 'Estimated long term health effects of the Chernobyl accident,' in *One Decade after Chernobyl – Summing up the Consequences of the Accident (Proc. EU/IAEA/WHO Conf. (Vienna, April, 1996)*, Vienna: IAEA, pp. 241–71.

Carpenter, A. T. (2013) 'Water and hydraulic fracturing,' *Journal: American Water Works Association*, 105(3): 56–9.

Carter, C., G. Rausser and A. Smith (2012) 'The effect of the U.S. ethanol mandate on corn prices,' PDF, agecon.ucdavis.edu/people/faculty/aaron-smith/docs/Carter_Rausser_Smith_Ethanol_Paper_submit.pdf, accessed 6 January 2014.

Carter, J. (1977) *National Energy Program Fact Sheet on the President's Program*, 20 April, The American Presidency Project, ed. J. Woolley and G. Peters, www.presidency.ucsb.edu/ws/?pid=7373, accessed 2 January 2014.

Cartlidge, E. (2011) 'Saving for a rainy day,' *Science*, 334: 922–4.

Casey, C. (2013) 'Is Brazil the energy power of the future (and always will be)?', *Americas Quarterly*, Summer, www.americasquarterly.org/is-brazil-the-energy-power-of-the-future, accessed 7 January 2014.

Ceccarelli, L. (2011) 'Manufactured scientific controversy: science, rhetoric, and public debate,' *Rhetoric & Public Affairs*, 14(2): 195–228.

Center for Ocean Solutions (n.d.) *Storm Intensity*, centerforoceansolutions.org/climate/impacts/cumulative-impacts/storm-intensity/, accessed 18 January 2014.

China Labour Bulletin (2013) 'HazardEx: China coal mine safety improves, but fatalities still high,' 9 May, www.clb.org.hk/en/content/hazardex-china-coal-mine-safety-improves-fatalities-still-high, accessed 2 January 2014.

City of Santa Monica (2013) *Landscape*, Office of Sustainability and the Environment, www.smgov.net/Departments/OSE/categories/landscape.aspx, accessed 23 December 2013.

Clark, C. E., A. J. Burnham, C. B. Harto and R. M. Horner (2012) 'Introduction: The technology and policy of hydraulic fracturing and potential environmental impacts of shale gas development,' *Environmental Practice*, 14(4): 249–61.

Clark, N. (2012) 'Energy policy in France divides governing coalition of Socialists and Greens,' *New York Times*, 14 September, www.nytimes.com/2012/09/15/world/europe/energy-policy-divides-governing-coalition-in-france.html?_r=0, accessed 31 December 2013.

Clark, P. (2013) '"Stern 2" to review economic costs of tackling climate change,' *Financial Times*, 24 September, www.ft.com/cms/s/0/cf2f2f6c-.2489-11e3-a8f7-00144feab7de.html#axzz2qtXn3scO, accessed 18 January 2014.

Conca, K. (2006) *Governing Water: Contentious Transnational Politics and Global Institution Building*, Cambridge, MA: MIT Press.

— (2008) 'The United States and international water policy,' *Journal of Environment & Development*, 17(3): 215–37.

Congressional Digest (1985) 'The controversy,' *Congressional Digest*, 64(2): 33–64.

Cook, J. et al. (2013) 'Quantifying the consensus on anthropogenic global warming in the scientific literature,' *Environmental Research Letters*, 8, doi: 10.1088/1748-9326/8/2/024024.

Council on Foreign Relations (2012) *World Opinion on Energy Security*, www.cfr.org/energy-policy/world-opinion-energy-security/p20063, accessed 30 December 2013.

Current Science (2009) 'Box oven wins prize,' *Current Science*, 95(7): 14–15.

Curry, A. (2009) 'Deadly flights,' *Science*, 24(325): 386–7.

Daily Show with Jon Stewart (2010) 'An energy independent future,' 16 June, www.thedailyshow.com/watch/wed-june-16-2010/an-energy-independent-future, accessed 27 December 2013.

Danish Energy Agency (2012) *Energy Policy in Denmark*, PDF, www.ukerc.ac.uk/support/tiki-download_file.php?fileId=3082, accessed 2 January 2014.

Danish Government (2011) *Energy Strategy 2050: From coal, oil, and gas to green energy (summary)*, PDF, Danish Ministry of Climate and Energy, marokko.um.dk/~/media/Marokko/Documents/Other/GBEnergistrategi2050sammenfatning.pdf, accessed 13 January 2014.

Danish Wind Industry Association (2013) 'Wind energy passes 30%,' *News*, 31 January, www.windpower.org/en/news/news.html#727, accessed 13 January 2014.

Davison, W. and A. Feteha (2014) 'Ethiopia reject Egypt proposal on Nile as dam talks falter,' *CyberEthiopia*, 9 January, cyberethiopia.com/2013/?p=670, accessed 10 January 2014.

De Chant, T. (2012) 'If the world's population lived like ...', *Per Square Mile*, 8 August, persquaremile.com/2012/08/08/if-the-worlds-population-lived-like/, accessed 14 August 2013.

DECC (Department of Energy & Climate Change) (2013) 'The Energy Act received Royal Assent on 18 December 2013,' 18 December, www.gov.uk/government/collections /energy-bill, accessed 7 January 2014.

DECC (Department of Energy & Climate Change) and Department of Transport (2013) 'Increasing the use of low-carbon technologies: Feed-in Tariff scheme,' 4 December, www.gov.uk/government/policies/increasing-the-use-of-low-carbon-technologies, accessed 7 January 2014.

Deets, S. (2009) 'Constituting interests and identities in a two-level game: understanding the Gabcikovo-Nagymaros dam conflict,' *Foreign Policy Analysis*, 5(1): 37–56.

Deichmann, N. and D. Giardini (2006) 'Earthquakes induced by stimulation of an enhanced geothermal system below Basel (Switzerland),' *Seismological Research Letters*, 80(5): 784–98.

Department of Infrastructure, Energy, and Resources (2013) *Major National Energy Policies*, State of Tasmania, Australia, www.dier.tas.gov.au/energy/energy_markets,_regulation_and_legislation/major_national_energy_policies, accessed 10 January 2014.

Department of State (2011) 'Foreign relations of the United States, 1969–1976, Volume XXXVI, energy crisis, 1969 to 1974,' Press release, Office of the Historian, 20 December, history.state.gov/historicaldocuments/frus1969-76v36/pressrelease, accessed 1 January 2014.

Diarra, S. T. (2011) 'West Africa: Niger river under pressure from dams,' Inter-Press Service News Agency, 31 October, www.ipsnews.net/2011/10/west-africa-niger-river-under-pressure-from-dams/, accessed 10 January 2014.

Doya, D. M. (2013) 'Kenya postpones renewable energy to reduce power costs,' Bloomberg, 27 November, www.bloomberg.com/news/2013-11-26/kenya-suspends-licensing-new-wind-farms-solar-plants-until-2017.html, accessed 16 January 2014.

DSIRE (Database of State Incentives for Renewables and Efficiency) (2013) *New York*, www.dsireusa.org/incentives/incentive.cfm?Incentive_Code=NY03R, accessed 13 January 2014.

Earth Policy Institute (2007) 'Crude oil price 1970–2007 (constant 2007 dollars),' www.earth-policy.org/datacenter/xls/update67_5.xls, accessed 4 January 2014.

Eaton, T. T. (2013) 'Science-based decision-making on complex issues: Marcellus shale gas hydrofracking and New York City water supply,' *Science of the Total Environment*, 461/462: 158–69.

Economist (2002) 'Dam shame,' *The Economist*, 4 July, www.economist.com/node/1216380, accessed 9 January 2014.

— (2013) 'How to lose half a trillion euros: Europe's electricity providers face an existential threat,' *The Economist*, 12 October, www.economist.com/news/briefing/21587782-europes-electricity-providers-face-existential-threat-how-lose-half-trillion-euros, accessed 10 January 2014.

Efstathiou, J., Jr (2013) 'Oil supply surge brings calls to ease US export ban,' Bloomberg, 17 December, www.bloomberg.com/news/2013-12-17/oil-supply-surge-brings-calls-to-ease-u-s-export-ban.html, accessed 31 December 2013.

Ellis, M. (2012) *Xeriscape Yard Adventure*, Blog, xeriscapeyard.wordpress.com, accessed 1 December 2013.

Elvan, O. D. and Y. O. Turker (2013) 'Geo-thermal energy capacity and legislation in Turkey,' *Journal of World Energy Law & Business*, 6(4): 300–13.

Energy Explorer (2013) *A–Z of Australia's Energy Sources*, Origin Energy, www.originenergy.com.au/energymix, accessed 10 January 2014.

Energy Regulatory Commission (2012) *Renewable Energy and Energy Efficiency Regulations (Public Notice)*, Kenya, www.renewable-energy.go.ke/index.php/news/3, accessed 15 January 2014.

EPA (Environmental Protection Agency) (2000) 'EPA decides mercury emissions from power plants must be reduced,' Press release, 14 December, yosemite.epa.gov/opa/admpress.nsf/8b75cea4165024c685257359003f022e/cd30963685856f30852569b5005ee740!OpenDocument, accessed 16 December 2013.

— (2009) *EPA Lifecycle Analysis of Greenhouse Gas Emissions from Renewable Fuels*, PDF, www.epa.gov/otaq/renewablefuels/420f10006.pdf, accessed 7 January 2014.

— (2011) 'EPA issues first national standards for mercury pollution from power plants/Historic "mercury and air toxics standards" meet 20-year old requirement to cut dangerous smokestack emissions,' Press release, 21 December, yosemite.epa.gov/opa/admpress.nsf/1e5ab1124055f3b28525781f0042ed40/bd8b3f37edf5716d8525796do05ddo86%21OpenDocument, accessed 14 January 2014.

— (2012) *About Yucca Mountain Standards*, www.epa.gov/radiation/yucca/about.html, accessed 15 January 2014.

— (2013) *Bilateral and International Agreements*, www.epa.gov/oita/air/agreements.htm, accessed 26 December 2013.

Erdogdu, E. (2009) 'A snapshot of geothermal energy potential and utilization in Turkey,' *Renewable and Sustainable Energy Reviews*, 13(9): 2535–43.

European Commission (2013) *Infringement of EU Law*, ec.europa.eu/eu_law/infringements/infringements_en.htm, accessed 8 January 2014.

European Parliament (2013) 'European Parliament backs switchover to advanced biofuels,' Press release, 11 September, www.europarl.europa.eu/news/en/news-room/content/20130906IPR18831/html/European-Parliament-backs-switchover-to-advanced-biofuels, accessed 8 January 2014.

EWEA (European Wind Energy Association) (2013) *Wind in Power*, PDF, www.ewea.org/fileadmin/files/library/publications/statistics/Wind_in_power_annual_statistics_2012.pdf, accessed 9 January 2014.

ExternE (2006) *Publications of ExternE*, ExternE – Externalities of Energy. A Research Project of the European Commission, www.externe.info/externe_2006/, accessed 26 January 2014.

ExxonMobil (2013) *Early Milestones*, www.exxonmobil.com/MENA-English/PA/about_who_history.aspx, accessed 31 December 2013.

Fackler, M. (2013) 'Former Japanese leader declares opposition to nuclear power,' *New York Times*, 2 October, www.nytimes.com/2013/10/03/world/asia/former-prime-minister-declares-opposition-to-nuclear-power-in-japan.html, accessed 31 December 2013.

Factbook (2013) 'Country studies,' *CIA World Factbook*, www.cia.gov/library/publications/the-world-factbook/, accessed 30 December 2013.

— (2014) 'Country studies,' *CIA World Factbook*, www.cia.gov/library/publications/the-world-factbook/, accessed 4 January 2014.

Federal Ministry for the Environment, Nature Conservation, and Nuclear Safety (2010) *Energy Concept for an Environmentally*

Sound, Reliable and Affordable Energy Supply, PDF, www.bmu.de/fileadmin/bmu-import/files/english/pdf/application/pdf/energie konzept_bundesregierung_en.pdf, accessed 10 January 2014.

Fincher, J. (2013) 'EWICON bladeless wind turbine generates electricity using charged water droplets,' Gizmag, 3 April, www.gizmag.com/ewicon-bladeless-wind-turbine/26907/, accessed 18 January 2014.

Firestone, J., W. Kempton and A. Kruger (2008) Delaware Opinion on Offshore Wind: Final report, PDF, University of Delaware College of Marine and Earth Studies, June, www.ceoe.udel.edu/windpower/docs/Final-DNRECOpinionReport.pdf, accessed 13 June 2014.

Fisher, J. (2013) 'Louisiana adds potential ethane cracker to its gas-inspired building boom,' Naturalgasintel, 24 December, www.naturalgasintel.com/articles/96846-louisiana-adds-potential-ethane-cracker-to-its-gas-inspired-building-boom, accessed 31 December 2013.

Fishkin, J. S. (2009) When the People Speak: Deliberative Democracy and Public Consultation, Oxford: Oxford University Press.

Ford, G. R. (1975a) Address on Energy Policy, Miller Center, University of Virginia, 27 May, millercenter.org/president/speeches/detail/3985, accessed 27 December 2013.

— (1975b) Statement on the Energy Policy and Conservation Act, 22 December, The American Presidency Project, ed. J. Woolley and G. Peters, www.presidency.ucsb.edu/ws/?pid=5452, accessed 2 January 2014.

Forum for the Future (2009) FT Climate Challenge: The 2009 Competition, www.forumforthefuture.org/project/ft-climate-challenge/overview, accessed 18 January 2014.

French Geological Survey (2012) 'Deep geothermal energy: the Soultz-sous-Forêts site has reached the sustainable production phase,' 15 July, www.brgm.eu/content/deep-geothermal-energy-soultz-sous-forets-site-has-reached-sustainable-production-phase, accessed 14 January 2014.

Freudenburg, W. R., R. Gramling and D. J. Davidson (2008) 'Scientific Certainty Argumentation Methods (SCAMs): science and the politics of doubt,' Sociological Inquiry, 78(1): 2–38.

Friedman, L. (2009) 'China, US give Copen-hagen negotiators some targets,' New York Times, 30 November, www.nytimes.com/cwire/2009/11/30/30climatewire-china-us-give-copenhagen-negotiators-some-ta-73618.html?pagewanted=all, accessed 2 January 2014.

Fröhlingsdorf, M. (2013) 'Turbine trouble: ill wind blows for German offshore industry,' Der Spiegel, 2 August, www.spiegel.de/international/germany/german-offshore-wind-industry-goes-from-boom-to-bust-a-914158.html, accessed 9 January 2014.

Fukushima Nuclear Accident Independent Investigation Commission (2012) The Official Report of The Fukushima Nuclear Accident Independent Investigation Commission, PDF, National Diet of Japan, www.nirs.org/fukushima/naiic_report.pdf, accessed 20 December 2013.

Galbraith, K. (2010) 'California: Jerry Brown kicked off clean energy revolution once, aims to do it again,' Gristmill, 24 June, grist.org/article/2010-06-24-jerry-brown-clean-energy-revolution-in-california-once-and-again/, accessed 13 January 2014.

Gardner, T. (2012) 'Water safe in town made famous by fracking-EPA,' Reuters, 11 May, uk.reuters.com/article/2012/05/11/usa-fracking-dimock-idUKL1E8GBVGN20120511, accessed 30 December 2013.

Gas in Focus (2013) Final Energy Consumption by Sector in France, www.gasinfocus.com/en/indicator/final-energy-consumption-by-sector-in-france/, accessed 25 January 2014.

General Assembly of the State of Delaware (2006) Electric Utility Retail Customer Supply Act of 2006, House Bill no. 6, legis.delaware.gov/LIS/lis143.nsf/vwLegislation/HB+6/$file/legis.html?open, accessed 15 January 2014.

Giddens, A. (2011) The Politics of Climate Change, 2nd edn, Cambridge, UK, and Malden, MA: Polity Press.

Gillis, J. (2013) 'Heat-trapping gas passes milestone, raising fears,' New York Times, 11 May, www.nytimes.com/2013/05/11/science/earth/carbon-dioxide-level-passes-long-feared-milestone.html?pagewanted=all&_r=0, accessed 2 June 2013.

Gold, R., B. Casselman and G. Chazan (2010) 'Leaking oil well lacked safeguard device,' Wall Street Journal, 28 April, online.wsj.com/news/articles/SB10001424052748270

4423504575212031417936798, accessed 17 December 2013.

Goldstone, J. A. (2011) 'Understanding the revolutions of 2011: weakness and resilience in Middle East autocracies,' *Foreign Affairs*, May/June, www.foreignaffairs.com/articles/67694/jack-a-goldstone/understanding-the-revolutions-of-2011, accessed 11 January 2014.

Gonzalez, M. and M. Lucky (2013) 'Fossil fuels dominate primary energy consumption,' *Vital Signs Online*, Worldwatch Institute, 24 October, www.worldwatch.org/fossil-fuels-dominate-primary-energy-consumption -1, accessed 16 December 2013.

Goodrich, L. and M. Lanthemann (2013) 'The past, present and future of Russian energy strategy,' *Stratfor Geopolitical Weekly*, 12 February, www.stratfor.com/weekly/past-present-and-future-russian-energy-strategy, accessed 6 January 2014.

Gordalla, B., E. Ewers and F. Frimmel (2013) 'Hydraulic fracturing: a toxicological threat for groundwater and drinking-water?', *Environmental Earth Sciences*, 70(8): 3875–93.

Gorst, I. and K. Lally (2013) 'Putin says he will pardon Yukos oil tycoon Mikhail Khodorkovsky,' *Washington Post*, 19 December, www.washingtonpost.com/world/putin-says-he-will-pardon-yukos-oil-tycoon-mikhail-khodorkovsky/2013/12/19/e48aca1c-68b6-11e3-8b5b-a77187b716a3_story.html, accessed 6 January 2014.

Guardian (2013) 'Dozens of Saudi Arabian women drive cars on day of protest against ban,' *Guardian*, 26 October, www.theguardian.com/world/2013/oct/26/saudi-arabia-woman-driving-car-ban, accessed 4 January 2014.

Gurgenci, H. (2011) 'What will make EGS geothermal energy a viable Australian energy option,' in A. R. Budd (ed.), *Proceedings of the Australian Geothermal Energy Conference*, Sebel Albert Park, Melbourne, 16–18 November, Canberra: Geoscience Australia, pp. 81–4.

GWEC (Global Wind Energy Council) (2013) *Global Wind Statistics*, PDF, www.gwec.net/wp-content/uploads/2013/02/GWEC-PRstats-2012_english.pdf, accessed 9 January 2014.

Hagström, E. and J. Adams (2012) 'Hydraulic fracturing: identifying and managing the risks,' *Environmental Claims Journal*, 24(2): 93–115.

Hall, C., J. G. Lambert and S. B. Balough (2014) 'EROI of different fuels and the implications for society,' *Energy Policy*, 64: 141–52.

Haluszczak, L., A. Rose and L. Kump (2013) 'Geochemical evaluation of flowback brine from Marcellus gas wells in Pennsylvania, USA,' *Applied Geochemistry*, 28: 55–61.

Hargraves, R. and R. Moir (2010) 'Liquid fluoride thermium reactors: an old idea in nuclear power gets reexamined,' *American Scientist*, 98(4), July/August.

Hastie, R. and R. M. Dawes (2010) *Rational Choice in an Uncertain World: The Psychology of Judgment and Decision Making*, 2nd edn, Thousand Oaks, CA: Sage Publications, Inc.

Hatzenbuhler, H. and T. Centner (2012) 'Regulation of water pollution from hydraulic fracturing in horizontally-drilled wells in the Marcellus Shale region, USA,' *Water*, 4(4): 983–94.

Heaton, E. (n.d.) *Factsheet – Biomass: Miscanthus*, PDF, Iowa State University Extension Department of Agronomy, www.extension.iastate.edu/publications/ag201.pdf, accessed 14 January 2014.

Hendrix, C. and S. Haggard (2007) *International Food Prices, Regime Type, and Protest in the Developing World*, PDF, cshendrix.files.wordpress.com/2007/03/hh_foodprices protest_forweb.pdf, accessed 11 January 2014.

Hernández-Moro, J. and J. Martínez-Duart (2013) 'Analytical model for solar PV and CSP electricity costs: present LCOE values and their future evolution,' *Renewable & Sustainable Energy Reviews*, 20: 119–32.

Hertel, T. W., A. Golub, A. D. Jones, M. O'Hare, R. J. Plevin and D. M. Kammen (2010) 'Global land use and greenhouse gas emissions impacts of U.S. maize ethanol: estimating market-mediated responses,' *BioScience*, 60(3): 223–31.

Herweyer, M. C. and A. Gupta (2008) 'Appendix D: Tar sands/oil sands,' *The Oil Drum*, www.theoildrum.com/node/3839, accessed 3 August 2014.

Hicks, C. (2004) 'Kenya slums turn sun into energy,' *BBC News*, 11 December, news.bbc.co.uk/go/pr/fr/-/2/hi/africa/4001061.stm, accessed 12 October 2009.

Holahan, R. and G. Arnold (2013) 'An institutional theory of hydraulic fracturing policy,' *Ecological Economics*, 94: 127–34.

IAEA-PRIS (2014) *Country Statistics: People's Republic of China*, International Atomic Energy Agency Power Reactor Information System, www.iaea.org/PRIS/Country-Statistics/CountryDetails.aspx?current=CN, accessed 2 August 2014.

ICJ (1997) *Case Concerning Gabčíkovo-Nagymaros Project (Hungary/Slovakia): Summary of the Judgment of 25 September 1997*, International Court of Justice, www.icj-cij.org/docket/index.php?sum=483&code=hs&p1=3&p2=3&case=%2092&k=8d&p3=5, accessed 15 January 2014.

IEA (2010a) *Energy Policies of IEA Countries: France 2009*, PDF, International Energy Agency, OECD Publishing, www.iea.org/publications/freepublications/publication/france2009.pdf, accessed 31 December 2013.

— (2010b) *Renewable Energy Essentials: Hydropower*, PDF, International Energy Agency, OECD Publishing, www.iea.org/publications/freepublications/publication/Hydropower_Essentials.pdf, accessed 8 January 2014.

— (2012) *Energy Policies of IEA Countries: Australia 2012 Review*, www.iea.org/publications/freepublications/publication/Australia2012_free.pdf, accessed 2 August 2014.

IEA-ETSAP and IRENA (2013) *Production of Liquid Biofuels: Technology Brief*, PDF, www.irena.org/DocumentDownloads/Publications/IRENA-ETSAP%20Tech%20Brief%20P10%20Production_of_Liquid%20Biofuels.pdf, accessed 8 January 2014.

Independent (2013) 'Delight in Aussie town over "trillion-dollar" oil find,' *Independent*, 25 January, p. 50.

Inman, M. (2013) 'The true cost of fossil fuels,' *Scientific American*, 308(4): 58–61.

International Commission for the Protection of the Danube River (n.d.) *Dams and Structures*, www.icpdr.org/main/issues/dams-structures, accessed 10 January 2014.

IPCC (2007a) 'Summary for policymakers,' in *Climate Change 2007: The Physical Science Basis*, Contribution of Working Group I to the Fourth Assessment Report of the Intergovernmental Panel on Climate Change, ed. S. Solomon, D. Qin, M. Manning, Z. Chen, M. Marquis, K. B. Averyt, M. Tignor and H. L. Miller, Cambridge and New York: Cambridge University Press.

— (2007b) 'Summary for Policymakers,' in *Climate Change 2007: Impacts, Adaptation and Vulnerability*, Contribution of Working Group II to the Fourth Assessment Report of the Intergovernmental Panel on Climate Change, ed. M. L. Parry, O. F. Canziani, J. P. Palutikof, P. J. van der Linden and C. E. Hanson, Cambridge and New York: Cambridge University Press, pp. 7–22.

— (2014) 'Summary for policymakers,' in *Climate Change 2014: Impacts, Adaptation, and Vulnerability*, Contribution of Working Group II to the Fifth Assessment Report of the Intergovernmental Panel on Climate Change, www.ipcc.ch/report/ar5/wg2/, accessed 2 April 2014.

Island President (2011) Film, dir. Jon Shenk, Afterimage Public Media ITVS and Actual Films, in association with Impact Partners.

ITU (2014) *Statistics – Time Series by Country*, International Telecommunications Union, www.itu.int/en/ITU-D/Statistics/Pages/stat/default.aspx, accessed 15 January 2014.

Jetter, J., Y. Zhao, K. R. Smith, B. Khan, T. Yelverton, P. DeCarlo and M. D. Hays (2012) 'Pollutant emissions and energy efficiency under controlled conditions for household biomass cookstoves and implications for metrics useful in setting international test standards,' *Environmental Science & Technology*, 46: 10827–34.

Jordan, M. and P. Finn (2006) 'Radioactive poison killed ex-spy,' *Washington Post Foreign Service*, 25 November, www.washingtonpost.com/wp-dyn/content/article/2006/11/24/AR2006112400410.html, accessed 30 December 2013.

K1 Team (2012) *France: A Study of French Nuclear Policy after Fukushima*, K=1 Criticality Project, Columbia University, k1project.org/france-a-study-of-french-nuclear-policy-after-fukushima/, accessed 2 August 2014.

Kammen, D. M. and S. Pacca (2004) 'Assessing the costs of electricity,' *Annual Review of Environment & Resources*, 29(1): 301-C-3.

Kanagawa, M. and T. Nakata (2008) 'Assessment of access to electricity and the socio-economic impacts in rural areas of developing countries,' *Energy Policy*, 36(6): 2016–29.

Kanter, J. (2012) 'Obstacles to Danish wind power,' *New York Times*, 22 January, www.nytimes.com/2012/01/23/business/global/obstacles-to-danish-wind-power.html?_r=0, accessed 13 January 2014.

Kelly-Detwiler, P. (2013) 'Denmark: 1,000 megawatts of offshore wind, and no signs of slowing down,' *Forbes energy blog*, 26 March, www.forbes.com/sites/peterdetwiler/2013/03/26/denmark-1000-megawatts-of-offshore-wind-and-no-signs-of-slowing-down/, accessed 13 January 2014.

Khan, M. (2013) 'Crucial water issues between Pakistan and India, CBMs, and the role of media,' *South Asian Studies*, 28(1): 213–21.

Kim, H., D. A. Boysen, J. M. Newhouse, B. L. Spatocco, B. Chung, P. J. Burke, D. J. Bradwell, K. Jiang, A. A. Tomaszowska, K. Wang, W. Wei, L. A. Ortiz, S. A. Barrliga, S. M. Poizeau and D. R. Sadoway (2013) 'Liquid metal batteries: past, present, and future,' *Chemical Reviews*, 113: 2075–99.

Kirubi, C., A. Jacobson, D. Kammen and A. Mills (2009) 'Community-based electric micro-grids can contribute to rural development: evidence from Kenya,' *World Development*, 37(7): 1208–21.

Koerth-Baker, M. (2012) *Before the Lights Go Out: Conquering the Energy Crisis Before It Conquers Us*, Hoboken, NJ: John Wiley & Sons, Inc.

KPMG (2013) 'Turkey taxes and incentives for renewable energy,' *KPMG Global Energy & Natural Resources*, 8 October, www.kpmg.com/global/en/issuesandinsights/articlespublications/taxes-and-incentives-for-renewable-energy/pages/turkey.aspx, accessed 14 January 2014.

Lagi, M., K. Z. Bertrand and Y. Bar-Yam (2011) *The Food Crises and Political Instability in North Africa and the Middle East*, PDF, 28 September, Cambridge, MA: New England Complex Systems Institute, necsi.edu/research/social/food_crises.pdf, accessed 11 January 2014.

LaMonica, M. (2013) 'A liquid metal battery for grid storage nears production,' *IEEE Spectrum*, 8 November, spectrum.ieee.org/energywise/energy/the-smarter-grid/a-liquid-metal-battery-for-grid-storage-nears-production, accessed 2 January 2014.

Laurenzi, I. and G. Jersey (2013) 'Life cycle greenhouse gas emissions and freshwater consumption of Marcellus Shale gas,' *Environmental Science & Technology*, 47(9): 4896–903.

Le, L., E. van Ierland, X. Zhu, J. Wesseler and G. Ngo (2013) 'Comparing the social costs of biofuels and fossil fuels: a case study of Vietnam,' *Biomass & Bioenergy*, 54: 227–38.

Leepa, C. and M. Unfried (2013) 'Effects of a cut-off in feed-in tariffs on photovoltaic capacity: evidence from Germany,' *Energy Policy*, 56: 536–42.

Leggett, J. (2014) *The Energy of Nations: Risk Blindness and the Road to Renaissance*, London: Earthscan.

Lenzen, M. (2008) 'Life cycle energy and greenhouse gas emissions of nuclear energy: a review,' *Energy Conversion and Management*, 49(8): 2178–99.

Lévêque, F. (2013) 'French early plant closure and nuclear cutbacks,' *EU Energy Policy blog*, 13 September, www.energypolicyblog.com/2013/09/30/french-early-plant-closure-and-nuclear-cutbacks/, accessed 31 December 2013.

Levinson, A. (2013) 'California energy efficiency: lessons for the rest of the world, or not?', National Bureau of Economic Research Working Paper no. 19123, www.nber.org/papers/w19123, accessed 21 January 2014.

Lindberg, A. (2013) '2014 Hyundai Tucson fuel cell: hydrogen-powered motoring for $499 a month,' *Car and Driver*, November, www.caranddriver.com/news/2014-hyundai-tucson-fuel-cell-photos-and-info-news, accessed 18 January 2014.

Logan, J. and S. M. Kaplan (2008) 'Wind power in the United States: technology, economic, and policy issues,' Congressional Research Service Report for Congress, 20 June, Order Code RL34546.

Lundin, J. (2013) *EROI of Crystalline Silicon Photovoltaics*, PDF, thesis, Uppsala University, www.diva-portal.org/smash/get/diva2:620665/FULLTEXT01.pdf, accessed 11 January 2014.

Machol, B. and S. Riz (2013) 'Economic value of U.S. fossil fuel electricity health impacts,' *Environment International*, 52: 75–80.

Mahdi, W. (2013) 'Billionaire prince questions Saudi energy policy amid shale threat,' *Financial Post*, 29 July, business.

financialpost.com/2013/07/29/billionaire-prince-questions-saudi-energy-policy/?__lsa=904e-a788, accessed 3 January 2014.

Mai, T., D. Sandor, R. Wiser and T. Schneider (2012) *Renewable Electricity Futures Study: Executive Summary*, NREL/TP-6A20-52409-ES, Golden, CO: National Renewable Energy Laboratory, www.nrel.gov/docs/fy13osti/52409-ES.pdf, accessed 9 January 2014.

Mall of America (2014) *About Mall of America: Green Initiatives*, www.mallofamerica.com/about/future-expansion/green-initiatives, accessed 17 January 2014.

Martínez-Alier, J., U. Pascual, V. Franck-Dominique and E. Zaccai (2010) 'Sustainable de-growth: mapping the context, criticisms, and future prospects of an emergent paradigm,' *Ecological Economics*, 69: 1741–7.

Marx, S. and E. U. Weber (2012) 'Decision making under climate uncertainty: the power of understanding judgment and decision processes,' in T. Dietz and D. C. Bidwell (eds), *Climate Change in the Great Lakes*, MSU Press, pp. 99–128.

Matthiesen, T. (2012) 'A "Saudi Spring"?: the Shi'a protest movement in the Eastern Province 2011–2012,' *Middle East Journal*, 66(4): 628–59.

McCaffrey, S. C. (n.d.) *Convention on the Law of the Non-Navigational Uses of International Watercourses*, Codification Division, Office of Legal Affairs, United Nations, legal.un.org/avl/ha/clnuiw/clnuiw.html, accessed 9 January 2014.

McCarthy, S. and R. Blackwell (2013) 'Canadians want Harper government to take leadership role on climate change, poll says,' *Globe and Mail*, 6 November, www.theglobeandmail.com/report-on-business/canadians-want-harper-government-to-take-leadership-role-on-climate-change-poll-says/article15281917/, accessed 28 December 2013.

McDonald, A. (2008) 'Nuclear power global status,' *IAEA Bulletin*, 49(2), March, www.iaea.org/Publications/Magazines/Bulletin/Bull492/, accessed 30 December 2013.

McKay, D. (2013) *Sustainable Energy – without the Hot Air*, PDF, www.withouthotair.com/download.html.

Mendonça, M., S. Lacey and F. Hvelplund (2009) 'Stability, participation and transparency in renewable energy policy: lessons from Denmark and the United States,' *Politics and Society*, 27(4): 379–98.

MEP (Ministry of Energy and Petroleum) (2013) *National Energy Policy: Final draft*, PDF, November, Republic of Kenya, www.energy.go.ke/index.php/events/finish/3-ministerial-documents/41-national-energy-policy-november-2013-draft, accessed 15 January 2014.

MERF (Ministry of Energy for the Russian Federation) (2010) *Energy Strategy of Russia: For the period up to 2030*, Moscow, www.energystrategy.ru/projects/docs/ES-2030_(Eng).pdf, accessed 18 January 2014.

METI (2010) *The Strategic Energy Plan of Japan – Meeting global challenges and securing energy futures (Summary)*, PDF, Ministry of Economy, Trade and Industry, Japan, June, www.meti.go.jp/english/press/data/pdf/20100618_08a.pdf, accessed 31 December 2013.

Milman, O. (2014) 'Australia has 2m small-scale renewable systems, says Clean Energy Regulator,' *Guardian Alpha*, www.theguardian.com/environment/2014/jan/09/australia-has-2m-small-scale-renewable-systems-says-clean-energy-regulator, accessed 12 January 2014.

Ministry for the Environment (2010) *Iceland's Fifth National Communication on Climate Change under the United Nations Framework Convention on Climate Change*, PDF, 3 May, unfccc.int/resource/docs/natc/isl_nc5_resubmit.pdf, accessed 14 January 2014.

Ministry of Foreign Affairs (2011) *Turkey's Energy Strategy*, Republic of Turkey, www.mfa.gov.tr/turkeys-energy-strategy.en.mfa, accessed 2 August 2014.

MIT (2006) *The Future of Geothermal Energy: Impact of Enhanced Geothermal Systems (EGS) on the United States in the 21st Century*, PDF, Assessment by an MIT-led interdisciplinary panel funded by the National Renewable Energy Laboratory (NREL), www1.eere.energy.gov/geothermal/egs_technology.html, accessed 11 January 2014.

Mitchel, B. (2013) 'Manufacturing trends in Australia,' *Economic Outlook* (blog), bilbo.economicoutlook.net/blog/?p=26092, accessed 13 January 2014.

Mitchell, T. (2002) 'McJihad: Islam in the US global order,' *Social Text*, Winter.

Moller, H. (2012) *Data Highlights: Hydropower Continues Steady Growth*, Earth Policy Institute, www.earth-policy.org/data_high lights/2012/highlights29, accessed 8 January 2014.

Monroe, R. (2013) 'What does 400ppm look like?', *The Keeling Curve: A daily record of atmospheric carbon dioxide from Scripps Institution of Oceanography at UC San Diego*, 25 April, keelingcurve.ucsd.edu/ what-does-400-ppm-look-like/, accessed 6 September 2013.

Morales, A. (2013) 'China sticks to carbon intensity target, dismisses CO_2 cap,' *Bloomberg News*, 4 June, www.bloomberg.com/ news/2013-06-04/china-sticks-to-carbon-intensity-target-while-dismissing-co2-cap. html, accessed 2 January 2014.

Moriarty, L. (2012) 'French sour on nuclear power,' *The World, on Public Radio International*, 24 April, pri.org/stories/2012-04-24/ french-sour-nuclear-power, accessed 31 December 2013.

Morse, E. L. and J. Richard (2002) 'The battle for energy dominance,' *Foreign Affairs*, March/April, pp. 16–31.

Moser, M. and A. Zammitt (2009) 'The High-Energy Diet: an interview with Michael Pollan,' *Powering a Nation*, www.power inganation.org/index.php/michael-pollan-interview.html, accessed 16 December 2013.

Mott MacDonald Inc. (2010) *UK Electricity Generation Costs Update*, www.gov.uk/ government/uploads/system/uploads/ attachment_data/file/65716/71-uk-electricity-generation-costs-update-.pdf, accessed 9 January 2014.

Murphy, D. J. and C. A. S. Hall (2010) 'Year in review – EROI or energy return on (energy) invested,' *Annals of the New York Academy of Sciences*, 1185: 102–18.

Murray, J. W. and J. Hansen (2013) 'Peak oil and energy independence: myth and reality,' *EOS, Transaction American Geophysical Union*, 94(28): 245–52.

NASA (2005) *What's the Difference Between Climate and Weather*, www.nasa.gov/ mission_pages/noaa-n/climate/climate_ weather.html, accessed 28 December 2013.

National Climatic Data Center (2013) *Billion-dollar Weather/Climate Disasters*, National Oceanic and Atmospheric Administration, www.ncdc.noaa.gov/billions/events, accessed 18 January 2014.

National Security Archive (2000) *The Secret CIA History of the Iran Coup, 1953*, Electronic Briefing Book no. 28, ed. Malcolm Byrne, www2.gwu.edu/~nsarchiv/NSAEBB/ NSAEBB28/, accessed 1 January 2014.

Nicot, J. and B. Scanlon (2012) 'Water use for shale-gas production in Texas, U.S.,' *Environmental Science & Technology*, 46(6): 3580–6.

Nissan (2013) 'Nissan announces battery replacement program for Leaf,' Press release, 20 June, nissannews.com/en-US/nissan/ usa/releases/nissan-announces-battery-replacement-program-for-leaf, accessed 26 January 2014.

Niu, S. et al. (2013) 'Electricity consumption and human development level: a comparative analysis based on panel data for 50 countries,' *Electrical Power and Energy Systems*, 53: 338–47.

Nixon, R. (1973) *Address to the Nation about National Energy Policy*, 25 November, The American Presidency Project, ed. J. Woolley and G. Peters, www.presidency.ucsb.edu/ ws/?pid=4051, accessed 27 December 2013.

Nobelprize.org (2013a) 'Henri Becquerel – facts,' Nobelprize.org, Nobel Media AB, www.nobelprize.org/nobel_prizes/physics/ laureates/1903/becquerel-facts.html, accessed 31 December 2013.

— (2013b) 'Marie Curie – biographical,' Nobelprize.org, Nobel Media AB, www. nobelprize.org/nobel_prizes/physics/ laureates/1903/marie-curie-bio.html, accessed 1 January 2014.

Normile D. (2012) 'Is nuclear power good for you?', *Science*, 337(27): 395.

NREL (2013) *US Department of Energy Commercial Reference Building Models of the National Building Stock*, PDF, Department of Energy, www.nrel.gov/docs/fy11osti/46861. pdf, accessed 10 January 2014.

NRG (2011) 'NRG to put offshore wind development on hold for the near term,' Press release, 12 December, www.nrgenergy.com/ nrgbluewaterwind/index.html, accessed 14 January 2014.

Nuclear Energy Institute (2013) *Quick Facts: Nuclear Energy in America*, August, www. nei.org/Master-Document-Folder/ Backgrounders/Fact-Sheets/Quick-Facts-

Nuclear-Energy-In-America, accessed 15 January 2014.

NYPA (2011) 'NY Power Authority trustees vote to end proposed Great Lakes offshore wind project,' Press release, 27 September, www.nypa.gov/Press/2011/110927b.html, accessed 14 January 2014.

OECD (n.d.) *Denmark: Inventory of Estimated Budgetary Support and Tax Expenditures for Fossil-fuels*, PDF, www.oecd.org/site/tadffss/DNK.pdf, accessed 13 January 2014.

— (2008) *OECD Reviews of Regulatory Reform: Brazil 2008 Strengthening Governance for Growth*, OECD Publishing, www.oecd.org/gov/regulatory-policy/oecdreviewsofregulatoryreform-brazilstrengtheninggovernanceforgrowth.htm, accessed 5 January 2014.

OECD/IEA (2013a) 'Four energy policies can keep the 2°C climate goal alive,' Press release, 10 June, www.iea.org/newsroomandevents/pressreleases/2013/june/name,38773,en.html, accessed 13 June 2013.

— (2013b) *World Energy Outlook Special Report: Redrawing the Energy-Climate Map©*, Paris: IEA Publications, www.iea.org/publications/freepublications/publication/name,38764,en.html, accessed 2 January 2014.

— (2013c) *Energy Security*, www.iea.org/topics/energysecurity/, accessed 14 August 2013.

Oimeke, R. P. (2013) 'Feed in Tariff policy in Kenya,' Energy Regulatory Commission, www.afurnet.org/index.php/.../95-en-pp04-afur-re-presentation-kenya, accessed 3 August 2014.

Oleck, J. (2010) 'Citing "secrecy," NY counties demand offshore wind details,' *InsideClimate News*, 14 October, insideclimatenews.org/print/5451, accessed 14 January 2014.

Olsson, O., D. Weichgrebe and K. Rosenwinkel (2013) 'Hydraulic fracturing wastewater in Germany: composition, treatment, concerns,' *Environmental Earth Sciences*, 70(8): 3895–906.

Ondraczek, J. (2013) 'The sun rises in the east (of Africa): a comparison of the development and status of the solar energy markets in Kenya and Tanzania,' *Energy Policy*, 56: 407–17.

OPEC (2013) *Our Mission*, Organization of the Petroleum Exporting Countries, www.opec.org/opec_web/en/about_us/23.htm, accessed 26 December 2013.

Oreskes, N. and E. M. Conway (2010) *Merchants of Doubt: How a Handful of Scientists Obscured the Truth on Issues from Tobacco Smoke to Global Warming*, New York: Bloomsbury.

Orkustofnun (2012) *Energy Statistics in Iceland 2012*, PDF, National Energy Authority, www.os.is/gogn/os-onnur-rit/orkutolur_2012-enska.pdf, accessed 2 August 2014.

Owen, A. D. (2004) 'Environmental externalities, market distortions and the economics of renewable energy technologies,' *Energy Journal*, 25(3): 127–56.

Parkison, G. (2013) *Geodynamics Writes Off Cooper Basin Geothermal Assets*, RenewEconomy, reneweconomy.com.au/2013/geodynamics-writes-cooper-basin-geothermal-assets-40047, accessed 10 January 2014.

Patrick, S. M. (2011) 'Public more willing than politicians to address climate change,' *The Internationalist blog*, Council on Foreign Relations, blogs.cfr.org/patrick/2011/11/30/public-more-willing-than-politicians-to-address-climate-change/, accessed 28 December 2013.

PBS (2008) 'Why do the French love nuclear power?', *Frontline: Heat*, www.pbs.org/wgbh/pages/frontline/heat/etc/frenchnuclear.html, accessed 31 December 2013.

— (2014) 'Everyday exposures to radiation,' *Frontline: Heat*, www.pbs.org/wgbh/pages/frontline/shows/reaction/interact/facts.html, accessed 18 January 2014.

Pearlman, J. (2013) 'Billions of barrels of oil in the Outback may turn Australia into new Saudi Arabia,' *Daily Telegraph*, 25 January, www.telegraph.co.uk/news/worldnews/australiaandthepacific/australia/9822955/Trillions-of-dollars-worth-of-oil-found-in-Australian-outback.html, accessed 21 January 2014.

Peckham, J. (2009) 'Cellulosic biofuels may not be ready; corn lobby could push its alternative: NRPA,' *Ethanol & Biodiesel News*, 21(12): 16.

Peixe, J. (2013) 'After 20 years the World Bank will begin to finance mega-dams again,' *Oil Price.com*, oilprice.com/Latest-Energy-News/World-News/After-20-Years-the-World-Bank-will-Begin-to-

Finance-Mega-Dams-Again.html, accessed 2 August 2014.

Pew Charitable Trusts (2012) *Who's Winning the Clean Energy Race?* 2011, www.pewtrusts.org/en/research-and-analysis/reports/2012/04/11/whos-winning-the-clean-energy-race-2011-edition, accessed 2 August 2014.

Pew Research Center (2012) *More Say There Is Evidence of Global Warming*, PDF, Pew Research Center for the People and the Press, 15 October, www.people-press.org/files/legacy-pdf/10-15-12%20Global%20Warming%20Release.pdf, accessed 24 July 2014.

— (2013a) 'Climate change: key data points from Pew Research,' 5 November, www.pewresearch.org/key-data-points/climate-change-key-data-points-from-pew-research/, accessed 28 December 2013.

— (2013b) 'Climate change and financial instability seen as top global threats,' Global Attitudes Project, 24 June, www.pewglobal.org/2013/06/24/climate-change-and-financial-instability-seen-as-top-global-threats/, accessed 28 December 2013.

Plevin, R. J., M. O'Hare, A. D. Jones, M. S. Torn and H. K. Gibbs (2010) 'Greenhouse gas emissions from biofuels' indirect land use changes are uncertain but may be much greater than previously estimated,' *Environmental Science & Technology*, 44: 8015–21.

PRC (People's Republic of China) (2012) *China's Energy Policy 2012*, Information Office of the State Council, english.gov.cn/official/2012-10/24/content_2250497.htm, accessed 2 January 2014.

Princen, T. (2014) 'The politics of urgent transition,' in Y. Wolinsky-Nahmias (ed.), *Climate Change Politics: U.S. Policies and Civic Action*, California: CQ Press.

Princen, T., M. Maniates and K. Conca (2002) *Confronting Consumption*, Cambridge, MA: MIT Press.

Pyper, J. (2013) 'Has the US reached peak gasoline?', *Scientific American and Climatewire*, www.scientificamerican.com/article.cfm?id=has-the-us-passed-peak-gasoline, accessed 28 December 2013.

Rahm, D. (2011) 'Regulating hydraulic fracturing in shale gas plays: the case of Texas,' *Energy Policy*, 39(5): 2974–81.

Randolph, E. (2010) 'Indian protest over Narmada Dam builds awareness of rights,' *The National*, 31 October, www.thenational.ae/news/world/south-asia/indian-protest-over-narmada-dam-builds-awareness-of-rights#page1, accessed 9 January 2014.

Reagan, R. (1981) *Message to the Congress Transmitting the National Energy Policy Plan*, 17July, The American Presidency Project, ed. J. Woolley and G. Peters, www.presidency.ucsb.edu/ws/?pid=44096, accessed 3 January 2014.

Reiche, D. (2010) 'Energy policies of Gulf Cooperation Council (GCC) countries – possibilities and limitations of ecological modernization in rentier states,' *Energy Policy*, 38(5): 2395–403.

Reiche, D. and M. Bechberger (2004) 'Policy differences in the promotion of renewable energies in the EU Member States,' *Energy Policy*, 32(7): 843–9.

REN21 (2013) *Renewables 2013 Global Status Report*, PDF, ren21.net/Resources/Publications/REN21Publications.aspx, accessed 14 January 2014.

Renewable Energy World (2013) *Belgium Plans to Build Island to Store Excess Wind Energy*, www.renewableenergyworld.com/rea/news/article/2013/01/belgium-plans-to-build-island-to-store-excess-wind-energy, accessed 13 January 2014.

Renewable Fuels Association (2014) *World Fuel Ethanol Production*, ethanolrfa.org/pages/World-Fuel-Ethanol-Production, accessed 8 January 2014.

REUK (2007) 'Lardarello: world's first geothermal power station,' Renewable Energy United Kingdom, www.reuk.co.uk/Lardarello-Worlds-First-Geothermal-Power-Station.htm, accessed 2 August 2014.

Roeb, M. and C. Sattler (2013) 'Isothermal water splitting,' *Science*, 341(6145): 470–1.

Rosenbaum, W. (2013) *Environmental Politics and Policy*, 9th edn, Thousand Oaks, CA: CQ Press.

Sáez, R. M. and L. J. Leal (1998) 'Assessment of the externalities of biomass energy, and a comparison of its full costs with coal,' *Biomass and Bioenergy*, 14(5/6): 469–78.

Saidur, R., M. R. Islam, N. A. Rahim and K. H. Solangi (2010) 'A review on global wind energy policy,' *Renewable and Sustainable Energy Reviews*, 14: 1744–62.

Sampson, A. (1980) *The Seven Sisters: The Great*

Oil Companies and The World They Shaped, New York: Bantam.

Schröder, C. (2012) 'Energy revolution hiccups: grid instability has industry scrambling for solutions,' *Spiegel Online International*, 16 August, www.spiegel.de/international/germany/instability-in-power-grid-comes-at-high-cost-for-german-industry-a-850419.html, accessed 2 August 2014.

Searchinger, T., R. Heimlich, R. A. Houghton, F. Dong, A. Elobeid, J. Fabiosa, S. Tokgoz, D. Hayes and T. H. Yu (2008) 'Use of U.S. croplands for biofuels increases greenhouse gases through emissions from land use change,' *Science*, 319(5867): 1238–40.

Secretariat of the Antarctic Treaty (2011) *The Protocol on Environmental Protection to the Antarctic Treaty*, www.ats.aq/e/ep.htm, accessed 25 December 2013.

Service, R. F. (2011) 'Turning over a new leaf,' *Science*, 334(6058): 925–7.

Shaffer, B. (2009) *Energy Politics*, Philadelphia: University of Pennsylvania Press.

Shankleman, J. (2012) 'Scotland opens first marine energy park,' *Guardian*, 30 July, www.theguardian.com/environment/2012/jul/30/scotland-first-marine-energy-park, accessed 7 April 2014.

Shariq, L. (2013) 'Uncertainties associated with the reuse of treated hydraulic fracturing wastewater for crop irrigation,' *Environmental Science & Technology*, 47(6): 2435–6.

Siluk, S. (2011) 'Combining three regional grids into one US-wide grid,' *IEEE Smartgrid*, April, smartgrid.ieee.org/april-2011/91-combining-three-regional-grids-into-one-us-wide-grid, accessed 18 January 2014.

Şimşek, H. A. and N. Şimşek (2013) 'Recent incentives for renewable energy in Turkey,' *Energy Policy*, 63: 521–30.

Skocpol, T. (1982) 'Rentier state and Shi'a Islam in the Iranian Revolution,' *Theory and Society*, 11(3): 265–83.

Smith, K. C. (2006) 'Russian energy policy and its challenge to Western policy makers,' Statement by Ambassador Keith C. Smith before the US House of Representatives Government Reform Subcommittee on Energy and Resources and the Subcommittee on National Security, Emerging Threats, and International Relations, 16 May: Washington, DC: Center for Strategic and International Studies.

Smith, Z. (2012) *The Environmental Policy Paradox*, 6th edn, Pearson.

Smith Stegan, K. (2011) 'Deconstructing the "energy weapon": Russia's threat to Europe as a case study,' *Energy Policy*, 39: 6505–13.

Solar Energy Industries Association (2014) *Solar Industry Data*, www.seia.org/research-resources/solar-industry-data, accessed 4 April 2014.

Soraghan, M. (2011) 'Pa. well blowout tests natural gas industry on voluntary fracking disclosure,' *New York Times*, 4 May, www.nytimes.com/gwire/ 2011/05/04/04green wire-pa-well-blowout-tests-natural-gas-industry-on-36297.html, accessed 27 December 2013.

Sorda, G., M. Banse and C. Kemfert (2010) 'An overview of biofuel policies around the world,' *Energy Policy*, 38(11): 6977–88.

Specter, M. (2013) 'Inherit the wind,' *New Yorker*, 20 May, pp. 72–6.

Statkraft (n.d.) *Hydropower*, www.statkraft.com/energy-sources/hydropower/, accessed 8 January 2014.

Stattman, S., O. Hospes and A. Mol (2013) 'Governing biofuels in Brazil: a comparison of ethanol and biodiesel policies,' *Energy Policy*, 61: 22–30.

Status of the Watercourses Convention (2013) International Water Law Project, 20 December, www.internationalwaterlaw.org/documents/intldocs/watercourse_status.html, accessed 9 January 2014.

Stern, N. (2007) *The Economics of Climate Change: The Stern Review*, Cambridge: Cambridge University Press.

Stop Gibe 3 Dam (2014) Website, www.stopgibe3.org/pages/doc.php, accessed 10 January 2014.

SUNY Oswego (2013) 'Green features "ingrained" in Shineman Center design, construction,' www.oswego.edu/news/index.php/site/news_archive/shineman_center_sustainability, accessed 25 January 2014.

Sveinsdottir, P. S. (2013) *Energy Statistics in Iceland 2013*, PDF, Orkustofnun, www.os.is/gogn/os-onnur-rit/orkutolur_2012-enska.pdf, accessed 10 January 2014.

Svenvold, M. (2008) 'Wind-power politics,' *New York Times Magazine*, 14 September, pp. 76–81.

Sverrisson, F. (2006) 'Missing in action:

Iceland's hydrogen economy,' *World Watch Magazine*, 19(6), November/December, www.worldwatch.org/node/4664, accessed 10 January 2014.

Tanigawa, K., Y. Hosoi, N. Hirohashi, Y. Iwasaki and K. Kamiya (2012) 'Loss of life after evacuation: lessons learned from the Fukushima accident,' *The Lancet*, 379(9819): 889–91.

Thiele, L. P. (2013) *Sustainability*, Cambridge: Polity Press.

Tu, K. J. and S. Johnson-Reiser (2012) *Understanding China's Rising Coal Imports*, PDF, Carnegie Endowment for International Peace, 16 February, carnegieendowment. org/files/china_coal.pdf, accessed 20 December 2013.

TurkishPress.com (2013) 'Turkey rediscovers potential in geothermal energy,' 25 April, www.turkishpress.com/news/384449/, accessed 2 August 2014.

Tveten, Å., T. Bolkesjø, T. Martinsen and H. Hvarnes (2013) 'Solar feed-in tariffs and the merit order effect: a study of the German electricity market,' *Energy Policy*, 61: 761–70.

Tyagi, W., N. A. A. Rahim, N. A. Rahim and J. A. Selvaraj (2013) 'Progress in solar PV (photovoltaic) technology: research and achievement,' *Energy Reviews*, 20: 443–61.

Tyson, P. (1994) 'Solar ovens heat up in the tropics,' *Technology Review*, 97(4): 16.

UNEP (n.d.) *The World Commission on Dams*, United Nations Environment Programme Dams and Development Project, www.unep. org/DAMS/WCD/, accessed 10 January 2014.

UNFCCC (United Nations Framework Convention on Climate Change) (2013a) Website, www.unfccc.int, accessed 25 December 2013.

— (2013b) *Opportunities for Parties included in Annex I to the Convention whose special circumstances are recognized by the Conference of Parties to benefit from support from relevant bodies and institutions to enhance mitigation, adaptation, technology, capacity-building and access to finance: technical paper*, PDF, 30 May, unfccc.int/resource/docs/2013/tp/03.pdf, accessed 14 January 2014.

United Nations (2014) *Transboundary Waters*, www.un.org/waterforlifedecade/transboundary_waters.shtml, accessed 9 January 2014.

US Department of Energy (2008) *20% Wind Energy by 2030: Increasing Wind Energy's Contribution to the U.S. Electricity Supply*, PDF, www1.eere.energy.gov/wind/pdfs/42864.pdf, accessed 11 January 2014.

— (2013a) 'First commercial, grid-connected, hydrokinetic tidal energy project in North America: Ocean Renewable Power Company's (ORPC) TidGen™ device has a rated capacity of 150 kilowatts and generates enough electricity annually to power 25 to 30 homes,' Office of Science, January, science.energy.gov/sbir/highlights/2013/sbir-2013-01-e/, accessed 9 January 2014.

— (2013b) *Installed Wind Capacity*, www.wind poweringamerica.gov/wind_installed_capacity.asp, accessed 14 December 2014.

US Energy Information Administration (2011) 'U.S. energy intensity projected to continue its steady decline through 2040,' *Today in Energy*, www.eia.gov/todayinenergy/detail.cfm?id=10191, accessed 20 January 2014.

— (2012) 'How much electricity is lost in transmission and distribution in the United States?', www.eia.gov/tools/faqs/faq.cfm?id=105&t=3, accessed 13 January 2014.

— (2013a) *Annual Energy Outlook 2013*, PDF, www.eia.gov/forecasts/aeo/pdf/0383(2013), accessed 31 December 2013.

— (2013b) 'How dependent is the United States on foreign oil?', www.eia.gov/tools/faqs/faq.cfm?id=32&t=6, accessed 31 December 2013.

— (2013c) *International Energy Outlook*, 25 July, www.eia.gov/forecasts/ieo/world.cfm, accessed 31 December 2013.

— (2013d) 'China consumes nearly as much coal as the rest of the world combined,' *Today in Energy*, 29 January, www.eia.gov/todayinenergy/detail.cfm?id=9751, accessed 1 January 2014.

— (2013e) *Russia Analysis*, 26 November, www.eia.gov/countries/cab.cfm?fips=rs, accessed 6 January 2014.

— (2013f) *Electric Monthly Power*, 20 December, www.eia.gov/electricity/monthly/epm_table_grapher.cfm?t=epmt_5_6_a, accessed 10 January 2014.

— (2013g) 'Heating and cooling no longer majority of U.S. home energy use,' *Today in Energy*, www.eia.gov/todayinenergy/detail.cfm?id=10271, accessed 10 January 2014.

— (2013h) 'Table 4.3 total generating capacity,'

www.eia.gov/electricity/annual/html/epa_04_03.html, accessed 22 April 2014.

— (2014) *International Energy Statistics*, www.eia.gov/cfapps/ipdbproject/IEDIndex3.cfm, accessed January 2014.

US Nuclear Regulatory Commission (2013a) *Measuring Radiation*, www.nrc.gov/about-nrc/radiation/health-effects/measuring-radiation.html, accessed 31 December 2013.

— (2013b) 'Backgrounder on the Three Mile Island accident,' www.nrc.gov/reading-rm/doc-collections/fact-sheets/3mile-isle.html, accessed 31 January 2013.

Vidic, R. D., S. L. Brantley, J. M. Vandenbossch, D. Yoxtheimer and J. D. Abad (2013) 'Impact of shale gas development on regional water quality,' *Science*, 340, dx.doi.org/10.1126/science.1235009, accessed 7 January 2014.

Vos, A. D. (1980) 'Detailed balance limit of the efficiency of tandem solar cells,' *Journal of Physics D: Applied Physics*, 13(5): 839.

Wachsman, E. D. and T. L. Kang (2011) 'Lowering the temperature of solid oxide fuel cells,' *Science*, 334: 935–9.

Wakker, P. P. (2004) 'On the composition of risk preference and belief,' *Psychological Review*, 111(1): 236–41.

Wang, M. Q., J. Han, Z. Haq, W. E. Tyner, M. Wu and A. Elgowainy (2011) 'Energy and greenhouse gas emission effects of corn and cellulosic ethanol with technology improvements and land use changes,' *Biomass and Bioenergy*, 35: 1885–96.

Warner, N. R., R. B. Jackson, T. H. Darrah, S. G. Osborn, A. Down, K. Zhao, A. White and A. Vengosh (2012) 'Geochemical evidence for possible natural migration of Marcellus Formation brine to shallow aquifers in Pennsylvania,' *Proceedings in the National Academy of Sciences in the US*, 109(30): 11961–6.

Washington Post (n.d.) 'Solyndra scandal,' *Washington Post Special Reports*, www.washingtonpost.com/2010/07/08/gIQAtAHYwO_page.html, accessed 28 December 2013.

WCD (World Commission on Dams) (2000) *Dams and Development: A New Framework for Decision-Making, the Report of the World Commission on Dams*, PDF, London and Sterling, VA: Earthscan Publishing, Ltd.

Wesoff, E. (2011) 'DOE closes two solar loans just before the deadline,' *Greentech Media*, 30 September, www.greentechmedia.com/articles/read/doe-closes-two-solar-loans-just-before-the-deadline, accessed 2 August 2014.

White House (2009) 'President Obama announces $3.4 billion investment to spur transition to smart energy grid,' Office of the Press Secretary, www.whitehouse.gov/the-press-office/president-obama-announces-34-billion-investment-spur-transition-smart-energy-grid, accessed 23 December 2013.

— (2011) *Blueprint for a Secure Energy Future*, PDF, 30 March, www.whitehouse.gov/sites/default/files/blueprint_secure_energy_future.pdf, accessed 30 December 2013.

WHO (World Health Organization) (2010) 'Exposure to air pollution: a major public health concern,' www.who.int/ipcs/features/air_pollution.pdf, accessed 9 January 2014.

— (2013) *Health risk assessment from the nuclear accident after the 2011 Great East Japan Earthquake and Tsunami, based on a preliminary dose estimation*, PDF, World Health Organization, apps.who.int/iris/bitstream/10665/78218/1/9789241505130_eng.pdf, accessed 5 January 2014.

Wilcoxen, P. J. (2009) *Facts about Energy*, wilcoxen.maxwell.insightworks.com/pages/135.html, accessed 24 January 2014.

World Bank (2012) *Integrated Safeguards Data Sheet: Concept Stage. Report No. ISDSC764 for Inga 3 and Mid-Size Hydropower Development*, PDF, www-wds.worldbank.org/external/default/WDSContentServer/WDSP/AFR/2012/08/22/3E4E9A32476380oC85257A62006E6788/1_0/Rendered/PDF/ISDSoPrintoP13022201201345665954480.pdf, accessed 9 January 2014.

— (2013a) *Kenya Overview*, October, www.worldbank.org/en/country/kenya/overview, accessed 15 January 2014.

— (2013b) *Data by Country: Kenya*, data.worldbank.org/indicator/EG.ELC.ACCS.ZS/countries/KE?display=graph, accessed 15 January 2014.

World Nuclear Association (2013a) *Nuclear Power in France*, www.world-nuclear.org/info/Country-Profiles/Countries-A-F/France/, accessed 30 December 2013.

— (2013b) *Nuclear Power in Japan*, www.world-nuclear.org/info/Country-Profiles/

Countries-G-N/Japan/, accessed 31 December 2013.

— (2013c) *Energy Analysis of Power Systems*, www.world-nuclear.org/info/Energy-and-Environment/Energy-Analysis-of-Power-Systems/, accessed 2 January 2014.

World Public Opinion (2006) '30-country poll finds worldwide consensus that climate change is a serious problem,' 25 April, worldpublicopinion.org/pipa/articles/btenvironmentra/187.php?lb=bte&pnt=187&nid=&id=, accessed 2 April 2014.

— (2009) *Publics Want More Government Action on Climate Change: Global Poll*, 29 July, worldpublicopinion.org/pipa/articles/btenvironmentra/631.php?lb=&pnt=631&nid=&id=, accessed 27 December 2013.

Wyre Tidal Energy (n.d.) *La Rance Barrage*, www.wyretidalenergy.com/tidal-barrage/la-rance-barrage, accessed 9 January 2014.

Yablonski, S. (2010) 'Legislature affirms opposition to wind farm project,' *Oswego County Today*, 12 March, oswegocountytoday.com/legislature-affirms-opposition-to-wind-farm-project/, accessed 14 January 2014.

Yardley, J. (2007) 'Chinese dam projects criticized for their human costs,' *New York Times*, 19 November, www.nytimes.com/2007/11/19/world/asia/19dam.html?pagewanted=all&_r=0, accessed 9 January 2014.

Yuxia, J. (ed.) (2007) 'China warns of environmental "catastrophe" from Three Gorges Dam,' Xinhua News Agency, 26 September, news.xinhuanet.com/english/2007-09/26/content_6796234.htm, accessed 9 January 2014.

Zenawi, A. M. (2011) *Address made by H.E. Ato Meles Zenawi, Prime Minister of the Federal Democratic Republic of Ethiopia*, PDF, Conference on Hydropower for Sustainable Development, Addis Ababa, 31 March, www.ethioembassy.org.uk/news_archive/Address%20of%20H%20E%20%20Meles_Zenawi.pdf, accessed 14 January 2014.

INDEX